Professional Practice in ELC

Josephine Donohoe
Eileen McDermott
Caroline Regan

Boru Press Ltd.
The Farmyard
Birdhill
Co. Tipperary
www.borupress.ie

© Josephine Donohoe, Eileen McDermott and Caroline Regan 2021

ISBN 978-1-8384134-4-6
Design by Sarah McCoy
Print origination by Carole Lynch
Illustrations by Andriy Yankovskyy
Printed by Printer Trento srl., Italy

The paper used in this book is made from wood pulp of managed forests.

All rights reserved. No part of this publication may be copied, reproduced or transmitted in any form or by any means without written permission of the publishers or else under the terms of any licence permitting limited copyright issued by the Irish Copyright Licensing Agency.

A CIP catalogue record for this book is available from the British Library. For permission to reproduce photographs and artworks, the author and publisher gratefully acknowledge the following:

© Alamy: 182 © Department of Health: 141 © Mindtools: 192 © QQI: 72 © Shutterstock: 16, 17, 20, 28, 35, 39, 41, 51, 62, 94, 113, 129, 140. 142, 149, 151, 158, 183, 185, 189, 190, 191, 203.

The author and publisher have made every effort to trace all copyright holders, but if any has been inadvertently overlooked we would be pleased to make the necessary arrangement at the first opportunity.

Boru Press in an independent publisher and is not associated with any education and training board.

Contents

Acknowledgements	v
Abbreviations	vi
Resource Documents and Publications	viii
Introduction	1

Section 1 • Professional Practice Preparation — 3

1	Academic writing	4
2	Writing for assessment	14
3	Information and communications technology (ICT)	28
4	Reflective practice	38
5	Personal and professional development	54
6	Planning, goal setting and portfolio production	66

Section 2 • Legislation, Regulations and National Frameworks — 75

7	Pre-school Regulations 2016 – *Quality and Regulatory Framework* (Tusla)	76
8	*Children First: National Guidance for the Protection and Welfare of Children* (2017)	92
9	*Síolta: The National Quality Framework for Early Childhood Education* (2006)	113
10	*Aistear: The Early Childhood Curriculum Framework* (2009)	121
11	The *Aistear Síolta Practice Guide* (2015)	132

Section 3 • Professional Practice Placement — 135

12	Preparation for placement	136
13	Knowledge, skills and competences	146
14	Professional practice placement	160
15	Personal presentation in professional practice placement	166
16	Employment legislation	176
17	Communication	187
18	Teamwork	202
19	Current developments in early learning and care	212

REFERENCES — 222

APPENDICES — 229

Appendix 1 Tusla Early Years Inspection Process — 230
Appendix 2 Tusla Child Safeguarding Statement Sample Template — 232
Appendix 3 Sample forms — 234

INDEX — 237

Acknowledgments

We would like to thank our families and friends who provided continuous support in the writing of this book.

To our colleagues (past and present) and to all the students with whom we have had the privilege to work with over many years, we are ever grateful for the stimulation, encouragement, support and learning which we experienced.

'Together Old and Young – TOY Project' and the section on Intergenerational Learning has been kindly provided by Dr Anne Fitzpatrick for inclusion in Chapter 19.

> **Dedication:**
> This book is dedicated to the memory of Fred Meaney who died on the 14th June 2021 – ever a supportive and encouraging colleague and a dynamic Principal who facilitated and enabled many developments in the Early Learning and Care (ELC) department in Sallynoggin College of Further Education.

Abbreviations

ABC	Area-Based Childhood Programme
ACS	Affordable Childcare Scheme
AIM	Access and Inclusion Model
ASCC	After School Childcare Scheme
ASD	Autism Spectrum Disorder
CCC	City/County Childcare Committee
CCS	Community Childcare Subvention
DCEDIY	Department of Children, Equality, Disability, Integration and Youth
DEIS	Delivering Equality of Education in Schools
DES	Department of Education and Skills
DLP	Designated Liaison Person
ECCE	Early Childhood Care and Education
ECEC	Early Childhood Education and Care
ECI	Early Childhood Ireland
ELC	Early Learning and Care
ESD	Education for Sustainable Development
ETB	Education and Training Board
EYC	Early Years Capital
EYEPU	Early Years Education Policy Unit
EYSPR	Early Years Sector Profile Report
HSE	Health Service Executive
LINC	Leadership for Inclusion in the Early Years
NCCA	National Council for Curriculum and Assessment
NCS	National Childcare Scheme

NFQ	National Framework of Qualifications
NQF	National Quality Framework
NSAI	National Síolta Aistear Initiative
PIP	Programmes Implementation Platform
QQI	Quality and Qualifications Ireland
TEC	Training and Employment Childcare
VCO	Voluntary Childcare Organisation

Resource Documents and Publications

The following is a list of important publications to be read in conjunction with this book.

Síolta

Centre for Early Childhood Development and Education (2006) *Síolta: The National Quality Framework for Early Childhood Education*. Dublin: CECDE. Available from https://www.siolta.ie/about.php

Aistear

National Council for Curriculum and Assessment (2009) *Aistear: The Early Childhood Curriculum Framework: Principles and Themes*. Dublin: NCCA. Available from http://www.ncca.biz/Aistear/pdfs/PrinciplesThemes_ENG/PrinciplesThemes_ENG.pdf

Children First

Department of Children and Youth Affairs (2017) *Children First: National Guidance for the Protection and Welfare of Children*. Dublin: Stationery Office. Available from https://www.tusla.ie/services/child-protection-welfare/children-first/

Pre-school Regulations

Tusla (2018) *Quality and Regulatory Framework: Full Day Care Service and Part-Time Day Care Service*. Dublin: Early Years Inspectorate. Available from https://www.tusla.ie/services/pre-school-services/early-years-quality-and-regulatory-framework/

Introduction

This book is written to facilitate and guide learners in developing their personal and professional skills to study and work in Early Learning and Care (ELC) services. Significant changes have taken place over the past couple of decades in early childhood policy, education and legislation as well as in the wider areas of social policy and equality legislation.

Since the launch of the Workforce Development Plan in 2010, it is acknowledged that the sector is now striving to become a graduate-led workforce by 2028. QQI has developed professional award criteria and guidelines for Initial Professional Education (Level 7 and Level 8) degree programmes for the ELC sector in Ireland. These criteria and guidelines have emerged from a long process of research and close consultation with stakeholders and with the higher education institutions who are producing high-quality graduates for the sector. QQI was represented on this working group to ensure alignment of the development of criteria and standards at Levels 4, 5 and 6 and to ensure coherence across all levels of the National Framework of Qualifications (NFQ). In 2019 a Programme Award Type Descriptor (PATD) was developed for an ELC award at Level 5 and 6 by a working group established by the Early Years Education Policy Unit (EYEPU). The development of content using the PATD document for major professional ELC awards at Stages 5 and 6 was closely aligned and mapped across to these criteria and guidelines.

There has also been considerable state investment in the ELC sector, with the Government now providing two years free pre-school – a recognition of the importance of ELC. This is in line with the Government's strategy on Education for Sustainable Development, in particular Goal 4, which aims for all young children to have access to high-quality free pre-school services. Not least among the developments has been the introduction of the *National Quality Framework for Early Childhood Education* (*Síolta* 2006) and *The Early Childhood Curriculum Framework* (*Aistear* 2009), now cornerstones of practice in ELC. These frameworks will be referenced throughout the book and it is hoped that you, the learner, will be familiar with the themes and a confident user of the material by the end of your course. This will be invaluable to you later as an ELC practitioner.

The material presented in this book is specifically relevant to becoming a professional ELC practitioner and includes relevant legislation pertaining to ELC services, equality and diversity guidelines, child protection and child safeguarding. This book is underpinned by the guiding principles of Síolta (2006) and Aistear (2009).

The book is divided into three sections. In Sections 1 and 3 a practical approach is taken in the presentation of the material. Definitions, activities, scenarios and 'think abouts' are interspersed throughout the text and are designed to provoke thinking, learning and discussion as appropriate. Some of these are designed to be used as assignments or as part of project work, and may be submitted for assessment, while others will certainly be useful in your professional practice placement.

Section 2 contains detailed information relating to regulations and frameworks and is faithful to the content and structure of those documents. The chapters in this section are designed to be used to support learning in the other two sections. They are structured slightly differently and are colour-coded in the same purple as the prelims and the end matter for ease of reference.

References at the end of the book should be useful to the learner who wishes to explore further. There are many other readily accessible resources online, in libraries and in bookshops. It should also be noted that the location of content contained in website references given in this book may change over time, but such content can usually be found under archived material on those websites.

All of the material presented in the book is underpinned by a commitment to principles of quality and equality, which we believe should be intrinsic to all work in ELC.

Section 1

Professional Practice Preparation

Academic Writing

This chapter will explore:
- approaches to writing
- research methods
- referencing.

Introduction

This chapter focuses on communication in written form such as creative writing, academic writing, reflective writing, report compilation, form completion, letter writing and research undertaking and writing.

Creative, academic and reflective writing

In creative writing we are free to express our opinions and emotions, to tell stories using different styles and techniques. There is a place for creative writing in the early learning profession. For example, you may wish to write stories for children, come up with fun rhymes to enable their learning or write simple plays for learning and entertainment. This example of creative writing is part of the first verse of a poem written by the famous nineteenth-century English writer Edward Lear.

>'The Jumblies'
>They went to sea in a Sieve, they did,
>In a Sieve they went to sea:
>In spite of all their friends could say,
>On a winter's morn, on a stormy day,
>In a Sieve they went to sea!
>
>(Extract from *The Jumblies* by Edward Lear)

In contrast, a formal report on the adventures of the Jumblies might go like this:

>The weather was bad on the morning the Jumblies set out and they were warned by numerous friends not to go. They went in a sieve which, having holes, was not a very safe craft for sailing.

Activity

For these three exercises you will need a pen, some sheets of paper and a stopwatch or timer to hand. When you start to write, do not stop to think; rather, just keep writing whatever comes into your head.

Exercise 1: Write a list of (at least six) foods that you associate with your childhood. Now pick one of them and write for two minutes on that food. It can be a description of the food, something that happened when you were eating that food – anything at all. Do not edit yourself or stop to think about the subject.

Exercise 2: Choose one of the topics from this list without thinking about it:

* The angry butterfly
* The hurried monkey
* The bruised banana
* The romantic kettle
* The energetic bicycle
* The tired chair.

Now write for two minutes on your chosen topic, again without editing yourself or stopping to think.

Exercise 3: Pick a number between one and 10. Write a story (about half a page) for a young child about the adventures of one of the numbers, again for two minutes without editing yourself or stopping to think.

Academic writing, on the other hand, is formal and focused. It is also structured according to the purpose for which it is written, which is usually to demonstrate your knowledge of a subject, for example a factual report on some event or organisation. Academic writing also allows the writer to express opinions, but these opinions must be based on facts or research already outlined elsewhere in the academic text. Academic writing does not require one to use long, complicated sentences or big words. In fact, the best academic writing often uses clear, simple language that allows anyone to understand the points being made or the information being given.

Reflective writing is also focused but perhaps less formal, and can use many formats. As a learner it is a useful tool to enable you to think about and evaluate what you do as an early learning and care (ELC) practitioner. The art of reflective writing will be dealt with in detail in Chapter 4.

It is important to appreciate that, just like swimming or running or playing the guitar, writing takes practice. One of the best things you can do at the beginning of your course is to take five or 10 minutes at the end of each day to write. It is probably easiest to focus on the day just gone and reflect on what you learned, on a conversation you had or on something that irritated you. Do not edit your thoughts. You can tear up your writings later if you wish.

Another important matter to appreciate is that whatever we set out to write, we will need to draft and redraft. Many people find it difficult to start an assignment, for example, because they expect to begin with the introduction, write sequentially and finish with the conclusion. However, it does not always work like this. It is better to start with whatever you find easiest to write about and then let the remainder flow naturally or form the remainder around the initial text. The introduction is often written at the end. Throughout all, it is important to redraft and revise.

Research methods

There are two types of research: primary and secondary.

PRIMARY RESEARCH

Primary research refers to all the information and data that the researcher has found out for him/herself. It includes surveys, questionnaires, case studies, checklists and interviews.

A **survey** is used to gather and collate information from a selection of the population. Questionnaires, interviews or checklists are common tools used when doing a survey.

A **questionnaire** is a set of printed or written questions with a choice of answers, devised for the purposes of a survey or statistical study. If using a questionnaire or undertaking an interview, you need to decide the following:

- What do I need to find out?
- What questions will I ask?
- How many people will be included in my research and how will I select them?
- Will I approach organisations?
- How much will it cost?
- How much time will I need for my primary research?

Designing and using a questionnaire

Decide: What information do I want?

Design: What questions will help obtain that information?

Write: Put the questions down in logical sequence on a form.

Select: Choose the people that you are going to question.

Ask: Put the questions to these people (online or in person).

Record: Record the answers in as much detail as possible.

Analyse: Analyse the answers using tick boxes, graphs or another suitable method that makes them easy to read. If using technology-aided research tools, the program will analyse the data for you.

Present: Present the findings in an appropriate way.

There are many online tools (some free) to help with carrying out surveys, for example SurveyMonkey, SoGoSurvey and ZoHo Survey. If you plan to carry out primary research using a questionnaire, you should always carry out a 'pilot' or small-scale run-through to test the quality of the questions, to ascertain which questions work, which are unclear, which require re-wording, which should be omitted or if any new question should be added.

A **case study** is a detailed profile of a person, a group, an organisation or even a country, usually used to illustrate a point of view or a theory.

A **checklist** is a list that shows items arranged in a logical order and which the researcher can check against.

Thinking about yourself, how often would you say you are able to …
(*put a cross in one box on each line*)

	most of the time	some of the time	not very often	never
… take responsibility?	☐	☐	☐	☐
… take advantage of an opportunity when you see one?	☐	☐	☐	☐
… show initiative?	☐	☐	☐	☐
… have confidence in what you do?	☐	☐	☐	☐
…not give up when faced with difficulties?	☐	☐	☐	☐
… agree to take on new things that are challenging?	☐	☐	☐	☐
… take a risk once you've thought things through?	☐	☐	☐	☐
… make decisions about how things should be done?	☐	☐	☐	☐
… learn from the times you have not been successful?	☐	☐	☐	☐
… compete against other people or groups?	☐	☐	☐	☐
… think up new, different ways of doing things?	☐	☐	☐	☐
… recognise when you need advice?	☐	☐	☐	☐
… set targets for yourself?	☐	☐	☐	☐

An **interview** is a conversation between a researcher and a respondent/interviewee with the purpose of eliciting information on a certain topic/area. Interviews can be recorded either as audio or video; note, however, that the consent of the interviewee for use of such recordings is required.

Activity

Working on your own or in a group, and using one of the free online tools available, make up a short questionnaire about a subject of your choice, email it to friends and analyse your results. Discuss how useful or clear the questions were or whether there were any ambiguous questions or answers.

SECONDARY RESEARCH

All sources of information and data by others that has been gathered to inform research are considered secondary resources and comprise secondary research. Although it is called secondary research, it is nearly always the first thing that a person does when commencing a project or a study! Books, TV programmes, magazines, reports and data from government departments or from organisations, podcasts, social media platforms, pictures, YouTube videos, music, etc. all fall into this category. Many of these sources are now available online but the researcher must always be careful that information found online is from authentic sources. It is highly recommended that information be accessed on and gathered from official and reputable websites. If information is found on a blog, for instance, the facts acquired should always be checked against another, more reputable source. We have a responsibility as digital citizens to ensure that information we publish or disseminate is based on well-researched facts.

 Some websites are designed to 'fact check' and will redirect one to the original source of the information. Examples of such websites currently available are Media Matters, Truth or Fiction, ProPublica and Snopes.

When conducting secondary research and collating secondary resources, always ask yourself these questions:

* How can I know if what I am reading is valid or trustworthy?
* When I read an article or document, how do I determine if a source is credible or trustworthy?
* How will I use what I have learned when scrolling through Facebook, YouTube and other social media posts and articles?

Secondary research gives you an insight into the subject of the study and allows you to decide what area requires further examination or what aspects are most interesting before you embark on primary research. It will also help you to decide which method of primary research is best suited to the study.

Qualitative and quantitative research

Pertaining to quality, **qualitative research** aims to gain deep insight through the study of individuals, for example through a lengthy individual interview or an in-depth case study. A child observation is a good example of qualitative research. It gives a deep and rich insight into the subject being studied.

Pertaining to quantity, **quantitative research** aims to study the relationship of one set of facts to another using scientific methods. A questionnaire sent out to 500 early learning centres seeking information about naptime habits of two-year-olds would be an example of quantitative research.

Both quantitative and qualitative research are valuable. Documentaries often use both research methods: the general information based on quantitative research will be stated at the outset – for example, 'Eighty-five per cent of two-years-olds require a comfort toy to settle for a nap'; then a close observation comprising qualitative research of a two-year-old child settling down for a nap may be given.

References and bibliography

A reference list is a list of the sources of all the references (either quotations or citations, explained below) that you use in your assignment or project. A bibliography is a list of all the sources that you have used while researching your subject, whether you have used direct references or not. This programme requires that you produce a reference list at the end of each piece of work.

An outline of the Harvard System of referencing is given here. There are other systems for referencing, but all methods are broadly similar. The important thing is to choose one system of referencing and adhere to it throughout to avoid confusion.

PLAGIARISM

Before looking at the nuts and bolts of referencing, it is important to understand why we **must always** supply a reference when using a secondary source.

> According to the Merriam-Webster online dictionary, to plagiarise means:
> * to steal and pass off (the ideas or words of another) as one's own
> * to use (another's production) without crediting the source
> * to commit literary theft
> * to present as new and original an idea or product derived from an existing source.

Plagiarism is an act of fraud. It involves stealing someone else's work or ideas and omitting to show where it came from. All colleges and centres will have a policy on plagiarism, and it is important that you read it carefully and check anything that you do not understand with your teachers. However, if you reference your work carefully, then you will avoid being guilty of plagiarism.

REFERENCING

QUOTATIONS AND CITATIONS

Quotations must be taken word for word from the original text. Short quotations (less than two lines) should be quoted exactly, inserted directly into the text without putting them on a new line, begin and end with single inverted commas ('/') and include the citation at the end with the full stop outside the closing bracket. For example:

> 'Communities, it is often said, are dense networks of human interactions accompanied by a strong sense of place'
>
> (O'Dwyer, 2018, p. 51).

Longer quotations (more than two lines) start on a new line, indented from the main text, do not include quotation marks and include the citation at the end. For example:

> It is sobering to keep in mind that other people see and hear you in action all the time. You are the only one excluded from this observational knowledge until you accept the opportunity to watch or listen to yourself …
>
> (Linden, 2012, p. 89)

Note that if there are more than three authors/editors, the first in-text citation should list all authors'/editors' surnames and year of publication; subsequent in-text citations list the first author/editor surname followed by '*et al.*', for example: Arnott *et al.*, 2017.

If you do not quote a sentence in full, you indicate this by the use of an ellipsis (...), as in the second example above.

Note that in the examples, the reference is placed in brackets at the end of the quote and consists of the author's surname followed by the year of publication and the page number (p. standing for page, pp. standing for pages).

If the author's or authors' names are part of the sentence, you should put the year of publication in brackets (parentheses) after the name/s.

> **Example:** Mhic Mhathúna and Taylor (2012) state that combining the word 'pedagogy' with the term 'nurture' is intended to strengthen the early years professional space.

REFERENCE LIST

At the end of the assignment or project, you will need to compile a list of all the references that you have used in-text. Make sure that you take note of each and every source of material and information you quote or use as you are composing any written material – do not leave it to the end to retrace your steps to locate the sources of material or quotes.

List the references by author surname in alphabetical order. Format the entries to have enough paragraph spacing between each entry so that the list is easy to read or authors/publications easy to find.

REFERENCING A BOOK
Author's surname, Initials. (Year of publication) *Title*. Place of publication: Publisher.

> **Example:** Kissinger, K. (2017) *Anti-bias Education in the Early Childhood Classroom*. London: Routledge.

REFERENCING AN EDITED BOOK
Editor's/Editors' surnames, Initials. (ed./eds) (Year of publication) *Title*. Place of publication: Publisher.

> **Example:** Forde, C., Kiely, E. and Meade, R. (eds) (2009) *Youth and Community Work Perspectives.* Dublin: Blackhall Publishing

REFERENCING A CHAPTER IN AN EDITED BOOK
Chapter author/s surname, Initials. (Year of publication) Title of Chapter. In: Editor's/Editors' names [first name/initial(s), surname] (ed./eds) *Title*. Place of publication: Publisher, page/page range.

> **Example:** Lillis, T.M. and Swann, J. (2003) Giving Feedback on Student Writing. In: C. Coffin, M.J. Curry, S. Goldman, A. Hewings, T. Lillis and J. Swann (eds) *Teaching Academic Writing: A Toolkit for Higher Education.* London: Routledge, pp. 101–129.

REFERENCING A JOURNAL ARTICLE
Author's surname, Initials. (Year of publication) Title of article. *Title of Journal*, Volume(Issue number), page range.

> **Example:** Seymour, K. (2015) Politics and positionality: engaging with maps of meaning. *Social Work Education: An International Journal,* 34(3), pp. 275–285.

REFERENCING ELECTRONIC SOURCES
Ebook: Author, Initials. (Year) *Title*. Place of publication: Publisher. Available from [full website address] [accessed 00 Month Year].

> **Example:** Anglia Ruskin University (2021) *The Harvard System of Referencing.* Available from https://library.aru.ac.uk/referencing/files/Harvard_referencing_201920.pdf [accessed 23 June 2021].

Note: It is important to print out the first page of electronic sources, as web pages change frequently or indeed may disappear altogether. You may put these pages in an appendix.

TV series/DVDs/downloads/online viewing: *Title* (Year) [download]. Place of publication: Publisher./Broadcast medium, Season, episode.

> **Example:** *Health for All Children 3: The Video* (2004) [download]. London: Child Growth Foundation.

YouTube video: Screen name of contributor (Year) Video title. *Series title* [download]. Available from [full website address] [accessed 00 Month Year].

> **Example:** Sir Ken Robinson (2007) Do schools kill creativity? *TEDTalks* [download]. Available from http://www.youtube.com/watch?v=iG9CE55wbtY [accessed 20 June 2021].

PDF file of government publication or similar: Authorship (Year) *Title of document*. Place of publication (if known): Publisher. Available from [full web address/file URL] [accessed 00 Month Year].

> **Example:** Tusla, Child and Family Agency (2015) *Child Protection Conference and the Child Protection Notification System. Information for Professionals*. Dublin: Tusla, Child and Family Agency. Available from http://www.tusla.ie/uploads/content/CPNS_Prof_Booklet.pdf [accessed 23 June 2021].

There are many finer points to be learned about referencing; only the basics are included here. The best way to learn how to reference is to take note of how references are presented in your textbooks and other books that feature reference lists.

 To make referencing and the compilation of bibliographies easier, there is a referencing tool on most software designed to produce documents. It is a good idea to learn to use them. If you are not familiar with this tool, it might be helpful to explore it in small groups.

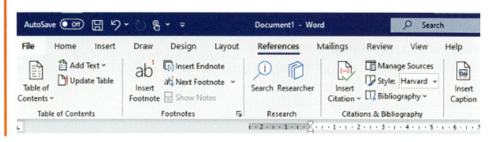

GLOSSARY AND INDEX

A glossary gives, in alphabetical order, the meaning of specialised words used in the book or report that may be unfamiliar to the reader. It serves as an easy reference dictionary for a specific subject and is usually placed at the beginning or end of the work.

A glossary is not the same as an index. An index is a list of words and topics (again in alphabetical order) and their corresponding page numbers so that the reader can easily locate content of interest.

APPENDIX

An appendix includes material not suitable for the main part of a study, for example newspaper cuttings, an observation, the questionnaire used, a copy of a table of statistics. An appendix should be numbered, so that it can be easily referred to in the main text.

Keep a record of all your planning notes. This is part of the research. Sometimes you will do a lot of background work, which will not be evident in your written submission. It is therefore recommended that you provide evidence of all your project work, as this can go in an appendix. However, an appendix is not to be used to dump material in the hope that the reader will make sense of it. It is up to the writer to contextualise the appendix and justify its existence.

RECAP QUESTIONS

1. What is the difference between primary and secondary research?
2. What is plagiarism and how can you avoid plagiarising the work of others?

Writing for assessment

This chapter will explore:
* writing formats and skills for various types of assignments
* production and completion of workplace documents.

Introduction

On early learning and care courses there may be a variety of approaches to assessment and depending on their function and intended readers, the style, structure and format may differ. What follows are some guidelines to writing:

1. an assignment or project
2. an observation of a child
3. a play activity
4. a child learning story.

1. An assignment or project

An academic assignment will contain the following sections.

* **Title page and contents page.** The title page is the first page of your assignment/project. Therefore, it is important to have a well-formatted title page that clearly represents your paper. This page should include all the information necessary for a reader to identify the contents of the assignment/project. A contents page should indicate the relevant page numbers. Pages should therefore be numbered. There may be no need for a contents page in a short assignment or project.

* **Introduction.** The introduction should: 1. be brief and clear; 2. give a broad overview of what will be covered in the essay/project, etc.; and 3. include some general background information, for example the particular issues that will be examined. For example:

This assignment (essay/project, etc.) studies the organisational profile in the structure, funding and staffing of an ELC service. It will examine the role of the ELC practitioner in a community where there are a high number of young economically disadvantaged families. Primary research will include ... An evaluation of the effectiveness of the service will be undertaken and recommendations made.

* **Aim and objectives.** Not all academic assignments will require these to be written down, but it is a good mental exercise in order to get started. There is an old proverb, 'If you don't know where you're going, any road will take you there.' With that in mind, the aim is where you want to get to and the objective is to learn how to read maps and to identify the most efficient or appropriate road to get you there. For example, considering the early years example, the aim might be:

    to examine the use of toys and equipment in the centre during free play with a view to improving play provision.

    The objectives might be:

    - to learn what toys might be appropriate to the stage of development of the age group, to match theory to practice
    - to understand what makes for a worthwhile/less useful activity (reflection, evaluation and analysis).

* **Methodology.** A methodology section should provide an outline of how the study was conducted. For example, where did you source your information (i.e. what did you read)? This is your secondary research. If you are doing primary research, you need to explain what type of research methods you used (e.g. questionnaire, survey, observation, case study, etc.). Detail regarding sample size (how many) might be relevant. (If you are doing a single case study, sample size is irrelevant.) Detail regarding sample choice – why and how you chose your sample – might also be relevant. Again, it might only be necessary to list methodology for larger projects or an assignment that involves research.

* **Content.** This is the main part of your assignment. There are no hard and fast rules, but you should first present your facts and figures, then brainstorm all the ideas that you think you might like to cover. Map them to your introduction, which should be mapped to the brief. Decide on some structure. Each paragraph should deal with one topic or question. If we consider the early years example given earlier, the following paragraphs might be planned:

    - A brief description of the community in which the service operates
    - The internal structure and staffing of the service
    - The numbers and characteristics (age, gender, etc.) of young children who attend the centre
    - A brief description of the programmes

- Funding
- The needs of children
- The role of the ELC practitioner
- The results of any primary research, e.g. questionnaire, interviews.

✱ **Presentation of findings.** Experiment with different ways of presenting your findings. Data from surveys and questionnaires need to be put into categories and groups so that the reader will be easily able to see patterns of difference or similarity and be able to extract significant information. Note that numerical data can be presented in many ways, e.g. tables, bar charts, histograms, graphs, which are the simplest methods of presenting your data. Some computer programs can facilitate the production of very detailed and clear presentations. Photographs, video or audio recordings may also be used.

When you have presented your findings, it is important to describe what you have found, drawing attention to significant points, what surprised you, which results were predictable, how your findings relate to the literature, etc. For example, if you study a group of five-year-olds using computers for learning over a period of time, you should be able to relate this to what is said in your textbooks about child development on the one hand and the effects of TEL (technology enhanced learning) on the other.

Next, analyse, criticise and evaluate, relate to theory, discuss, compare and make recommendations. Again, what you do should be guided by the brief and the marking sheet. Be critical of yourself and your methodology and indicate improvements you could make if you were doing the project again.

— Were you surprised by anything you discovered while doing your project?

— Comment on possible bias and any ethical issues that have arisen.

— Suggest ways that you feel the research area could be extended.

In your evaluation, do not be afraid to be critical, admitting, for example, 'In my questionnaire, answers given to question no. 1 revealed nothing material to the study because I had phrased the question badly.' By admitting such failings, you will demonstrate that you have acquired an insight into the skill of devising questions. However, if you try to cover up a failing or do not mention it in the hope that it will go unnoticed, you will be displaying that you have gained little insight or skill or that your research was dishonest.

✱ **Conclusion.** In your conclusion, summarise, clarify and recommend. In simple language, state what it was you were looking for, what you found and what it means. Set out the main points but do not go into long repetitious detail of what has already been stated. Before writing the conclusion, it is a good idea to look again at the key terms and tasks as set out in the assignment brief. Do not be tempted to include opinions and hunches that were not evident in the research; in other words, do not introduce any new information in the conclusion. Finally, look to the future or pose a question. Referring to the early years example above, the following conclusion might be given:

> **This assignment found that although the structure and organisation were effective and all ELC staff were trained and committed, cutbacks in funding affected programmes, and rising unemployment in the area means that more and more young parents in the community are struggling. Therefore, the whole community may feel the effects of this in increasing social and psychological problems in the future.**

* **References**: See pages 9–13.
* **Appendices**: See page 13.

2. An observation of a child

When writing an observation, it is advisable to use a format that clearly sets out the necessary background information and clarifies for both the observer and reader who is being observed, where and why. The observation could contain the following information:

1. Observation number
2. Date
3. Method and media used
4. Time started/finished
5. Number of children present
6. Number of adults present
7. From whom permission was obtained
8. The setting
9. The immediate context
10. Child observed
11. Brief description of the child observed
12. The observation aim and rationale

13. The observation
14. The evaluation
15. Reflection on personal learning
16. Recommendations
17. Reference list
18. Signatures.

1. OBSERVATION NUMBER/2. DATE

When observations are carried out regularly in an early years setting as part of ELC practice, it is important that they are numbered and dated, as this can help give both staff and parents a picture of a child's progression within a particular area over time.

In the case of a learner who is presenting a portfolio of observations for assessment, it is usual to number and date them in sequence. This helps when preparing an overview of the portfolio contents and indicates which criteria have been met within the work.

3. METHOD AND MEDIA USED

The method chosen (e.g. narrative, checklist, time sample, etc.) should be appropriate to the information being sought in the observation. The media used will vary depending on the particular observation being carried out. Media can be pen and paper or recording (either audio or video). It is important to remember child safeguarding policies and procedures when using any material that might identify a child.

4. TIME STARTED/FINISHED

Start and finish times should be indicated precisely. In some cases, for example with a narrative, the observation will last for a number of minutes only. A time sample may take place over half a day, while a checklist or event sample may be carried out over a number of days.

5. NUMBER OF CHILDREN PRESENT/6. NUMBER OF ADULTS PRESENT

It is important to record this data because if the ratio of children to adults is high, it may affect the observer's ability to remain uninvolved, either because a child is interacting with the observer or because the observer may have to set the observation aside and become involved with the children. It may also help to put some of the child's actions/reactions into context.

7. FROM WHOM PERMISSION WAS OBTAINED

It is essential that permission is sought either directly from the child's parent/guardian, or indirectly through the workplace supervisor. In the interests of confidentiality, the person's role rather than name should be used, e.g. the Child's Mother, or the Nursery Supervisor, rather than Ms Smith or Mr O'Reilly.

8. THE SETTING

This refers to the type of centre in which the observation is to be carried out, e.g. a primary school, playgroup, early learning centre, etc. For example, a description of the setting could read:

> The observation took place in a community playgroup which is open for three hours per day, five days per week, and caters for 12 children, whose ages range from three years to four years six months.

9. THE IMMEDIATE CONTEXT

This is a description of exactly where in the setting the observation took place. It defines the context in which the child is observed, and should contain information on what she/he is doing, who she/he is with and, if necessary, what has just occurred. For example:

> The child M is playing in the kitchen corner with two other children, F and C. M has invited the other two children over to play with him and has just announced that he will be the dad and the others the children. The three children are sitting at a table with some cups, saucers and plates. There is a large cardboard box on the floor beside them, which M has referred to as the dishwasher.

10. CHILD OBSERVED

When a learner is completing an observation, the child's actual name should not be used. For reasons of confidentiality, either an initial or the code TC (Target Child) is acceptable.

11. BRIEF DESCRIPTION OF THE CHILD OBSERVED

This should include details of the child's sex, age in years and months and any other factual information relevant to the observation, such as details of the child's health, family details (if known) such as place in family, number of siblings, how long she has been attending the centre and staff concerns, if any. For example:

> TC is female, aged 3 years and 4 months. She has been attending the centre for five mornings a week since she was 2 years old. She is in good health generally and rarely misses a day. She lives locally with her mother, father and her younger brother who attends the toddler section of the centre twice a week. She drops in to see him from time to time. Both her parents are in full-time employment, and she spends the afternoons along with her brother in the house of a local childminder who collects her at around 1.00 p.m. It is planned that she will start primary school in September of next year.

12. THE OBSERVATION AIM AND RATIONALE

This should explain what it is you hope to learn from carrying out the observation and why you are carrying it out. It should clearly relate to the child being observed and to the specific situation the child is in at that particular time. For example:

> My aim is to assess the language development of the child M while he is involved in a role play in the kitchen corner. I am doing this because M seems to spend a lot of time in role play situations at the moment. Role play offers many opportunities for language development and I hope to assess both verbal and non-verbal communication, as well as noting how he uses language to socialise.

13. THE OBSERVATION

The main body of the observation should be focused on the child. What you write down will depend on the observation method chosen. There are numerous methods of observing children, for example narrative, checklist, time sample, child story, event sampling, and so on. You will need to mention what the adult is doing only if it directly affects the child and what is happening during the observation. Essentially, in a running narrative observation, you are recording in detail the actions, interactions and language of the child. For example, 'The child is playing with the ball' is very general – what exactly is the child doing? If video recording is used, then it can be seen exactly what the child is doing with the ball. However, if the written word is being used to record, then the description should be vivid and as accurate as possible, avoiding vague, judgmental or value-laden language.

14. THE EVALUATION

This is where you analyse and reflect on what you have observed. It is useful to start by briefly summarising your aim, i.e. what you were looking for. This will help to focus the evaluation. You then need to ask what you found during the observation. This involves careful re-reading of the observation with the aim in mind. For example, if you had aimed to observe the child's physical development, then you would look for examples of where this is demonstrated, including gross motor skills, fine manipulative skills and eye–hand coordination.

The next stage is to ask what all this means in terms of the child's present stage of development. The usual way to make sense of what you have observed is to compare it with what is considered appropriate for the age, using a developmental checklist or guide. It is essential that you use acknowledged sources which are clearly referenced, and **not** what *you* think is normal. Most textbooks that deal with holistic child development contain such information, giving a detailed guide to expected developmental milestones at each stage, helping you to make valid assessments and demonstrating that there is a wide range of behaviour, learning, skills and development within the norm.

> **DEFINITION**
>
> **Developmental norms** (also known as developmental milestones) refer to the normal timeline of mental and physical growth and development as the child gets older. For example, the norm for walking is 12 months; however, this does not mean that all children walk at 12 months. Some will walk as early as nine months and others as late as 16 months, but they are still within the 'norm'.

Depending on what source is used, the information may be organised in different ways, but essentially will cover one or more of the areas of development.

Reference to child development theory is important here. Look for examples of where your observation appears to either agree with or contradict a theory that you have studied. For example, you have observed that a child of 18 months has put an object in and out of the same container several times. Your reading of child development tells you that children learn through repeating actions. Your evaluation here could refer to Jean Piaget, whose cognitive development theory was based on the notion of the child as an active learner, who needs first-hand experiences of objects to inform him of what they can do, and what he can do with them. You have seen evidence of this in the child's repetitive actions.

You could also examine aspects of whatever play the child is engaged in. Your discussion could include consideration of why a particular activity is provided for the child, whether it is suitable for the child's stage of development, the type of play and stage of play the child is engaged in.

15. REFLECTION ON PERSONAL LEARNING

In this section the focus is on what you, the observer, have learned by carrying out the observation. This can cover learning about:

* the age group of the child observed
* child development in general, and the application of theory in practice
* the play provision available to the children
* the difficulties and distractions encountered in carrying out an observation
* the advantages or limitations of the observation method used.

In fact, it can cover just about any kind of learning that has taken place but should not repeat information that was previously known about the child.

16. RECOMMENDATIONS

This section offers an opportunity for the observer to make recommendations or suggestions about how the child's development could be supported and how to highlight the growing culture of inclusive pedagogy in ELC. This could include areas such as the provision of specific play materials or equipment to enrich play or to enhance learning in a particular area, opportunities for specific experiences such as outings or outdoor play, or a strategy to encourage positive behaviour and continually plan inclusive activities for all children

17. REFERENCE LIST

(See pp. 9–13.)

18. SIGNATURES

The work should always be signed and dated by the observer and then by the workplace supervisor. This authenticates the work and verifies that it has been carried out as stated.

The observation can be an element of planning age- and stage-appropriate activities for the child or for a group of children.

3. A play activity

'Play is children's work' is wisdom imparted by both Piaget and Montessori. The toys are the tools and the work that they are doing is learning, but this play needs to be organised, planned and scaffolded.

> **DEFINITION**
>
> **Scaffolding** describes the process by which adults (and more capable peers) support and guide children's learning, enabling children to reach the next level of ability, beyond their own personal capability at that particular time (NCCA, 2009).

The concepts of scaffolding and 'Zone of Proximal Development', developed by Vygotsky, basically refer to the idea that, with support from and interaction with an adult and more knowledgeable peer, a child can accomplish more than they would be able to do on their own; they can more easily expand their knowledge and skill set with 'scaffolding'. Even free play sessions have to have an element of thought and planning if they are to be productive and enjoyable rather than chaotic and confusing.

For our purposes, we will concentrate on writing up a plan for a focused activity containing the following information:

1. Name of activity/Focus of activity
2. Date, time and duration of activity
3. Number of adults
4. Number of children
5. Age range of children
6. Materials required including space/room
7. Cost of materials
8. Health and safety issues
9. Equality, diversity and inclusion
10. Description of activity
11. Reflection on learning and development for the children
12. Reflection on personal learning
13. References and bibliography
14. Signatures.

1. NAME OF ACTIVITY/FOCUS OF ACTIVITY

This should clearly state the activity planned, linked to children's learning using Aistear themes. An example might be 'Planting seeds', linking to the four themes of Aistear.

2. DATE, TIME AND DURATION OF ACTIVITY

Obviously, the activity has to fit into the schedule of the service. The length of time necessary for the activity from beginning to completion (including cleaning up and transitioning/tidying) should be negotiated with the manager/supervisor.

3. NUMBER OF ADULTS

It is important to establish at the planning stage the number of adults to be involved as it may affect the outcome of the activity for the children. Is there a need for high input/scaffolding from adults or is this an activity that the children will be able to engage in independently?

4. NUMBER OF CHILDREN

The number of children involved will have an impact on space, material required and will dictate the number of adults required to support the activity. Sometimes it may be a more positive experience for all if children engage in the activity in several small groups at different times rather than trying to carry it out in one large group.

5. AGE RANGE OF CHILDREN

This will have an impact on planning. The developmental stage of children and children with additional needs should also be noted.

6. MATERIALS REQUIRED INCLUDING SPACE/ROOM

It is important to have sufficient materials/space for all the children to engage fully with the activity. An activity can be disappointing if some essential element has been forgotten. If a child needs a left-handed scissors to carry out a task, for example, they should be provided with one. Younger children should not be expected to 'wait their turn' too often or for too long.

7. COST OF MATERIALS

It is important to negotiate cost of materials with management. A clear idea of what materials will need to be purchased over and above what is already available in the service is required. There may also be delays in purchasing because of rules and regulations within the service.

8. HEALTH AND SAFETY ISSUES

Many services today will have a 'risk assessment checklist' for most activities that are facilitated in the service. Surfaces, hygiene, toxicity, allergies, potentially dangerous equipment (e.g. scissors), protective clothing required, etc. all have to be considered.

9. EQUALITY, DIVERSITY AND INCLUSION

Ensure that the activity can be fully enjoyed by all the children involved irrespective of their age or abilities. While some adaptations may be required to facilitate a child with a particular additional need, forethought and planning should strive to plan inclusive activities suitable for all children. Also, if appropriate, it should be ensured that the activity embraces diversity and promotes an anti-bias element.

10. DESCRIPTION OF ACTIVITY

The activity should be recorded in detail using visual recording if appropriate. Record language and activity during the process. Do not omit the tidying and transitioning stage.

> **DEFINITIONS**
>
> The **process** is the learning that happens during the activity.
>
> The **product** is the end result.

11. REFLECTION ON LEARNING AND DEVELOPMENT FOR THE CHILDREN

Reference to the child's/children's development and the Aistear themes is important in this section. What areas of the child's/children's development was supported and stimulated by the activity? What were the opportunities for learning and for new experiences offered to the children during the activity? Use the Aistear theme chart to identify and explain how the activity incorporated this learning.

Aistear Themes

Wellbeing	Identity/Belonging	Communication	Exploring/Thinking
Interest	Friendship	Language	Ideas
Fun	Interpersonal skills	Non-verbal language	Questioning
Energy	Self-esteem	Creative	Logic
Physical development	Self-image	Express feelings	Problem solving
Independence	Cooperation	Self- and other regulation	Maths
Competence	Helpfulness	Ideas	Science
Confidence	Involvement	Collaboration	Examining
Resilience	Accepted	Mark-making	Predicting
Persistence	Culture		Creativity

12. REFLECTION ON PERSONAL LEARNING

Evaluation of your own learning should:

* **assess** what has been learned from planning and carrying out the activity about the child/children and about yourself
* **identify what** you would do differently if you were to plan this activity again, and **why**
* **recommend** follow-on activities to extend the children's learning and development.

See Chapter 4 for more information on reflective practice.

13. REFERENCE LIST

(See pp. 9–13.)

14. SIGNATURES

The work should always be signed and dated by the observer and then by the workplace supervisor. This authenticates the work and verifies that it has been carried out as stated.

4. A child learning story

The importance of play in young children's learning and development is a key concept for ELC educators. Assessing children's understanding and progress as they play, either alone or with others, is a crucial activity in ELC settings.

Learning stories are very different from traditional observational assessments that use fragmented evidence. They are a form of 'assessment for learning' rather than 'assessment of learning' (formative assessment versus summative assessment).

> **DEFINITIONS**
>
> **Formative assessment** is used to assess and extrapolate ongoing learning.
>
> **Summative assessment** is used at the end of something to assess a stage or what has been learned; typical summative assessment is an examination.

The storytelling format is written in the child's words, written about the child or written to the child. This allows the storyteller to capture the learning without the confinement of a list or a definite structure, and because the stories are simple and written from the storyteller's perspective they are entertaining and compelling reading for the parent/family. Learning stories are made for sharing with the child and with their family. The child/children and family interpret the event in the story, reflect and collaborate on next steps for the child.

LEARNING STORY FORMAT

Each story has a main event and highlights skills, habits and dispositions displayed by the child.

* The story/observation – generally with images and/or video.
* Collaboration with the child to garner an understanding of what the child's understanding is rather than personal thoughts on what is happening for the child. This can be recorded alongside the images.
* Reflection and interpretation of the learning (recognising 'What learning is happening here?')
* Next steps (opportunities and possibilities, 'What's next?')
* Linking the story to Aistear as part of assessment of learning.

Stories are often documented in paper books or digitally using an e-portfolio, which can be very easy to share. There is an argument that a paper book/hard copy is easier for the child to access, take home, share with friends or siblings, add to or look at later.

There are many examples of learning stories, and Early Childhood Ireland has examples on its website. See https://www.earlychildhoodireland.ie/work/quality-practice/awards/learning-stories/current-learning-story-winners/.

LEARNING STORY IMPACT

Learning stories have many impacts, including the following:

* Positively influences the child's sense of identity
* Contributes to family engagement, interpretation and contribution
* Directs the children's perspective – children see what they are learning
* Intensifies practitioners' noticing skills
* Helps children feel that they are making a contribution
* Integrates teaching, learning and assessment.

The *Aistear Síolta Practice Guide* has many ideas, templates and samples to help you observe children, plan activities and document their learning. The templates offer various alternative ideas about recording, documenting, assessing and linking your practice to the Aistear themes. Go to https://www.aistearsiolta.ie/en/planning-and-assessing-using-aistears-themes/. Further guidance on the use of the practice guide can be found in Chapter 11.

Information and Communications Technology (ICT)

3

> **This chapter will explore:**
> * online information and internet searches
> * information and communications technology (ICT)
> * technology-enhanced learning (TEL)
> * General Data Protection Regulation (GDPR).

Introduction

This chapter will examine the contribution of ICT, especially its use in and contribution to early learning and care (ELC). Issues relating to copyright and GDPR will also be considered.

Online information and internet searches

There is so much information available now, literally at the click of a mouse, that it is difficult to know what is the most suitable or relevant, what is true and what is fake, what is out of date and what is current, what is gossip and what is as a result of thorough research. For a moment, think about when there was no internet, and then consider the following:

* A group of teenagers are talking about the best trainers to buy and are discussing their preferences, price and so on.
* A group of adults are having a conversation over lunch about young people and drug use.

* An older person relays the method of rubbing 'a little brandy' on a baby's gums to help with teething.

In all the above scenarios, there is context with which to judge the reliability and validity of the information. However, website information comes without such immediate context. Therefore, information found online needs to be thoroughly considered and investigated before a decision is made as to whether the information gleaned is valid and useful.

When looking something up online, be aware of the following:

* All browsers use algorithms that determine the arrangement of the responses to an initial search, but they may not be the most appropriate or useful results for the purposes of the initial request.
* Many websites invest in search engine optimisation (SEO) to improve their visibility in search results. Results occurring further down the list should be considered. (According to some research, over 80 per cent of people never scroll past the first page of their search result.)
* The words used in the search will influence the result of that search.

Think about

When next on a TV or movie streaming website, take note of the percentage match given for a recently viewed series or film. Then search for something you would never usually watch. Take note of the percentage match given for this new search. It will likely be much lower. Consider why this is.

If you visit a library, you are able to go the relevant section, for example 'Education', and scan titles and their contents pages to ascertain which ones are most relevant to your search. So it is with internet searches: use slightly different keywords, refine your search, scroll down the pages to see and consider all the results. (Of course, there is also the danger of scrolling endlessly without finding relevant content!)

Activity

1. Working as part of group, each individual uses a different search engine to look up 'Italy' (or another topic of your choice). Compare your results.
2. Go around to different courses and ask one student on each course to do a search on a particular word or topic. Take note of the first site that comes up in each person's search. As a group, discuss why different people get different results. Discuss how this might affect academic research.

STEPS FOR A SUCCESSFUL INTERNET SEARCH

1. First, clarify the information for which you are looking. This might involve referring to your class notes or going directly to a site that you know is 'official' or derives from a recognised organisation or expert.

2. Use simple terms in your search and be as specific as possible. Know that the results are not always objective and may not be the best answer to your research. This is for you to determine.

3. Evaluate the information on the site. The information is not just the content but also the name of the site – its URL. Does the URL contain a reputable domain name, e.g. '.gov' or '.edu'? Is it sponsored (advertised) content? Crosscheck the validity of any potentially relevant information on other websites. (As mentioned earlier, there are sites available to fact check information.) Consider the date of publication, the author/organisation, and so on.

4. Remember that any information sourced online must also be referenced.

Activity

Carry out some internet searches on subjects about which you are informed and then critically consider the results.

Record-keeping and administrative forms

In order to effectively operate an efficient and compliant ELC service, there are numerous forms to be filled and records to be retained. The following is just a sample of the many forms and administrative documents essential to the running of an ELC service:

* Registration with Tusla
* Fire safety
* Child protection
* Attendance
* Accident and incident forms (see Appendix 3)
* Medicine administration form
* Routines
* Child's daily record (see Appendix 3)
* Child's safeguarding statement.

Go to the Tusla website and examine the samples and templates given there: https://www.tusla.ie/services/pre-school-services/early-years-quality-and-regulatory-framework/sample-policies-and-templates/

Activity

Using the samples/templates available on the Tusla website, write out a policy on food safety (or another topic of your choice). Write out a selective sample of procedures that would support this policy.

DEFINITIONS

A **policy** is an overarching statement of the principles by which all the decisions and actions in an organisation will be guided.

A **procedure** is a step-by-step practical guide on how to act and interact in certain circumstances and in keeping with the policy of the organisation.

ICT and technology-enhanced learning (TEL)

Today, most of the information listed above will be stored online on the ELC service's website so it is important that every employee has some basic ICT skills. It is also a fact that we are living in a digital age when children are able to navigate online resources from a very early age. Every ELC practitioner needs to:

* develop the necessary ICT skills to fill forms and extract information online
* become familiar with TEL to support children's learning experience
* understand the issues that arise from the use of ICT – confidentiality and security, and awareness of the relevant laws and regulations.

WHAT IS ICT?

Information and communications technology (ICT) refers to computer hardware and software, digital cameras and video cameras, the internet, telecommunication tools, programmable toys, e-books, robots and many other devices and resources. It is an ever-expanding area. Numerous studies support the assertion that the use of ICT can enhance and reinforce learning.

While most of us now have basic keyboard skills and can browse the internet, it is important to review what ICT is and know how to use its resources in a formal manner. ICT is an invaluable resource in ELC and can be used in three main ways:

1. In administration and management, to record, maintain and store information electronically, to create databases and to share information with other agencies and organisations
2. To support and communicate with parents and families
3. To support and extend children's learning.

1. IN ADMINISTRATION AND MANAGEMENT

The vast majority of businesses and organisations today share information through their websites. Most form-filling can be accessed and completed online, and with the introduction of electronic signatures administrative tasks such as registration with Tusla, Garda clearance and reporting child protection concerns can now also be completed online.

All children's records (including background information, medical history, daily records and tracking of development) can be stored electronically, which makes it easier for those persons relevant to the child's care and education in ELC to access them.

The collection of data within the centre can be an invaluable aid to the planning and development of the service itself, for example:

* to map attendance – of both staff and children
* to keep track of dietary patterns and issues
* to examine patterns in the use of play equipment, indoor/outdoor play, etc.

How ICT resources are used in any one centre is important. If data is collected merely for the sake of collection, with no clear objectives as to how it is to be used, it can become just another burdensome task for ELC practitioners. Similarly, if resources and access to resources are limited, it can lead to frustration.

Probably most important, all ELC staff should be familiar with the hardware and software available to them, or if such familiarity is not evident, should be facilitated to participate in training.

> There is evidence that most Early Years practitioners have their own mobile phones and computers. They word process and use the email and the internet. Most can use digital audio players (DAPs), CD-ROM and DVD players, and programmable toys. They are, however, less confident in using software for spreadsheets and editing and downloading digital images, still and moving. Not all are confident with interactive whiteboards. (Aubrey and Dahl, 2008, p. 4)

It is important to develop basic ICT skills, which can then be easily transferable for use with different programs.

Activity

1. Learn/revise basic IT skills such as creating, typing, naming and saving a document.
2. Use a spreadsheet to create a table.
3. Use basic word processing skills to create a document. Give it a title page and write a short report using bold, italics, underline, bullets and numbering. Save the document, attach it to an email and send it.

2. TO SUPPORT AND COMMUNICATE WITH PARENTS AND FAMILIES

The obvious use of ICT is to keep in touch with parents on a daily basis, to inform staff of any concerns when children arrive in the centre and to provide a report on the child's day.

Additionally, the organisation website and Facebook page, flyers, newsletters and information leaflets all serve to keep parents informed. These information resources will not replace or supersede personal conversation, but in the course of their busy lives many parents will be able to review the information at a time that suits them. It should also be noted that information shared electronically is less likely to get lost in a busy household.

There are also apps and programs that enable ELC staff to share 'snapshots' during the child's day, which can serve as reassurance for an anxious parent as well as allowing them to feel and be more involved in their child's learning and development.

3. TO SUPPORT AND EXTEND CHILDREN'S LEARNING

In a 2005 survey of 1,852 English parents and carers of children aged 0–6 years, Marsh *et al.* indicated that young children had access to a wide range of media and technologies. Since then, the digital and audio-visual landscape has changed significantly and irrevocably.

The term 'technology-enhanced learning' (TEL) is used to describe the application of technology to teaching and learning. In other words, TEL is any technology that enhances the learning experience. 'Smart' or IoToys ('Internet of Toys'), dance mats, electronic microscopes, robots, interactive whiteboards, drawing pads and touch screens are just some of the resources available to the current generation of children and the adults involved in their education. Learning games and apps abound where one can learn/explore 'virtually' anything. Various research studies have shown that many children can navigate an electronic toy before they can walk. Therefore, it seems reasonable that we move beyond debates about the appropriateness or otherwise of the inclusion of ICT/TEL in children's lives and towards ensuring that these resources become valuable tools in the learning environment.

> ### DEFINITION
> A **smart** or **IoToy** is a device consisting of a physical component – a doll or a teddy bear, for instance – that connects to one or more toy-computing services through Bluetooth or the internet to facilitate cloud gameplay. The toy will also have sensory technology to enhance functions.

There are many benefits to be gained from incorporating ICT into the learning environment. ICT can:

- support children's cognitive and emotional development
- promote the development of social and cooperative skills
- assist in the emergence of early literacy and mathematical thinking

- 'level the playing field' for children with additional learning needs
- enhance and strengthen relationships between children and adults
- give adults new ways to gain insight into children's thinking or their interests, thereby providing opportunities to better support and scaffold children's learning
- facilitate the emergence of 'new literacies' or 'multiliteracies' in children.

(Hill and Broadhurst, 2001; Pastor and Kerns, 1997)

ICT can indeed enhance learning, but as with any other resource or piece of equipment, it is how it is used that will enhance the child's experience and relationships. Therefore, it is incumbent upon those facilitating use of these ICT resources in TEL to apply a process of pedagogical planning.

The Developmentally Appropriate Technology in Early Childhood (DATEC) Project, 'Principles for Developmental Appropriateness of ICT', offers eight general principles for determining the appropriateness of ICT applications to be used in the early years:

1. Ensure an educational purpose.
2. Encourage collaboration.
3. Integrate with other aspects of the curriculum: that is, if children are to understand ICT, they need to see it used in a meaningful context, and for real purposes. This includes allowing for ICT to feature in children's play.
4. The child should be in control: that is, the ICT application should not control the child's interaction through programmed learning or any other behaviourist device.
5. Choose applications that are transparent and intuitive. The 'drag and drop' facility on a computer screen is a good example.
6. Avoid applications that contain violence or stereotyping.
7. Be aware of health and safety issues.
8. Encourage the educational involvement of parents.

(Siraj-Blatchford, I. and Siraj-Blatchford, J., 2000)

In relation to point 4, it is worth noting the difficulty of the child being in control of the application. It is in the nature of the design of devices and programmes that they try to elicit certain responses. In relation to point 6, while it may be easy to spot inappropriate violence, stereotyping is much more insidious. Therefore, ELC practitioners have to be as vigilant about this in relation to ICT/TEL as when using any book or toy.

Some additional benefits to be derived from the appropriate use of TEL including the following:

- Word processors offer the facility to be able to write without having to master the art of pen control.
- TEL can be used with learning stories, where children can be involved in the story, contributing pictures and narrative.

* The environment can be structured in inclusive ways that would have been more difficult without the use of technology. An obvious example is in the area of language, where a child can see the picture and then the word in their native language as well as in the majority language.

ROBOTICS

Robotics is another growing area of TEL. It not only marries new technology with traditional learning methods (trial and error) but also expands the understanding of TEL. The word 'robot' was not coined until the twentieth century, but humans have been dreaming about, making and using robots for hundreds of years, as seen in an exhibition in the Science Museum in London, where the development of robots was traced and the future of robotics examined. One exhibit that gave rise to much discussion was the use of robots in the young child's environment.  The exhibit showed humanoid robots involved with children in various ways: reading a story, playing a board game, and so on. It was evident that the robot could respond (in limited ways) to the child – a big step on from a child listening to an audiobook, for example.

Other benefits of robotics have been identified. Research has shown that 'beginning in pre-kindergarten, children were able to master basic robotics and programming skills, while the older children were able to master increasingly complex concepts using the same robotics kit in the same amount of time' (Sullivan and Bers, 2015, p. 1). In addition to developing computational thinking, educational robots promote the development of other cognitive skills among children and young people.

* **Learning from mistakes:** Children discover that errors are not final, but a source of new conclusions – a valuable lesson for the future.
* **Teamwork:** The group challenge approach encourages socialisation and collaboration.
* **Adaptation:** Because of the growing use of automation and intelligent devices, becoming familiar with the use of robots will help children adapt to the world of tomorrow more easily.
* **Creativity:** The search for solutions and the freedom to assign new functions to these robots stimulates imagination and creativity.
* **Self-esteem:** Achieving success in a new field improves children's self-awareness.
* **Proactive spirit:** In addition to boosting their self-esteem, success in one field stimulates children to take on new tasks in other fields.
* **Self-assessment:** By being able to see the results of their actions instantly, without the need for an adult to tell them whether they have done well or badly, children learn to assess their own performance.

* **Practical applications:** Applying the mathematical or physical knowledge learned in school motivates children and young people to continue studying these subjects.

    (https://www.iberdrola.com/innovation/educational-robots)

ISSUES ARISING FROM THE USE OF ICT IN ELC SETTINGS

Specific areas of concern often raised in relation to TEL and children's ICT use are as follows:

* **Physical effects:** The detrimental physical effect of children's prolonged computer use is often flagged, with the most commonly cited consequences being repetitive strain injury and postural effects from sitting at consoles or computers for long periods.
* **Social effects:** Negative impacts on children's social development are cited, with concerns that computer use will encourage anti-social behaviour, foster isolation or lead to aggressive behaviour.
* **Educational effects:** Educational concerns are raised that computer use can interfere with aspects of children's cognitive development.
* **Emotional effects:** The serious concern is raised about children's exposure to unsuitable content, for example material of a sexual or violent nature, or containing inappropriate gender, cultural or social stereotypes.
* **Behavioural effects:** Concerns are raised that computer use may displace other important learning and play activities.

Activity

Access and read the Barnardos booklet on 'Children and Technology': **https://www.barnardos.ie/media/1496/chidlren-and-technology.pdf**

In relation to the concerns listed therein, think about what safeguards can be put in place. Are there other concerns that might arise in each area? Devise a 'Risk Assessment Checklist' that could be used for ICT in an ELC service.

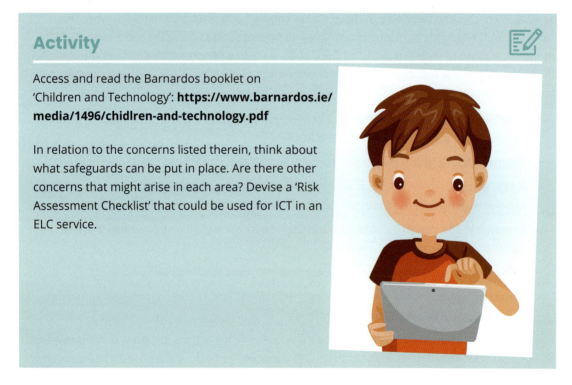

Data protection and GDPR

The General Data Protection Regulation, or GDPR, came into effect in May 2018. It is the main instrument through which the issues of the storage of information and data, information usage, privacy and security breaches are dealt with. All businesses with an online presence that collect and store customer information must comply with GDPR regulations or face considerable penalties.

Parents and guardians are responsible for safeguarding their children's data. Parents are therefore entitled to withhold information if they see fit, and also have corresponding rights:

1. The **Right to Information** about why the service needs the information
2. The **Right of Access** to any details held on file about them or their child
3. The **Right to Rectification** whereby they can request that information be modified if it is incorrect or incomplete
4. The **Right to Erasure** whereby they can ask that some information be deleted
5. The **Right to Restriction of Processing** whereby they can say what can or cannot be done with the information

Adapted from Fogg (2019) *GDPR for Dummies: Simple GDPR Guide for Beginners*

6. The **Right to Data Portability** whereby the service has the ability to share information at the request of the parents with themselves or another service safely and securely
7. The **Right to Object** to any content that is deemed unsuitable, irrelevant or prejudicial
8. The **Right to Avoid Automated Decision-making** whereby profiling or decisions are not made solely based on computed information and without any human involvement.

RECAP QUESTIONS

1. What do the following acronyms stand for? ICT, TEL, GDPR.
2. Identify two ways in which TEL might be used to support a child with an additional need.

Reflective practice

4

> **This chapter will explore:**
> * engaging in reflective practice
> * models of reflective practice
> * Gibbs' Reflective Cycle
> * Kolb's Experiential Learning Cycle
> * Schön's Reflective Model
> * reflective writing.

Introduction

'We do not learn from experience … we learn from reflecting on our experience.'

(John Dewey)

This chapter will focus on how, through use of self-reflection and evaluation, skills and knowledge can be continuously examined, adjusted and improved upon. This helps keep practice fresh and vibrant but also ensures the practitioner is up to date with the constantly evolving trends and research in ELC and that such trends and research are incorporated into the work practice. Models of reflective practice and their integration in ELC work will be investigated. Research indicates that reflective practice is key to personal and professional learning and development. Therefore, approaches to developing this skill using a model of reflection will be addressed.

What is reflective practice?

If we brainstorm the word 'reflection', several images come to mind, for example mirror, thinking, religion, water, photograph. To take the first example: most of us look in the mirror every morning. While doing so, we may fix our hair or straighten our collar. When we are going out to do something important, we are more critical and very conscious of how we look, as we want people to see the best possible version of ourselves.

Reflective practice is, in its simplest form, thinking about or reflecting on what you do. It is directly linked to the concept of learning from experience, in that you think about what you did, how you felt, and then decide from these feelings what you would do differently next time, if indeed you would do anything differently. It is also essential that we reflect when things go well and not get into the habit of only reflecting on an experience when something goes wrong.

> "Reflection is an important human activity in which people recapture their experience, think about it, mull it over and evaluate it. It is this working with experience that is important in learning."
>
> (Boud, Keogh and Walker, 1985, p. 19)

Thinking about what happened is part of being human. However, the difference between casual 'thinking' and 'reflective practice' is that reflective practice requires a conscious effort to think about events/incidents and to develop insights into them. The good news is that reflective practice is a skill which can be learned and developed and once you get into the habit of using reflective practice, you will find it enhances both your professional and personal life.

(https://www.skillsyouneed.com/)

Reflective practice promotes

* greater self-awareness
* emotional intelligence
* questioning of your values, beliefs and attitudes
* informed decision-making
* understanding of the ethical nature of working in ELC
* critical examination of theories underpinning practice
* continuous engagement in a cycle of inquiry and improvement
* challenging practices which are often taken for granted
* identification of gaps in professional knowledge
* the importance of engaging in continuous professional development (CPD).

To become a reflective ELC practitioner, you must

* have an open mind
* be open to new ideas, and willing to change your ways of working
* be proactive in improving your own professional learning and development through observation, cooperation and discussion with other practitioners.

> " Without reflection, we go blindly on our own way, creating more unintended consequences, and failing to achieve anything useful. "
>
> (Wheatley, 2005, p. 262)

Initiatives that support becoming a reflective practitioner

There have been several initiatives in recent years aimed at improving ELC, including two national frameworks – *Síolta* (2006) and *Aistear* (2009) – as well as the introduction of a state-funded pre-school scheme (ECCE) for all young children (2010). (For more information, see Section 2.) Initiatives continue to emerge as the sector moves towards a recognised professional status. Key to many of the initiatives is the need for qualified staff to provide high-quality services. Becoming a reflective practitioner is linked to professionalism and is now considered a professional responsibility of all ELC practitioners.

SÍOLTA AND REFLECTIVE PRACTICE

Síolta proposes that quality early childhood practice is built upon the unique role of the adult. The competencies, qualifications, dispositions and experience of adults, in addition to their capacity to reflect upon their role, are essential components in supporting and ensuring quality experiences for each child.

Standard 11 Professional Practice states:

> Practising in a professional manner requires that individuals have skills, knowledge, values and attitudes appropriate to their role and responsibility within the setting. In addition, it requires regular reflection upon practice and engagement in supported, ongoing professional development. (*Síolta Research Digest* Standard 11 Professional Practice)

Síolta recommends that services support and promote regular opportunities for practitioners to reflect upon and review their practice and contribute positively to the development of quality practice in the setting.

AISTEAR AND REFLECTIVE PRACTICE

Aistear proposes that the role of the adult in early childhood is central because adults enhance learning through a respectful understanding of the child's uniqueness. Early learning takes place through a reciprocal relationship between the adult and the child; sometimes the adult leads the learning, and at other times the child leads. The adult alters the type and amount of support as the child grows in confidence and competence and achieves new things (NCCA, 2009).

Ongoing observation and assessment of what children do, say and make, and reflection on these experiences enables practitioners to plan more developmentally appropriate and meaningful learning experiences for children. This also enables practitioners to improve their own practice. The need to engage in reflective practice is a key message from the Aistear framework. This message is further developed in the *Aistear Síolta Practice Guide* **http://aistearsiolta.ie/en/**.

AISTEAR SÍOLTA PRACTICE GUIDE

The *Aistear Síolta Practice Guide* was developed in 2015 by the National Council for Curriculum and Assessment (NCCA) to support professionals to work with Aistear and Síolta together. It includes examples of quality practice along with self-assessment tools and templates that support reflection and analysis of professional practice (see section 2). As already noted, the practitioner's role is fundamental in supporting all children to learn and develop to their full potential. However, the demands of this role can often be overlooked or misunderstood by parents, other professionals, the community and wider society. The way in which practitioners view, describe and explain their role impacts on how it is seen by others. This image and sense of identity as a professional can, in turn, influence how practitioners feel about their own role, carry out their daily work with children and interact with parents and other professionals.

Activity

This activity is designed to help you as a practitioner to reflect on the importance and complexity of your role in supporting children's early learning and development. It supports you to develop a description of your role which you can share with others. Part 1 of the activity supports you to consider your own role. Part 2 explores your understanding of the role as part of a team or profession.

1. Download and complete the *Aistear Síolta Practice Guide* template (go to **https://www.aistearsiolta.ie/en/** and search 'Activity A Professional Role' to access this PDF file).

2. In groups, discuss and compare your answers, identify similarities and differences and reflect on your answers in comparison to others.

The *Code of Professional Responsibility and Code of Ethics for Early Years Educators* (2020), published by the Professionalisation Sub-Group of the Early Years Forum, outlines the values and ethics that should underpin the duties and responsibilities of those working in the ELC sector. One of these values is to 'engage in critical reflection' (p. 22). This document also notes the important of collaboration with colleagues to 'generate a culture of continual reflection and renewal of best practices in early childhood education and care' (p. 18). Therefore, reflective practice should include individual and group reflection within services.

The *Code of Professional Responsibility and Code of Ethics for Early Years Educators* (2020) is available from http://www.limerickchildcare.ie/wp-content/uploads/2015/06/Code-of-Professional-Responsibilities-and-Code-of-Ethics-for-Early-Years-Educators.pdf.

Models of reflective practice

The models of reflective practice described here are useful learning tools to enable you to become familiar with the process of reflection.

GIBBS' REFLECTIVE CYCLE

In order to use this cycle, think of a personal event or activity that you have been involved in and apply the following reflective steps.

STEP 1: DESCRIPTION

During this step, you describe the event in detail, without drawing any immediate conclusions. The most common questions that can help create an objective description are:

* What happened?
* When did it happen?
* Where did it happen?
* Who was involved?
* What did I do myself?
* What did other people do?
* What was the result of these actions?

All details of the event are vital, including why other people were involved and their role, as this will provide a better understanding of what happened. Otherwise, the practitioner may make choices about what they think is important while leaving out vital information. All information that is key to a better understanding of the event is relevant.

STEP 2: FEELINGS

This phase is about the feelings that the event triggered, as well as what your thoughts were as described in Step 1. The intention is not to discuss the feelings in detail or comment on them directly. Emotions do not need to be evaluated or judged at this stage. Awareness is the most critical goal of this phase. Helpful questions include:

* What did I feel leading up to the event?
* What did I feel during the event?
* What did I feel after the event?
* How do I look back on this event?
* What do I think other people felt during the event?
* How do I think others feel about the event now?

Because people often have difficulty talking about their feelings, it helps that they are encouraged by the questions or someone asking these questions. This also demonstrates that Gibbs' Reflective Cycle can be used in an individual setting or in a mentoring or supervision setting. The final two questions also allow one to see the event from other people's perspectives.

STEP 3: EVALUATION

In this step, you ask yourself whether the experience of the event in Step 1 was good or bad. Which approach worked well and why? Which approach did not work as well and why? It can be difficult for people to be objective about an event. To conduct a proper evaluation, the following questions may be helpful:

- What went well during the event?
- Why was that?
- What did not go so well?
- Why was that?
- What was my contribution?
- What contribution did other people make?

It is worth evaluating good and bad experiences, and the subsequent steps in this Reflective Cycle help people learn from such experiences.

STEP 4: ANALYSIS

This analysis is often done together alongside Step 3 and concerns what you have learned from the event. Because of the experience, you now know what to do in similar future situations. This means that both positive and negative things and/or problems you experienced will be written down and analysed individually. People with a growth mindset often learn more when things go wrong.

STEP 5: CONCLUSION

Here you take a step back and look at yourself from a distance, asking what else you could have done during the event. The information gathered earlier is very valuable in this step and can encourage you to come to a useful conclusion. The following questions may be helpful:

- To what positive experience did the event lead?
- To what negative experience did the event lead?
- What would I do differently if the event were to happen again in the future?
- Which skills do I need to develop for a similar event in the future?

STEP 6: ACTION PLAN

In this final step, actions are developed for future events. Based on the conclusions reached in Step 5, people make concrete promises to themselves. The intention is to keep these promises. If everything went well, you could promise yourself to act the same way next time. In areas where things did not go so well, you can promise yourself not to make the same mistakes again, asking yourself what would be a more effective approach and which change will lead to actual improvement. In addition to an action plan, it is wise to plan on how to encourage yourself to stick to these promises.

(Adapted from *What is Gibbs Reflective Cycle?*: https://www.toolshero.com/management/gibbs-reflective-cycle-graham-gibbs/)

Thinking about one's own experience can help us to perform better or to do things differently in the future. As the above shows, these experiences do not have to be positive; negative experiences are also helpful. Gibbs' Reflective Cycle stimulates you to think long and hard about how to do things better next time – the core of reflective practice. People do not just learn to understand certain events better, but also learn to judge how the same event can be handled in different ways in the future.

Activity

Working in groups, read the following scenario and then devise a template based on Gibbs' Reflective Cycle that you could use to reflect on Jenny's experience. Adapt the template as required based on your own personal experiences in ELC.

> Jenny was looking forward to her placement and had planned to make playdough with the children. However, on her arrival at her placement she realised she had forgotten the recipe provided by her teacher. She decided to go ahead, but the result was a very wet, sticky dough, which was soon unmanageable for the children. Jenny was disappointed with the outcome and felt she had let herself and her placement down.

KOLB'S EXPERIENTIAL LEARNING CYCLE

Concrete experience
(doing/having an experience)

Reflective observation
(reviewing/reflecting on the experience)

Abstract conceptualisation
(concluding/learning from the experience)

Active experimentation
(planning/trying out what you have learned)

Kolb's Experiential Learning Cycle emphasises the central role that experience plays in the learning process. Just as Jean Piaget proposed that children are active agents in their own learning, Kolb's model proposes that adults are active agents in their own learning. This learning cycle involves four stages.

Stage 1: The cycle begins with a **Concrete Experience** as a result of doing something.

Stage 2: The second stage of **Reflective Observation** means taking time out from 'doing', stepping back from the task and reviewing what has been done and experienced. At this point, lots of questions can be asked of self and others as to how the experience went.

Stage 3: The third stage of **Abstract Conceptualisation** is the process of making sense of what has happened and interpreting the activity or event based on whether or not you were satisfied with the outcome.

Stage 4: The final stage of **Active Experimentation** is where the learner considers how they are going to put what they have learned into practice. If everything went well, it may mean refining the activity/event to make it even better; if things did not go well, this is the time to plan how you will undertake the activity/event in the future to try to improve the outcome.

In summary, three elements are central to Kolb's model:

1. Emphasis is on the 'here and now' of concrete experiences.
2. Ideas are not fixed and unchangeable but are formed and re-formed again through reflecting on experiences.
3. Feedback from experienced practitioners and your placement supervisor can provide the basis for continuous learning and further evaluation of your work.

SCHÖN'S REFLECTIVE MODEL

REFLECTION IN ACTION

Reflecting as something happens
* Consider the situation
* Decide how to act
* Act immediately

REFLECTION ON ACTION

Reflecting after something happens
* Reconsider the situation
* Think about what needs changing for the future

Another approach is the work of Donald Schön. Schön (1991) distinguishes between 'reflection in action' and 'reflection on action'.

'Reflection in action' is reflection during the 'doing' stage; that is, reflecting on the incident while it can still benefit your learning. This is carried out during an activity/event rather than after the event when you might reflect on how you would do things differently in the future. This is an efficient method of reflection as it allows you to react and change an incident/event at the time it happens.

For example, you may be reading a story to the children and you can see they are not as interested as you would like them to be. Your reflection in action may prompt you to make the story more appealing for the children by changing your voice for the various characters in the book, which may help the children pay more attention.

At the end of the storytelling, you may reflect again on whether or not your strategy worked. This is called 'reflection on action'. Based on this, you may decide to rehearse how you will read the story and think of how props can also be used to further sustain the children's interest.

Reflective practice in ELC

OBSERVING MORE EXPERIENCED PRACTITIONERS

Attending professional practice placement is key to developing your ELC professional skills. There is no doubt that this may be a daunting prospect but, as many learners report, this is often the most satisfying part of their course. The combination of academic learning and placement in an ELC service is without question the most active method of learning. Observing and learning from more experienced practitioners is central to your professional development. Some of these practitioners will have worked in ELC for several years and may display a level of expertise in their work from which you can learn, and which can support you in bringing your academic learning to life in a positive way for you and the children. It is worth noting that services will welcome the new ideas and ways of working that you bring with you based on your studies.

WORKING WITH BABIES, TODDLERS AND YOUNG CHILDREN

Your course of study will require you to carry out and evaluate observation of babies, toddlers and young children. In preparation for this it is important that you work in a way that helps you to become familiar with the children and their routines. The children will be curious about you too, and learners often report children becoming attached simply because they are a new and friendly face in the service. It is a known fact that children like novelty, and you will be a novelty for them until they get used to you being there. As you carry out observations of the children, you will have the opportunity to link theory to practice, which is how you will gain a deeper understanding of children's overall growth and development and how you can contribute to their holistic wellbeing. When we speak of children's holistic development, we are referring to their physical, intellectual, language, emotional, social, moral and spiritual needs. These areas of development are closely linked to the Aistear themes of wellbeing, identity and belonging, communicating, and exploring and thinking. Again, careful observation helps you to reflect on and learn from others the most effective ways of meeting children's needs.

Physical	Gross and fine motor skills
Intellectual	Also referred to as cognitive development; includes thinking, memory and problem solving
Language	Speech and body language
Emotional	Feelings and sense of wellbeing
Social	Playing, sharing and taking turns with other children
Moral	Understanding the difference between right and wrong
Spiritual	Seeing the beauty in nature and the environment

As you work with babies, toddlers and young children, you must support their development in each of these areas. You can do this by linking theory to your practice and through observation and reflection on your experiences in placement.

OBSERVING FAMILY MEMBERS AND THEIR INTERACTIONS WITH CHILDREN AND STAFF IN ELC

It is a well-understood concept that parents are the primary educators of their children and that primary socialisation occurs within the family. Secondary socialisation occurs in ELC services. Bronfenbrenner's bioecological theory outlines the importance of working in partnership with families in the care of children.

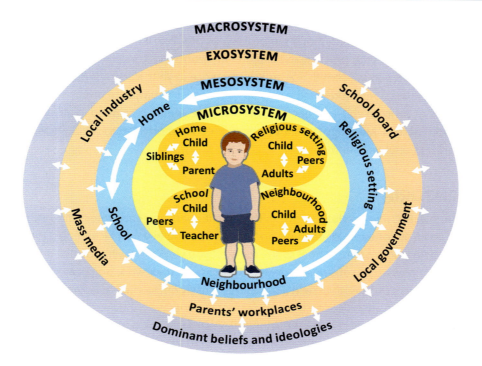

Bronfenbrenner's theory

Like fish in the ocean, people exist as part of an ecosystem, with each person having their own immediate social microsystem (Landon, 2014). Parents, families and ELC staff all form part of a child's 'microsystem' and positive interactions between all involved will create a good balance for children's sense of wellbeing and belonging. As an ELC professional, you should observe the interactions between parents/guardians, children and staff as they arrive and depart the service. These interactions are vital learning points for all concerned and how children relate to these transitions should be noted. It is important that children enter the service feeling safe and secure, as we know this can build children's confidence in their surroundings. A warm welcome first thing in the morning provides opportunities for building positive relationships for all concerned, while ending the day on a positive note is equally good for all. It is not unknown for children to ignore their parents when they arrive to collect them and reassuring parents that this reaction is okay is important.

> Partnership involves parents, families and practitioners working together to benefit children. Each recognises, respects and values what the other does and says. Partnership involves responsibility on both sides. (NCCA, 2009, p. 7)

LEARNING FROM SUPERVISION WHILE ON PROFESSIONAL PRACTICE PLACEMENT

As part of your professional practice placement, you will have regular supervision with your supervisor to support you in your work. This one-to-one support is a valuable method of promoting effective practice. This is a specially dedicated time for the supervisor to support and listen to you, which in turn enables you to continuously improve your practice. It provides you with an opportunity to reflect on your practice and explore any worries or concerns you may have and contributes to you developing confidence and competence in your work. It is important that you contribute to these sessions by keeping a journal of the areas you wish to discuss and to seek advice for areas of concern you may have. A time and date should be agreed in advance that is suitable for both parties. Meetings should be documented and referred to regularly to reflect on continuing professional development.

PEER MENTORING

Peer mentoring in ELC involves learning from the practitioners you encounter daily in your placement/s and from other students both on your course and in your placement/s. Whether in a baby room, toddler room or pre-school room, the staff you work with will provide you with valuable learning opportunities as you observe, reflect and learn from their work practices. Further discussion with others on your course in a structured classroom session, where learners individually and collectively reflect on their placement experiences, is invaluable as you learn from each other how different services operate. In this way, possible solutions can be found if you experience difficulties in your service.

The following are some peer reflection activities that can be completed on a regular basis using the model of reflective practice chosen by the college/centre.

Activity 1

This activity can be utilised on a regular basis to include post-placement discussions or discussion on activities to be carried out on placement. In small groups and using active listening skills, discuss your first placement experience under the following headings:

* Induction
* Type of service
* Number of children
* Number of staff
* Various rooms for children and age groups
* Supervision experience
* Your experience and learning
* Your feelings
* Action plans for the future.

Now feedback the information gathered in your group to the wider class.

Activity 2

In small groups and using active listening skills, discuss your placement experience under the following headings:

* What went well?
* What did not go well?
* What were your feelings?
* Who was there when the activity/event was going on?
* How will you change things in the future?
* What was your overall learning?

Now feedback the information gathered in your group to the wider class.

It is good to remember that learners who attentively listen to and support each other in the ELC course will help to make the journey to becoming an ELC professional a more engaging, enjoyable and rewarding one for everyone.

REFLECTIVE LEARNING JOURNAL

Many ELC courses will require learners to present a reflective learning journal as part of their assessment. This journal could include:

1. Reflection on the daily timetable/routines. Would you change anything?
2. Reflection on Aistear/Siolta in action
3. Reflection on communication and teamwork in the setting
4. Reflection on your supervision experience
5. Reflection on your own personal learning and development.

The evidence for each entry will include a reflection using the stages of a chosen model of reflective practice.

There are various structures to adhere to when reflecting on your work or learning, but for the purposes of this chapter the focus will be on writing a reflective journal. The structure of a reflective learning journal is flexible, and you can be creative and take an approach that suits your style. However, reflective writing should include an examination of the following:

1. Description of the task
2. The learner's feelings, attitudes and values
3. The key learning that took place
4. Changes as a result of the reflection.

1. DESCRIPTION OF THE TASK

Consider these two descriptions of the one task by the same practitioner.

> **Description 1:** I placed four chairs in a circle and I selected a number of books. Then I invited the children to come and sit down. Together we chose which book to read. It was *Farmer Duck*.

> **Description 2:** I placed the chairs in a circle for the children to sit in. I then went to choose some books, and this took quite a while as I was feeling uncertain about what the children might like. When choosing which book to read, all the children were shouting out different choices. I was feeling a bit panicky as I had no experience on how to move the children forward. I knew the story of *Farmer Duck* so I suggested we might start with that and the children agreed.

Both descriptions of the task could have continued to include a synopsis of the story, how the children reacted and so on. Dialogue could also be recorded.

As demonstrated in the second description, an account of feelings (subjective) can be an integral part of the recount of what happened. It does not have to stick to objective facts.

2. THE LEARNER'S FEELINGS, ATTITUDES AND VALUES

This is where you might explain the reasons why you did what you did, the way you did it and why you were feeling the way you did.

For example, considering the sample descriptions above, why were only four chairs chosen? Perhaps the activity was planned that way; perhaps only four children were present in the room. Why was the particular book selected? Why were the children not involved in selecting the book? Why might there have been feelings of uncertainty as to what the children might like? Why were there feelings of panic? Was there fear that some children would be upset, that the situation would get out of hand? Was the supervisor looking in on the activity and causing feelings of nervousness?

Description 2 demonstrates that the practitioner took control by deciding what to read; description 1 does not show this.

Skills of interpretation might be strengthened here by examining how child development theory might interpret the event. Did the children have choices or control? In this case, they did not. You could even analyse the story that was chosen (in this instance, in which the animals also had no choice at first!).

3. THE KEY LEARNING THAT TOOK PLACE

The following terms may be helpful prompts in considering and discussing key learning:

* Looking back ...
* I now understand that ...
* Having experienced ...
* I now realise ...
* I will need to ... in future
* Faced with a similar situation in the future I would ...

4. CHANGES AS A RESULT OF THE REFLECTION

In relation to the example above, you might now understand that the practitioner was new in the placement and should have consulted more with the room supervisor at the planning stage. You might also recognise that the practitioner did not want to seem needy or lacking in confidence so wanted to showcase their skills. You might also recognise that consulting with the children about the choice of book earlier might have made for an easier reading session. In future, the practitioner might plan to give themselves more time observing colleagues before embarking on an activity. They might consider taking on activities about which they feel very confident in order to allow time for their confidence to grow in other areas.

As noted in Chapter 1, writing takes practice, and reflective writing is no different. It is good practice to take a few minutes at the end of the day to reflect on classes: what you learned, what was interesting and why you were particularly interested, what was boring and why. Alternatively, reflect on an event outside college that you did or did not enjoy.

When doing your reflective journal for your assessment tasks, take notes at each stage of the activity or event, from planning to afterwards. It may not all be used, but it will help you to reflect on what actually happened. Even a few hours after an event, things are seen and remembered differently and consequently interpreted differently. It is important to remember that, irrespective of assessment, reflection now and throughout your career is essential to your continued growth as a professional.

RECAP QUESTIONS

1. Name and describe how two national initiatives that support engaging in reflective practice.
2. Discuss three models of reflective practice.

Personal and professional development

5

This chapter will explore:
* personal and professional development
* personal wellbeing
* values, beliefs and mindsets
* qualities and skills
* skills audit.

Introduction

In the ELC programme, the learner will complete a course of study consisting of centre-based directed learning, self-directed learning and work-based learning. While personal and professional development is an ongoing process, it can be said that work-based learning draws out real-life learning where practical, hands-on experience is really authenticated.

Supervised professional practice placements are an integral part of ELC training programmes and they foster the development of personal and professional competence in learners. Professional practice placements offer opportunities to observe experienced practitioners, children, families and other learners. As part of experiential learning, the learner will have opportunities to apply theory to practice, carry out child observations, implement inclusive activities, demonstrate care skills, try new experiences and reflect individually and as a part of a group.

The combination of work-based and centre-based active learning will provide the foundations for the development of the learner's personal and professional knowledge, skills and competence.

> " To learn something new, apply it in your work and seeing a resulting benefit for a child is rewarding, not just for the child but for you as a professional – to know that you have truly made a difference in that child's life. "
>
> (Graham and McDermott, 2010, p. 2)

Personal and professional development

In any work that involves us interacting and working with others, our personal qualities and skills are as important as our theoretical knowledge and professional skills. It is true to say that both personal development and professional development are equally important; in fact, they are interdependent, particularly in the ELC sector where the landscape of learning is ever-changing for both the practitioners and the children. The professional skills and knowledge that you acquire through training and studying and how they are incorporated into your practice is very much influenced by your personal skill set. Your personal skill set is in turn influenced by your values and beliefs. This chapter will explore values, beliefs, mindsets, qualities and skills. It is also essential for your professional development that you engage with the themes and guidelines for good practice as outlined in Aistear and the principles, standards and components of quality as reflected in Síolta.

In the *Aistear Principles and Themes* document, the section 'Children's connections with others' is particularly relevant to the topic of personal and professional development because it defines the adult's role.

> **Early learning takes place through a reciprocal relationship between the adult and the child – sometimes the adult leads the learning and sometimes the child leads. The adult enhances learning through a respectful understanding of the child's uniqueness. He/she alters the type and amount of support as the child grows in confidence and competence and achieves new things.** (NCCA, 2009, p. 9)

This principle clearly states that the adult's relationship with the child is hugely important, and in order to enhance the development of this relationship the adult must be very aware of their own personal and professional competencies. *Síolta* (2006) is also based on principles and these principles are the core values that guide the way we work in ELC services, how we organise our services, how we relate to children, families and each other, the content of what we teach and the way in which it is taught. *Síolta* Standard 11 Professional Practice is most relevant to the topic of personal and professional development.

> **Practising in a professional manner requires that individuals have skills, knowledge, values and attitudes appropriate to their role and responsibility within the setting. In addition, it requires regular reflection upon practice and engagement in supported, ongoing professional development.** (*Síolta Research Digest* **Standard 11 Professional Practice**)

From this it is clear to see that Aistear and Síolta have the same philosophy even though their focus is different. Both frameworks primarily support the adult's role in providing early learning and care for babies, toddlers and young children. Both frameworks are invaluable and should be used on a daily basis and be integral to all policy and decision-making in ELC settings.

> **DEFINITIONS**
>
> **Personal development** is an ongoing process of identifying, challenging and improving one's qualities, beliefs and values.
>
> **Professional development** is an ongoing process of identifying, challenging and improving one's knowledge, skills and competencies.

Personal and professional development is an integral part of the lifelong learning process. The effectiveness of our personal and professional development depends largely on our desire to grow and develop as a person. People choose many different methods of self-development, for example attending courses, referring to self-help books, websites, apps, etc. This chapter introduces just two approaches: the 'High Five' principles and *ikigai*.

THE 'HIGH FIVE' PRINCIPLES

Dealing constructively with stress both in our personal and working life is essential to our personal wellbeing. We all need certain levels of stress to help us perform to the best of our ability, but too much stress and anxiety can have the opposite effect. The 'High Five' principles provide a way of thinking that may help us to cope and deal with the pressures of life.

1. CHANGE IS CONSTANT

'To change is difficult, not to change can be fatal.' (William Pollard)

By accepting change is going to happen in our future, we are taking the first steps towards addressing any stress or anxiety associated with that change. When we are not amenable to change, we are much more likely to complain and have feelings of helplessness, leading to feelings of stress and anxiety. It is worth noting that while we cannot control changes in life, we can control how we react.

2. LEARNING IS LIFELONG

'Education is no load to carry.' (Proverb)

Learning should be looked at as a journey that never ends. In order to handle the challenges that a changing world can bring, it makes sense to constantly update our understanding of the world.

3. FOCUS ON THE JOURNEY

Get to know yourself and do not get too obsessed with your destination. Try to enjoy the process of getting to your destination. There will be opportunities, relationships, situations and possibilities that can bring you joy and fulfillment; for example, working in an ELC setting will offer you rewards that you may never have experienced before.

4. SEEK SUPPORT

'It's okay not to be okay.' (World Mental Health campaign)

Learn how to ask for help. It is very important to be able to talk to somebody if you are not okay. Share your experiences with others and ask for support if you need it. Common humanity means that we will all need compassion at some points in our lives. Sometimes we are giving support and other times we will receive support.

5. FOLLOW YOUR HEART

Dare to dream and anything is possible. Sometimes your dreams can be threatened by your self-doubts and pressures from society; however, the more effort you make to know yourself and believe in yourself the stronger you become. Be compassionate and kind to yourself.

(Adapted from *Reach+: Career and College Preparation Programme*, 2020)

IKIGAI

'Essentially, *ikigai* is the reason why you get up in the morning.' (Yukari Mitsuhashi)

As well as dealing with pressures in our lives and trying to live our lives as the best versions of ourselves, we all need motivation, whether from within or external to ourselves. To be motivated requires setting goals, but first we must know what we want to achieve and why. *Ikigai* is a very old Japanese concept that essentially means we all need a reason to get up every day and have a sense of purpose, meaning and direction to where our lives may take us. *Ikigai* has four core concepts related to work and other practices in life: passion, mission, vocation and payment.

Activity

Working on your own, look at each of the four concepts of *ikigai* and answer honestly in relation to your own life and work.

* Passion: What do you love to do? For example, 'Education and learning'.
* Mission: What are you good at? For example, 'I like caring, helping, teaching children'.
* Vocation: Does society need what you are good at?
* Payment: Can you get paid for it?

Values, beliefs and mindsets

Our underlying beliefs contribute to our values, and our mindset is a collection of our beliefs. As we go through our lives, our beliefs and values may change but they are largely influenced by our socialisation: family, friends, culture, education and religion.

Our core beliefs are ideas or philosophies that we hold very strongly and deeply. They are referred to as being 'core' as they are deeply held ideas at the centre of our belief system. These ideas are usually developed in childhood or early in adult life. Good and bad experiences of life and of other people generally lead to the development of positive or negative ideas about yourself. Core beliefs fall into three categories: beliefs about yourself, beliefs about other people and beliefs about the world.

Our values are basically derived from our long-held and fundamental beliefs. Values become the standards by which we judge people, actions or social movements. Our personal values are what we consider to be fundamentally important to ourselves. They could be family, friendship, success, kindness; the list is endless. Our moral values are those by which we judge whether something or someone is right or wrong. If we live according to our beliefs and values, we tend to be happier and less stressed than if we act against them, which might lead to us feeling dissatisfied or guilty.

To value something means it has importance. For example, if you value the concept of fostering positive relationships with children based on mutual respect, then your behaviour as an early years practitioner will be very different than it will be if you place more value on your ability to control and regulate children so that you have an orderly room where everyone does as they are told.

To explore our core beliefs and values, we need to examine them.

Activity

Have a look at the diagram on the following page and then consider the following areas and your own core beliefs and values in relation to them:

* your childhood
* your adolescence
* your loved ones
* your friends
* your community
* your leisure activities.

What did you value in the past? What do you value now?

What did you believe in the past? What do you believe now?

Have your beliefs and values changed? If so, why?

Write down what your values are today and what you believe is a true way to live your life.

How do the beliefs and values you have just identified affect your attitudes and behaviour as an early years professional?

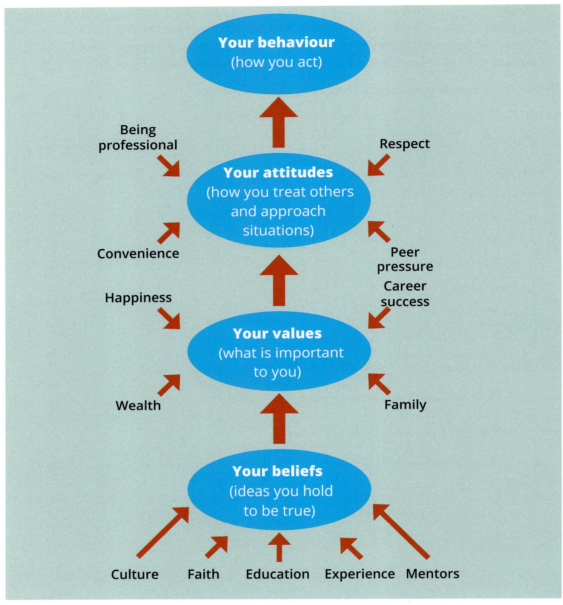

Our needs also affect our behaviour and how we act (or fail to act) on our beliefs and values. Abraham Maslow first introduced the idea of a hierarchy of needs in 1943. It is a motivational theory in psychology comprising a five-tier model of human needs, often depicted as hierarchical levels within a pyramid. From the bottom up, the needs are:

* Physiological (food and clothing)
* Safety (job security)
* Love and belonging (friendship)
* Esteem
* Self-actualisation.

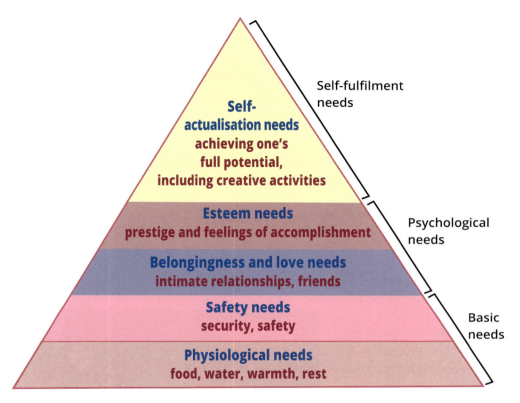

Think about and Discuss

Think about and discuss this statement as a group: 'It is the belief that needs lower down in the hierarchy must be satisfied before you can attend to needs higher up.'

This model explains the forces that motivate people. The more motivated you feel, the more inclined you are to push yourself through that which may be holding you back and hence climb to the next level.

For example, when you find yourself in a new social group, such as in college, you can expect to feel anxious because at this moment you are at Maslow's third level, needing to feel accepted in this new group. Some may be motivated to gain the respect of their peers because of their need for social esteem. It is important to remember that everyone in the classroom is on some level of Maslow's hierarchy and is therefore feeling the need for acceptance to some degree, and to be conscious of the different types of personalities that exist within a group. Having the solid grounding of your own beliefs and values will help you to navigate the various demands that people or situations make on you

The order of needs as defined by Maslow may or may not tally with your own beliefs and ideas, which may trigger a thought process whereby you consider your own beliefs and values.

Activity

Working on your own, consider your responses to these questions:

1. What makes you happiest? What makes you sad?
2. What makes you feel good?
3. What kind of material on social media makes you feel uncomfortable and why?
4. If you could change three things about the world, what would they be?

What beliefs and values can you identify from your answers?

Mindsets

The term 'mindset' refers to a way of thinking about ourselves and the world. It is a collection of our own thoughts and beliefs. The view we adopt for ourselves or about ourselves profoundly affects the way we lead our lives. It can determine whether we set ourselves up for success or failure. Dweck (2017) distinguishes between two important mindsets: a fixed mindset and a growth mindset

People who have a fixed mindset believe that intelligence is fixed and static. They believe that intelligence is determined at birth and cannot be changed. People with a growth mindset believe that intelligence can be developed and increased. They have a focus on a desire to learn and embrace challenges. They are open to learning from criticism.

Somebody with a fixed mindset may be scared to challenge themselves lest they fail, as anything that challenges a fixed intelligence challenges self-worth or self-esteem. For example, a child with a fixed mindset might give up a difficult jigsaw, as they believe that if they were smart enough they should be able to complete it without much effort. Other children welcome such challenges. Dweck maintains that praising children for being bright, smart or clever inculcates a fixed mindset, and rather that praising children for working hard, learning from mistakes and being open to learning new ways of doing things creates or moves them towards a growth mindset. Research has shown that if you grade a child or a student with a 'not yet' grade instead of a fail grade, they are more likely to try again and succeed. Of course, most of us have a mixture of these two mindsets.

A fixed mindset may be developed into a growth mindset in the following ways:

* Embrace challenges.
* See challenges as opportunities for learning.

- Persist in the face of setbacks.
- Understand that the effort is part of the journey.
- Tap into your 'calling': why did you choose this career or vocation?

People skills and qualities

People skills are a combination of interpersonal and intrapersonal skills. Interpersonal skills are a combination of the skills one needs to be able to work well with others. Examples include verbal and non-verbal communication, organisation, negotiation, teamwork, time management, self-awareness, conflict management, empathy and diplomacy. Intrapersonal skills are a combination of the skills one needs to be able to manage one's own attitudes and emotions. Examples include emotional intelligence, empathy, reflection, self-regulation and perseverance.

Activity

Working on your own, rate and then reflect on your responses to these 15 statements as 'not at all', 'rarely', 'sometimes', 'often' or 'very often'.

1. I can recognise my emotions as I experience them.
2. I lose my temper when I feel frustrated.
3. People have told me that I'm a good listener.
4. I know how to calm myself down when I feel anxious or upset.
5. I enjoy organising groups.
6. I find it hard to focus on something over the long term.
7. I find it difficult to move on when I feel frustrated or unhappy.
8. I know my strengths and weaknesses.
9. I avoid conflict and negotiations.
10. I feel that I don't enjoy my work.
11. I ask people for feedback on what I do well and how I can improve.
12. I set long-term goals and review my progress regularly.
13. I find it difficult to read other people's emotions.
14. I struggle to build rapport with others.
15. I use active listening skills when people speak to me.

(https://positivepsychology.com/emotional-intelligence-tests/)

Transversal skills are skills that can be used in a wide variety of situations and work settings. They are often referred to as core skills, basic skills or soft skills, and are the cornerstone for the personal development of an individual. Examples include organisation, planning, creativity, problem solving, critical thinking, effective communication, teamwork, patience and using initiative.

A quality is a distinctive attribute or characteristic possessed by someone or something. Examples include dependability, loyalty, open-mindedness, creativity, adaptability, willingness to learn, empathy, patience, honesty, charisma and passion.

> A skills audit is a written document that clearly lays out all the skills you currently have and how advanced those skills are. It will also document what skills you need for your chosen career, where the gaps are in your skill set and how you can gain the skills you need.
>
> Each and every one of us has people skills, transversal skills, qualities, values and beliefs. Some of these are stronger than others and some may need to be challenged in order to develop personally and professionally.
>
> The origin of your skills, qualities, values and beliefs, whether acquired through work, education or leisure, is irrelevant. It is how they are used that is important. The fact that you may have learned them in one area and are capable of transferring to another context is also invaluable.

A skills audit and goal setting could be facilitated using *Aistear Síolta Practice Guide* templates (Curriculum Foundations: Element 4; Professional Practice; Activity D); alternatively, other templates can be found online, for example at www.jobs.ie.

Activity

Identify the skills required in the following job description and match them with your skill set. (Two have been completed for you.)

JOB DESCRIPTION: ELC QQI LEVEL 5

Role: To support and assist in the provision of full-time day care of the highest quality in a holistic setting for children from birth to six years

Reports to: The supervisor

Duties and Responsibilities

- Be willing to work with children of various ages from babies to after-school children
- Perform a variety of tasks, such as nappy changing, toileting, sterilising, feeding, nap supervision and engaging in play
- Conduct observations of children under the direction of the room leader
- Follow the policies and procedures of the service at all times
- Clean, tidy and put away equipment and toys after use

- Coordinate the implementation of activities suitable for different age groups
- Maintain room and equipment, to ensure the health and safety of children at all times
- Ensure a good standard of hygiene
- Organise materials and toys to the benefit of children
- Support children's development – emotional, social, physical and cognitive – in carrying out activities
- Attend meetings and undergo training as required
- Be aware of child protection procedures and advise manager should you have any concerns about a child
- Maintain strict confidentiality
- Perform other reasonable and relevant duties as may be assigned from time to time

Person specifications
- Minimum QQI Level 5 in ELC
- Minimum one year's work experience with different ages of children
- Ability to work as part of a team
- Kindness, warmth and responsiveness to the needs of children
- Good communication and relating skills with children, staff and parents
- Sense of humour
- Knowledge of relevant legislation and regulations
- First aid
- Complete Garda vetting

(Adapted from https://www.earlychildhoodireland.ie/wp-content/uploads/2015/08/Job-Description-Early-Childhood-Educator.pdf)

Skills required for job	My skills
Organise materials and toys to the benefit of children	I have excellent organisational skills. I am very aware of how important it is to organise the materials and toys so the children can access them easily and play with their favourite toy.
Attend meetings and undergo training as required	I am quite shy and may need to work on this.

RECAP QUESTIONS

1. Outline the difference between personal and professional development.
2. Give some examples of qualities and skills you may need to work in the ELC sector.

Planning, goal setting and portfolio production

This chapter will explore:
- planning
- goal setting
- professional practice portfolio
- continucus professional development
- ongoing developments in the sector.

Introduction – The importance of planning

Planning is the process of making plans for something. It is a thinking process that is open to change, and it provides direction for action.

The importance of planning cannot be overemphasised; from starting your own career to the last stages of your working life, planning will be the most important tool that you use throughout each stage. You may be familiar with the saying: 'Fail to prepare, prepare to fail' (Benjamin Franklin). It is a simple concept but very true. When you plan ahead, you can anticipate what is going to happen and be prepared. For example, if you are going to a meeting where you will discuss your progress to date with the professional practice placement supervisor you must be prepared.

How do you prepare? Your planning for this can start weeks ahead by ensuring you are being competent in all areas and also ensuring that you are organising and implementing the required activities on placement. If, for example, you are unsure if you are competent in a certain area, you could ask your supervisor for some advice or guidance. This will also help you progress in your professional practice placement.

There are three types of planning: **short**, **medium** and **long term**.

* Short-term planning is the type of planning that one does every 2–3 days.
* Medium-term planning is planning within a 2–3-week period.
* Long-term planning is a yearly plan.

Career goals

Part of your professional development plan is setting career goals. Goals should be set using a short-, medium- and long-term planning approach and using clear objectives. Once your goals or intended outcomes are set, you should adopt the SMART technique to turn the intended outcome into an action. Both planning and objectives are important because they give you a focus and also draw on your skills, competence, personal strengths, experiences and interests. Examples of planning include the following:

* A short-term goal (over a period of 4–6 days) might be: 'I am going to get to know the names of all the children in the room I am working in during the first week of my professional practice placement.'
* A medium-term goal (over a period of 4–6 weeks) might be: 'I am going to plan and implement an inclusive activity for a small group of children in the room I am working in on my professional practice placement.'
* A long-term goal (over a period of a year) might be: 'I am going to complete all my assignments in college and attend the required hours in ELC placement.'

Let's take a look at the short-term goal and apply the SMART technique.

Specific: I will get to know the children's first names in my first week of professional practice placement.

Measurable: I will try to remember at least three names each day and build up my memory by writing them down and recalling something about each child whose name I remember.

Achievable: I can practise by talking to the children and using their first name each time.

Realistic: I will be in the professional practice placement for at least four hours per day working with the same group of children.

Time-bound: I will know all their names by the end of the first week.

S	**specific**
M	**measurable**
A	**achievable**
R	**realistic**
T	**time-bound**

Continuous professional development (CPD)

When considering the importance of CPD in the ELC sector, think about a car mechanic who has trained in the 1970s but has no knowledge or experience of working with electric cars. Would that mechanic be able to work effectively with this modern mechanism? Only if they had continually updated their knowledge and skills and knew of recent developments in the car manufacturing industry (Graham and McDermott, 2010).

Similarly, there have been huge developments in the ELC sector, with vast amounts of research giving us a greater understanding of children's abilities and needs. Therefore, it is incumbent upon ELC professionals to keep up to date with new theories and improved practices when working with babies, toddlers and young children. This is very evident in the area of TEL, which was unheard of when the Child Care Act was passed in 1991. (For information on TEL, see Chapter 3, pages 33–35.)

As with all other workforces, ELC poses challenges and opportunities, so it is important to be able to adapt to move forward on your career path. Keeping up to date and upskilling is very important. There are a number of ways you can do this:

1. Becoming a member of a professional ELC organisation
2. Following organisations on social media platforms
3. Becoming a member of a voluntary childcare organisations, for example:
   * Childminding Ireland – National Childminding Association of Ireland
   * Early Childhood Ireland (ECI)
   * Irish Steiner Waldorf Early Childhood Association
   * National Childhood Network
   * National Parents Council
   * St Nicholas Montessori Teachers' Association.

Showcasing personal and professional development

Showcasing personal and professional development using a professional practice portfolio is an invaluable method of keeping records of your development over time. It should be a combination of your formal and non-formal professional development. People also need ways to keep track of their learning experiences. Individuals are continually accumulating assets (e.g. skills, contacts) through learning events, but few people develop a habit by which they can identify, record and organise these assets. Consequently, they often do not recognise that they have undergone a tremendous amount of learning.

Formal professional development refers to completing or participating in a structured activity either as a learner, speaker, panel member, an employee/employer or other. This includes but is not limited to conferences, seminars, webinars, training courses (classroom or online), workshops, panels, committees and councils.

Non-formal professional development refers to completing other activities associated with your work that contribute to your development as a professional but are not necessarily designed as professional development, such as field trips, listening to podcasts, volunteering.

In your portfolio you should have:

* an up-to-date CV
* Garda clearance letter/certificate
* two references
* a Tusla *Children First* e-learning certificate
* any other documentation to showcase your achievements; examples include:
  - a certificate in manual handling
  - a certificate in paediatric first aid
  - a certificate of attendance at an Aistear or Síolta workshop
  - a certificate of attendance at a literacy and numeracy workshop and/or a play-based workshop
  - documentation including pictures of interesting field trips, for example to a forest school.

Keeping a CPD record as you attend to each form of professional development is very helpful because we often forget what we did, whether it was formal or non-formal professional development. A CPD record will represent your training and education in ELC and should show that you are passionate about this sector and interested in lifelong learning. An example of a table to record your CPD is given on the next page.

My Continuous Professional Development Record

DATE	NAME OF CPD	TYPE OF CPD (FORMAL OR NON-FORMAL)	KEY AREAS COVERED	CERTIFICATE OF ATTENDANCE OR QUALIFICATION

(Adapted from Graham and McDermott, 2010)

Professionalising the ELC sector

Ireland has seen a rapid increase in the development of the ELC sector in the past few years, motivated by the following:

1. The increased understanding of the value of quality ELC experiences for young children
2. The national Síolta/Aistear initiatives, currently being implemented by the Department of Education and Skills in collaboration with the Department of Children, Equality, Disability, Integration and Youth
3. State involvement through regulation:
   * Introduction of a minimum qualification requirement in the sector
   * Updated Pre-school Regulations
   * New *Quality and Regulatory Framework* by Tusla
   * National Tusla Early Years Inspectorate and the rollout of education-focused inspections by the Inspectorate at the Department of Education and Skills for the ECCE scheme.

4. State investment in the sector:
   * Introduction of the free pre-school year (ECCE) scheme in 2010 and its extension to a second year in 2016, which has increased professional expectations of the ELC workforce.

This evolving policy and practice landscape has led to an increase in the level of qualifications achieved by staff in ELC settings. Higher capitation grants are awarded to ELC settings in the ECCE programme that employ staff with higher qualifications in the role of pre-school leader (Level 7 qualification on the National Framework of Qualifications (NFQ), and three years of post-qualification experience). The *First 5* strategy has also set a target for the ELC workforce that by 2028, 'A graduate-led ELC workforce, with at least 50% of staff (i.e. all room leaders, assistant manager and managers), will be working directly with children in centre-based ELC settings' (*Workforce Development Plan for the ELC/SAC Sector*, p. 4).

From these developments it is clear that

> "We need to future-proof and professionalise the qualifications on offer to the current and future early learning and care workforce, so that we can be assured that they are prepared for the responsibility to deliver high-quality learning and care experiences for their young charges."
>
> (Minister for Children, Katherine Zappone, 2019)

> "Fortunately, as a result of much effort, professional awards in ELC at QQI level 5 and 6 are now recognised and aligned to the Level 7 and 8 degree programmes for ELC in Ireland.
>
> For the first time in the history of the ELC sector, the workforce will have access to a suite of professional awards from entry level qualifications at Level 5 to honours degree level, that recognise the value of professionals at all these levels working in ELC settings across the country."
>
> (Minister for Education & Skills, Joe McHugh, 2019)

The previous Workforce Development Plan for the Early Childhood Care and Education Sector (Department of Education and Skills (DES), 2010) in Ireland was also committed to the development of the sector. The plan acknowledged the strong evidence base that early childhood experiences have a critical impact on the wellbeing, learning and development of children and that the skills, knowledge, competencies, values and attitudes of the workforce delivering ELC services is a determining factor in the quality of those experiences. Relevant to the area of professional development, the plan includes a commitment to

* professionalising the sector; and
* identifying occupational roles in the ELC with terms and conditions of employment.

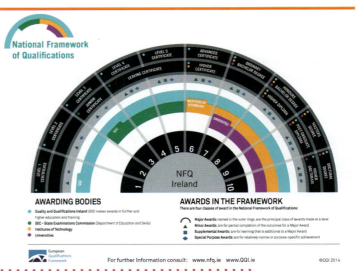

> The most effective practice is found in settings with well-trained, well-informed staff, familiar with child development and subject material, who recognise and respond to the dynamic and individual nature of development in the early years and who can work with an emerging curriculum driven by the interests and experiences of children and the opportunities afforded by the environment.
>
> (Hayes, O'Toole and Halpenny, 2017, p. 142)

A collation of the skills and competencies believed to be a current requirement for the delivery of quality ELC services in Ireland is available in the document *Skills and Competencies Framework for Early Years Professionals* (2016) prepared by the National Childhood Network (NCN) and the Crann Support Group. This document is intended as a potential guide for all early years settings whatever the management structure or type of service, with cognisance being given to *Síolta* (2006), *Aistear* (2009), Tusla's *Quality and Regulatory Framework*, Child Care Act 1991 (Early Years Services) Regulations 2016 and the Department of Education and Skills, which has more recently been involved in voluntary Early Years Education Inspections (EYEI). It should also be noted that the work has been informed by:

* Department of Justice, Equality and Law Reform (2002) *Quality Childcare and Lifelong Learning: Model Framework for Education, Training and Professional Development in the Early Childhood Care and Education Sector*
* CORE (2012) *Competencies Requirements in Early Childhood Education and Care*
* Ministry of Social and Family Development, Singapore (2012) *Achieving Excellence through Continuing Professional Development: A CPD Framework for Early Childhood Educators.*

 Skills and Competencies Framework for Early Years' Professionals https://www.ncn.ie/images/PDFs/Proposed-Core-Skills-and-Competencies-Framework-071116.pdf

While waiting for an agreement of titles for ELC professionals, which will take place as part of the forthcoming workforce development planning process, it is hoped that this *Skills and Competencies Framework* document will generate discussion and debate with all relevant stakeholders and will in turn lead to an agreement on a national skills and competencies framework that will be supported by a comprehensive national CPD system and an agreed national salary scale. With the numbers employed in the sector now approaching 30,000, it is time for a national agreement to be made.

According to the *Skills and Competencies Framework* document, the early years/childhood professional:

* takes delight and interest in how children learn and develop
* acknowledges, appreciates and provides support for the unique role of parents/carers in their children's lives
* acknowledges play as the main medium through which young children learn
* demonstrates enthusiasm when offered opportunities to obtain new knowledge and skills that provide support for children's development and learning
* models the positive behaviours and attitudes that are valued in childhood
* sees negative behaviour as an opportunity for a child's learning and development
* celebrates diversity that occurs among children, their families and their community
* asks for help, observes and learns from others and welcomes constructive criticism
* engages in reflective practice to address personal beliefs and values that may influence his/her own attitudes and beliefs
* is accountable for his/her own actions
* demonstrates respect for children and families and understands the need to maintain confidentiality
* communicates clearly, respectfully and effectively with children and adults
* responds to challenges and changes with positivity, flexibility, perseverance and cooperation
* expresses his/her emotions in healthy and productive ways
* appreciates and nurtures resilience, determination, risk taking, imagination, creativity and play in children
* displays a professional manner at work and in all interactions with others
* demonstrates a team player attitude.

(Crann Support Group and National Childhood Network, 2016, p. 6)

RECAP QUESTIONS

1. Explain why it is important to set career goals.
2. Describe in your own words what you understand by the term 'continuous professional development'.

Section 2

Legislation, Regulations and National Frameworks

Pre-school Regulations 2016 – *Quality and Regulatory Framework (Tusla)*

Introduction

The Pre-school Regulations (Part VII of the Child Care Act 1991) first appeared in 1996. The regulations have since been reviewed and updated, with the current specifics regarding regulation of pre-school childcare services set out in the Child Care Act 1991 (Early Years Services) Regulations 2016. Tusla's Early Years Inspectorate is the independent statutory regulator of ELC services and has published a *Quality and Regulatory Framework* (QRF) (2018).

> The QRF aims to support registered providers in achieving compliance with the regulations and enhance the safety and care of children who attend these services. The QRF is child-centred, with a specific focus on the quality and safety of the care provided directly to children using the services. (https://www.tusla.ie/services/pre-school-services/early-years-quality-and-regulatory-framework/)

The QRF details regulations relating to:

* full- and part-time day care services
* sessional pre-school services
* childminding
* pre-school service in a drop-in centre
* overnight pre-school services.

For the purposes of this text, only full- and part-time day care services will be covered in detail. There will be considerable overlap with the other four categories but some differences too.

 To familiarise yourself with all five categories, consult the QRF document: https://www.tusla.ie/services/pre-school-services/early-years-quality-and-regulatory-framework/

Overall responsibility for the oversight of ELC services in Ireland lies with the Department of Children, Equality, Disability, Integration and Youth (DCEDIY). The main purpose of the regulations is to ensure that standards are in place to safeguard the health and welfare of children in all ELC services and to promote their development through the provision of developmentally and culturally appropriate materials, experiences, activities and interactions. The regulations affect the full range of groups in pre-school provision, ranging from voluntary and community through to full day care private sector provision, and require that all those who provide an ELC service be registered with Tusla and undergo inspections to ensure that they are compliant with the regulations.

All employers and employees are also protected at work by the Safety, Health and Welfare at Work Act 2005 (see Chapter 16, p. 176), which imposes duties and responsibilities on both parties to maintain safe practices.

DEFINITIONS

A **pre-school child** is a child under six years who is not attending a national school or a school providing an educational programme similar to a national school.

An **early years/pre-school service** is any pre-school, playgroup, day nursery, crèche, day care or other similar service that caters for pre-school children. These include sessional, full-time and drop-in services and childminders who are registered.

Relating to pre-school services, the main provisions of the Act direct that pre-school providers notify Tusla that they are operating or intend to operate an ELC service, whereupon the Tusla inspectorate is obliged to inspect and register the service. The following services may be excluded from the provisions of the Act:

* The care of one or more children undertaken by a relative of the child or children or the spouse of such relative
* A person taking care of one or more children of the same family and no other children (other than the person's own children) in their own home
* A person taking care of no more than three children of different families (other than that person's own children aged under six years) in that person's home.

As set out in the QRF, the regulations broadly cover the areas of:

* governance
* health, welfare and development of the child
* safety
* premises and facilities.

It is not intended to give a full detailed description of all regulations here, but rather to give a broad overview, which indicates their range and general content. Where specific detail is required, the Tusla website – specifically the QRF documents – should be consulted.

Overview of regulations

The inspection process is designed to monitor and protect the health, welfare and safety of children in pre-school services and to promote their development. It ensures that services comply with all legal/statutory requirements, including the pre-school regulations. Inspectors are appointed by Tusla and visit the premises to view how the service is being run, taking detailed account of a wide range of aspects of provision, as set out in the regulations.

Anyone who plans to start a service must make an application to Tusla three months prior to the commencement of the service. Services that are in operation must apply for re-registration every three years.

A written report is issued to the service provider and adequate time is allowed in the event that issues need to be addressed or improvements made. A follow-up inspection is then usually carried out. The report of the inspector, known as the Outcome Inspection Report, is made available to the public by Tusla to facilitate parents and families in making informed decisions when choosing childcare.

See appendix 1 for details of the inspection process.

1. GOVERNANCE

(i) Management: There must be a clear, effective and competent management structure in place. A pre-school service should have a designated person in charge and a designated deputy, one of whom should be on the premises at all times. There should be an adequate number of competent adults working directly with the children at all times. (Ratios are set out on pages 79–81.)

A competent adult is defined as a person aged over 18 years who has appropriate experience in the field and an appropriate qualification. All staff should have an appropriate qualification. There should be written policies on management, recruitment, training and staff absences. Staff, students and volunteers, indeed anyone with access to children, must be Garda-vetted and two recent work references should be validated.

(ii) Policies, procedures and statements of a pre-school service: Policies and procedures are required in order to ensure consistency and standardisation within the practice and to ensure that the service is implementing 'best practice'. Management is required to develop and approve policies, procedures and statements on specific areas relating to service provision, such as:

- statement of purpose and function
- complaints policy
- policy on administration of medication
- policy on infection control
- policy on managing behaviour
- policy on safe sleep
- fire safety policy
- inclusion policy
- outings policy
- policy on accidents and incidents
- policy on authorisation to collect children
- policy on healthy eating
- policy on outdoor play (if applicable)
- policy on staff absences
- policy on the use of the internet and photographic and recording devices
- recruitment policy
- risk management policy
- settling-in policy
- staff training policy
- staff supervision policy.

All of these are required to be made available to parents, guardians and staff in hard and soft copy. Parents and guardians should sign a declaration that they have read, understood and accepted the policies and statements

(iii) Staffing: The regulations relating to staffing specify that an adequate number of trained and competent staff must be available at all times. There are specific staff ratios laid out in the regulations. Rosters should be available and there should be a clear policy on staff absences and replacement.

Adult:Child ratios – Full day care and part-time day care services	
Age range	Adult:Child ratio
0–1 year	**1:3**
	1–3 children: one adult
	4–6 children: two adults
	7–9 children: three adults

Adult:Child ratios – Full day care and part-time day care services	
Age range	Adult:Child ratio
1–2 years	**1:5**
	1–5 children: one adult
	6–10 children: two adults
2–3 years	**1:6**
	1–6 children: one adult
	7–12 children: two adults
3–6 years	**1:8**
	1–8 children: one adult
	9–16 children: two adults
	17–24 children: three adults

The adult:child ratios are 1:11 for any child availing of the Early Childhood Care and Education (ECCE) scheme and attending a Sessional Pre-school Service (up to 3.5 hours). A child attending on a full day care basis avails of an ECCE scheme once a day only.

The adult:child ratio of 1:8 or 1:6 is effective after 3.5 hours (when the ECCE Sessional Pre-school Service has finished) and the child is staying on in the full day care service for the rest of the day. At least two adults are on the premises at all times. (QRF, 2018, p. 9)

Adult:Child ratios – Sessional pre-school service	
Age range	Adult:Child ratio
0–1 year	**1:3**
	1–3 children: one adult
	4–6 children: two adults
	7–9 children: three adults
1–2.5 years	**1:5**
	1–5 children: one adult
	6–10 children: two adults
2.5–6 years	**1:11**
	1–11 children: one adult
	12–22 children: two adults

In a sessional group, no more than 25 per cent of children should be under three years, and no more than 20 children should be catered for in one room.

Adult:Child ratios – Full day care and part-time day care services	
Age range	Adult:Child ratio
Full age integration	1:4
0–6 years	24 (maximum number of children at one time)

There should be a maximum of two children under 15 months to one adult, and no more than 24 children should attend a drop-in service at any one time. A sole operator must ensure that another adult is available in case of an emergency.

Adult:Child ratios – Overnight pre-school service	
Age range	Adult:Child ratio
0–1 year	1:3
1–6 years	1:5

Childminding service: A childminder should look after not more than five pre-school children, including her own, and no more than two of these should be under 15 months old (except in cases of multiple births or siblings). There should be a telephone on the premises and a second person available in case of emergency.

In the interests of child safety and quality care, Tusla may determine the maximum number of children to be catered for in any pre-school service.

(iv) Formal assessment: There must be a formal assessment of the services and policies at least once a year. This review should be held with a view to making changes and improvements if necessary.

(v) Record of a pre-school child: Records containing relevant information should be maintained on each child attending the service. Such information would include details of health, relevant family details, who is authorised to collect the child, and so on. Confidentiality must be maintained and records should be stored safely (see GDPR, p. 37). They should be shared with parents and guardians and the consent of a parent or guardian is required to share such records with anyone else. Records should be kept for two years after the child has left the service.

(vi) Record in relation to a pre-school service: Records must be kept in relation to the service; such records would include details of staffing and rosters, ratios, roles and responsibilities, etc. Confidential information in relation to individuals must be stored safely as per GDPR.

(vii) Information for parents: Such information should be provided in an accessible manner. Information should be updated and disseminated as appropriate (emails, newsletter, posters, etc.). Information would include the following:

* Staff/child ratios
* Maximum number of children catered for
* Type of service and age range
* Care programme provided
* Facilities provided

- Opening hours and fees
- Policies and procedures
- Daily staff rosters
- Record of programmes, activities and opportunities offered to children, based on individual needs and interests.

Additionally, the following information is made available as appropriate:

- All accidents, no matter how minor, recorded and notified to parents
- Details of medicine administered to children.

All records should be updated regularly and should be available for inspection as required. Relevant information should be made available to the parent/guardian of a child proposing to attend a service. The following information should be publicly displayed at all times:

- the registered provider's name
- the service's Tusla registration certificate
- contact name and number for the service
- contact details for emergency medical assistance
- the process to be followed, evacuation routes and procedures if there is a fire or other emergency.

(viii) Notification of incidents: The service must have policies and procedures in place to manage the notification of incidents or accidents, whether of a child or a member of staff, to the inspectorate and, if required, to Tusla, the Gardaí or the Health Authority. There are forms of notification on the various websites. The following must be notified:

- Death or serious injury to a child
- The incidence of an infectious disease
- An accident or incident which required the service to close for any length of time
- A child going missing.

(ix) Complaints: A system must be in place to deal with complaints in an open, fair, consistent and unbiased manner.

2. HEALTH, WELFARE AND DEVELOPMENT OF THE CHILD

This requires the provision of age-appropriate and culturally appropriate opportunities, activities, experiences, interactions and materials for all children attending an ELC service. There is a clear statement here acknowledging the value of play as a powerful learning vehicle for young children, as well as the importance of the relationships and environment they are engaged in. The regulations are laid out under the following specific areas.

A) BASIC AND INDIVIDUAL CARE NEEDS OF ALL CHILDREN

* Eating and drinking
  - Healthy eating is encouraged and promoted.
  - Children are encouraged but not forced to eat a variety of foods.
  - There is an emphasis on comfort, enjoyment and interaction during snack and mealtimes.
  - Children should be encouraged to feed themselves independently in line with stage of development.

* Toileting and nappy changing
  - Privacy and dignity are respected at all times.
  - Children's routines are handled sensitively.
  - Children are supported and encouraged to be independent in line with the stage of development and readiness.
  - Toilet training is in agreement with and supported by parents and guardians.

* Self-care routines
  - Children are supported and encouraged to participate or take charge of their own personal care as age and stage appropriate, for example brushing teeth, dressing, putting on coats, etc.

* Rest
  - There should be provision for each child's need for sleep and rest as required.
  - Naps and rest should be in response to individual's children's needs rather than at set times.
  - Sleep areas should be in quiet, restful areas.
  - Sleeping babies should be supervised.

* Mobility: There should be adequate, appropriate and safe space, indoor and outdoor, for children to move around freely and unencumbered whether crawling or walking.

B) SUPPORT OF RELATIONSHIPS AND INTERACTIONS AROUND CHILDREN

* Staff develop positive relationships with children through respecting, listening and encouraging the child, by being positive, responding to each individual and spending time getting actively involved. Where possible, a key worker might be assigned to each child.

* Children's relationships with siblings and peers are supported by facilitating time and space and encouraging interaction.

* Children who are new to the service, who have additional needs or perhaps are not fluent in the majority language are supported.

* Relationships with parents and guardians are supported by open communication, responding to fears and worries, offering opportunities to become involved and respecting all.

* Information and knowledge is shared.
* Children are integrated into the local community as far as possible – visits to the library, the park, inviting local community members to 'events', 'funds of community knowledge'.
* Teamwork is demonstrated through positive and warm relationships, showing how to work together and displaying mutual respect with a team spirit.

C) SUPPORT OF INCLUSION, DIVERSITY AND TRANSITION

* Service supports inclusion, diversity and children's transitions and there is clear evidence of an inclusion policy being implemented.
* The service uses a child-centred approach, catering for the individual needs of all children.
* All children are encouraged to reach their full potential, taking cognisance of their background and developmental stage and additional needs.
* Children are given equal opportunities through the provision of a diverse range of experiences and facilities designed to meet their needs.
* All children are encouraged to embrace diversity and be respectful. They are encouraged to be critical thinkers and to be able to respond to bias and discrimination as appropriate.
* A sense of belonging is fostered in the service.
* A settling-in policy should ease every child's entry to the service.
* Policies and procedures should also facilitate and ease children's transitions within the service and out of the service to school or other services.

D) BEHAVIOUR POLICY

* There is evidence of a robust behaviour policy being implemented.
* Children's positive behaviour is supported, and the needs of all children are responded to in a positive, caring way.
* Babies and young children especially are attended to when they cry.
* Children are supported in developing recognition and control of their emotions as developmentally appropriate.
* Written policies and procedures should be in place to deal with challenging behaviour in a caring, constructive and developmentally appropriate way. Children with ongoing challenging behaviour are supported and helped to control their emotions and distress.
* Corporal punishment, physical intervention and any practices that are disrespectful, degrading, humiliating, harmful or neglectful are prohibited.

E) SUPPORT OF LEARNING, DEVELOPMENT AND WELLBEING

* The environment supports the learning, development and wellbeing of each child.
* A flexible and responsive environment should be designed and resourced in a way that supports and encourages the development of every individual child.

- The indoor environment should be pleasing, comfortable and varied. It should allow for active and quiet play. Materials should be visible and accessible to the children. Interest areas should be grouped together.
- The outdoor environment should extend the opportunities for learning and development. Children should be facilitated to be outdoors as much as is possible. There should be areas suitable and equipped for active play, for engaging with nature, for exploration and experimentation, for education about risk and for engagement in team games.

F) DELIVERY OF EFFECTIVE PROGRAMME AND CARE PRACTICES

- The service should ensure the delivery of an effective programme and effective care practices.
- The service should be child-centred and flexible, taking into account age and stage of development, health and safety requirements, learning needs and interests and choices of individual children. There should be ample staffing resources to facilitate ongoing observations and assessments both of individuals, groups and resources.
- If individual care plans are required, these should specify how the service will meet the child's needs.

G) USE OF TECHNOLOGY

- The service should use technology, including the internet and photographic and recording devices, with the clear purpose of providing appropriate resources that will extend and enhance children's learning and development.
- Children with additional needs should be especially supported to use technology suitable to their needs.
- Staff must be aware of safety and security in relation to images and recordings and these should be handled and stored in line with GDPR (see page 37).
- Consent for use of images in public spaces, e.g. in newsletters, must be given by parents and guardians.

H) FACILITIES FOR REST AND PLAY

REST

- In general, the facilities should support the individual child's sleep and rest requirements. The rest areas should be well ventilated, clean and quiet with appropriate soft lighting and space for supervising staff to move around to check on or attend to each child. (The requirements of sleep areas for those under two years and those over two years of age are outlined below.)
- Room temperatures should be maintained between 16 and 20 degrees Celsius.
- A maximum of six children under two should be accommodated in one room, with 4.2 square metres' space allowed per child.

Child's age (approx.)	Number of cots
6 months	1 cot for each child
9 months	Cots available for two-thirds of children in this age range
18 months–2 years	Cots available for half the children in this age range

Children over two years should have access to comfortable sleeping mats or beds in a suitable area (e.g. a quiet area of the playroom). Of course, all bedding for all ages should be clean and cleaned between uses. It should meet the relevant safety standards and be maintained in good condition. It is prohibited to use the following items to accommodate sleeping children:

* car seats, buggies, strollers and infant carriers
* inflatable mattresses, inflatable beds or waterbeds
* beanbags
* couches, sofas, settees and chairs
* travel cots or portable cribs
* bunk cots or stackable cots
* pillows and cushions as a base to sleep on.

PLAY

* **Indoor play:** The indoor play space should be clean, uncluttered and divided into different interest areas. All the resources should be accessible to all children and adaptable for those who may have additional needs.

* **Outdoor play**
    — All services registered after June 2016 are required to have an outdoor space that is accessible on a daily basis. Services registered prior to June 2016 should have an outdoor space available separate from the premises, in which case the outings policy must be implemented and a risk assessment carried out prior to every visit to the space.

    — While the outdoor space should be safe, it also needs to provide opportunities for challenging and fun play.

    — The materials and equipment need to be of high standard and meet the relevant safety requirements. All equipment and surfaces need to be installed in line with manufacturers' guidance.

    — Where outdoor space is not attached to the premises, additional attention has to be paid to hazards and potential risks including risks from members of the public.

Services who registered a premises on or after 30 June 2016, and those who moved premises on or after the 30 June 2016 require a suitable, safe and secure outdoor space on the premises that is accessible to the children on a daily basis. Services registered before 30 June 2016 require access on a daily basis, to an outdoor space, either on or off the premises. (QRF, 2018, p. 49)

Activity

In small groups, read the scenario below. Identify what needs to be considered to take account of:

* the children's needs
* safety considerations
* consultation with parents
* integration into the local community.

Identify a number of local amenities that might be suitable.

> Since the new regulations relating to outdoor play have come into force, Play Zone ELC service has been availing of a small local outdoor space attached to a large building mostly used for offices. Staff have decided that they need to find a more suitable space where they can take larger numbers of children on each outing.

FOOD AND DRINK

* Children in full day care – that is, for more than five hours – have at least two meals and two snacks offered to them, one of which is a hot meal.
* Children in day care for up to a maximum of a five-hour session are offered at least two meals and one snack. It is not necessary to have a hot meal.
* Children in day care for up to a 3.5-hour session have one meal and one snack.
* Clean and safe drinking water is available and accessible to children at all times.
* Water used for infants under one year is boiled and cooled before use.
* Children are supported to self-serve as appropriate.
* Water and milk are the only drinks offered.
* The meals and snacks are of appropriate textures for infants.
* Breastfeeding supports are provided where required.
* Powdered infant formula is managed appropriately in the service.
* Food safety provisions include:
  — safe facilities to store food, including a fridge for perishable foodstuffs
  — a system where all food and drinks brought from the child's home are identifiable to the child.
* Special occasions like birthday parties are in line with the service's policy on healthy eating.

3 SAFEGUARDING THE SAFETY, HEALTH AND WELFARE OF THE CHILD

This section of the regulations has extensive guidelines with regard to safety and welfare in the context of

* the building/premises itself
* all equipment, both indoor and outdoor
* hygiene
* choking hazards
* toxic substances
* thermostat control of heaters and water
* medication
* outings
* infection control
* fire safety and fire drills

and so on.

As with all of the regulations, for all of the above there needs to be evidence of various relevant policies being implemented, staff training, awareness and understanding of their roles and responsibilities.

Activity

Plan an activity in the arts and crafts area, and as part of the planning devise a 'Health and Safety' checklist.

4 CHECKING IN AND OUT AND RECORDS OF ATTENDANCE

* Authorisation for collection of children – children should only be released into the care of people who have been authorised by the parents.
* Daily attendance records should be maintained securely.
* In addition to attendance records of the children, a record of all who enter/visit the premises must be kept including relevant contact details and purpose of visit.

FIRST AID

All ELC services are required to provide a suitably equipped first aid box for children, with recommended contents. It should be stored safely and should be taken on outings. Medicines should be clearly labelled in original containers and inaccessible to children. A person trained in first aid for children should be on the premises at all times and should accompany the children on outings. Arrangements should be in place to obtain medical assistance for a child in an emergency and written parental permission should be in place for this. There should also be a procedure for the administration of medicine to children where required, and parental consent should also be in place here.

Emergency medical assistance contact details should be publicly displayed.

All incidents of administration of first aid should be recorded.

FIRE SAFETY MEASURES

ELC services should comply with all fire safety responsibilities under the Fire Services Act (1981 and 2003). Procedures to be followed in the event of fire should be displayed prominently throughout the premises. Records of fire drills should be maintained, as well as details and maintenance records of fire-fighting equipment and smoke alarms. Records should be open to inspection by parents, staff and other authorised persons.

SUPERVISION

Careful and appropriate supervision by a qualified member of staff while maintaining the rights and dignity of each individual is a must at all times and should be more constant and careful at times when risks are higher such as when involved in boisterous and vigorous play or when:

1. Asleep: An adult may remain with children while they are asleep, or the children should be carefully observed at least every 10 minutes and this observation should be recorded. Sound monitors may increase supervision but should never replace direct supervision by a member of staff.
2. Eating and drinking.

INSURANCE

The service must be adequately insured, and this insurance should cover:

* public liability
* fire and theft
* buildings
* outings
* motors used in the service
* and other, depending on the nature of the service.

EQUIPMENT AND MATERIALS

The service provider must ensure as follows:

* There is sufficient and suitable furniture, play and work equipment, including materials available to the staff and children at all times: 'A wide variety of age and developmentally appropriate equipment is available indoors and outdoors for children throughout the day.'
* There is access to a sufficient quantity of safe, well-maintained, high-quality materials and equipment, toys and furniture for all children.
* Equipment and materials facilitate all types of play and learning, engage all children and keep them active and involved, while supporting and encouraging each child to experiment and explore.
* Natural materials are accessible to the children.
* The materials, equipment and toys support and reflect the identity of children who are attending the service, their families and also the wider community.
* Children with additional needs see themselves represented in the materials and the environment.
* Materials, equipment and toys provide a rich and varied environment with regard to gender, race, culture, ethnicity and additional needs, to encourage respect for diversity, equality and inclusion.
* Furnishings, equipment and materials, where required, allow children with additional needs to participate fully in the service.
* If the service provides outdoor play equipment and materials, they are accessible to each child and are of suitable design and size for early years children.
* Furniture and equipment should meet the needs of the children but also those of the staff.
* Materials should be organised in such a way as to encourage children to use them independently.
* All furniture and equipment should be made of material which facilitates cleaning and hygiene and should be maintained in good condition.

SPACE REQUIREMENTS

The space requirements relate to clear floor space per child, i.e. the area available for play, work and movement. This does not include the space taken up by furniture and fixtures. Kitchens, toilets and sleep areas are not included when calculating space per child.

Full- and part-time day care services	
Age of child	Floor area per child
0–1 year	3.5 sq metres
1–2 years	2.8 sq metres
2–3 years	2.35 sq metres
3–6 years	2.3 sq metres
Sessional pre-school services and drop-in centres	
A minimum of 1.818 square metres of clear floor space per child is required for the duration of the sessional service for the children attending that service.	

Premises should have laundry facilities and separate safe storage space for personal belongings of staff and children. There should also be a space for storing confidential information and for staff breaks. There should be adequate, suitable and hygienic sanitary accommodation:

* nappy-changing facilities
* separate toilet facilities for adults
* wash basins with running cold and thermostatically controlled hot water, soap and suitable hand-drying for children
* safe and hygienic disposal of soiled nappies

Full day care facilities should have a shower/bath facility with thermostatically controlled hot water, and a designated area for sluicing soiled garments.

Toilets and nappy-changing areas should not communicate directly with any occupied room, except by means of a ventilated space such as a hall.

Requirements for toilets and wash basins		
Number of persons	Toilets	Wash basins
Every 10 toilet-using children	1	1
Every eight adults	1	1

There are also regulations on heating, lighting, ventilation, drainage and sewage disposal, waste storage and disposal, as well as a requirement to have adequate insurance and to pay an annual fee to Tusla towards the cost of inspection.

8

Children First: National Guidance for the Protection and Welfare of Children (2017)

Introduction

The rights of children have gained increasing recognition since the Child Care Act was passed in 1991 and it is now firmly established that all children in Ireland have a fundamental right to protection and safety.

> **DEFINITIONS**
>
> **Child safeguarding** is about keeping all children safe from harm and ensuring that they grow up in an environment that enables them to reach their full potential.
>
> **Child protection** is part of the safeguarding process, with the focus being on protecting individual children identified as suffering or likely to suffer significant harm and responding effectively and promptly to any concerns that arise.

The primary aim of this section is to provide basic information on law, policy and procedure in line with *Children First: National Guidance for the Protection and Welfare of Children* (2017). It will also set out the statutory responsibilities for mandated persons and organisations under the Children First Act 2015 and will provide information about how to act and respond if you are concerned in any way about the welfare of a child.

However, as this is an introduction it is not intended to explore all areas in depth, and the learner should extend their knowledge and confidence by reading the various documents and guides which will be referenced throughout the section, but particularly the following, all of which are available online:

* *Children First: National Guidance for the Protection and Welfare of Children* (Department of Children and Youth Affairs, 2017)
* *Guidance on Developing a Child Safeguarding Statement* (Tusla, 2017)
* *Child Safeguarding: A Guide for Policy, Procedure and Practice* (Tusla, 2017).

Furthermore, learners can complete Tusla's e-learning training on child protection prior to undertaking their professional practice placement.

Tusla *Children First* e-Learning Programme
https://www.tusla.ie/children-first/children-first-e-learning-programme/

Principles of best practice in safeguarding children

* The safety and welfare of children is everyone's responsibility.
* The best interests of the child should be paramount.
* The overall aim in all dealings with children and their families is to intervene proportionately to support families to keep children safe from harm.
* Interventions by the State should build on existing strengths and protective factors in the family.
* Early intervention is key to getting better outcomes.
* Where it is necessary for the State to intervene to keep children safe, the minimum intervention necessary should be used.
* Children should only be separated from parents/guardians when alternative means of protecting them have been exhausted.
* Children have a right to be heard, listened to and taken seriously.
* Taking account of their age and understanding, they should be consulted and involved in all matters and decisions that may affect their lives.
* Parents/guardians have a right to respect, and should be consulted and involved in matters that concern their family.
* A proper balance must be struck between protecting children and respecting the rights and needs of parents/guardians and families.
* Where there is conflict, the child's welfare must come first.
* Child protection is a multiagency, multidisciplinary activity.

* Agencies and professionals must work together in the interests of children.
* Any intervention should take account of diversity in families and lifestyles.
* Training for effective child protection is mandatory in all establishments which care for children.
* Roles and responsibilities should be clearly defined and understood within organisations and services for children.

(Adapted from *Children First: National Guidance for the Protection and Welfare of Children*, 2017, pp. 3–4)

Definitions of child abuse

Different types of abuse are defined separately in the following, but in reality they are not easy to distinguish. Where a child is being physically abused within a family, that child is also being emotionally abused. Likewise, a child who is experiencing sexual abuse is being emotionally abused and physically abused. The following definitions are as set out in the *Children First* (2017) guidance document.

DEFINITIONS

Physical abuse is any form of non-accidental injury, or injury which results from wilful or neglectful failure to protect a child. Examples include shaking, hitting, punching, use of excessive force, poisoning, suffocating, allowing or creating substantial risk of significant harm to the child, and female genital mutilation. Disciplining a child by physical means is no longer defensible by the argument of 'reasonable chastisement' and is considered an assault on the child's person in the same way that hitting an adult would be considered physical assault.

Emotional abuse is normally to be found in the relationship between a caregiver and a child rather than in a specific event or pattern of events. It occurs when a child's needs for affection, approval, consistency and security are not met. Examples would include persistent criticism, sarcasm, hostility, conditional parenting, unresponsiveness, inconsistency, unrealistic expectations, under- and over-protection, or rejection of the child. Emotional abuse is not always easy to identify and therefore tends to be reported less than other concerns because the effects are not so easily recognised.

Neglect is the most frequently reported category of abuse both in Ireland and internationally. It is normally defined in terms of an omission, where a child suffers significant harm or impairment of development by being deprived of food, clothing, warmth, hygiene, intellectual stimulation, supervision and safety, attachment to and affection from adults, or medical care.

Sexual abuse occurs when a child is used by another person for his or her gratification or sexual arousal, or for that of others, e.g. masturbation or exposure in the presence of a child, inappropriate touching, intercourse, sexual exploitation as in the taking of photographs for sexual gratification purposes and distribution of pornography.

SIGNS AND INDICATORS OF PHYSICAL ABUSE

(Note that the following list of signs and indicators of abuse is not exhaustive.)

PHYSICAL

- Bruising in areas where bruises are not readily sustained, i.e. soft tissue areas
- Explanations for injuries where the explanation is not consistent with the injury
- Facial bruising
- Hand or finger marks/pressure bruises
- Bite marks
- Burns (especially cigarette), scalds
- Unexplained and frequent fractures
- Frequent and severe lacerations and abrasions
- Failure to thrive.

BEHAVIOURAL

- Fearful and shying away from physical contact
- Frozen watchfulness
- Withdrawn or aggressive behaviour
- Sudden changes in behaviour.

SIGNS AND INDICATORS OF EMOTIONAL ABUSE

BEHAVIOURAL

- Attention-seeking behaviour
- Withdrawn or aggressive behaviour
- Inability to have fun
- Low self-esteem
- Tantrums — beyond normal developmental age for same
- Indiscriminately affectionate.

SIGNS AND INDICATORS OF CHILD NEGLECT

PHYSICAL

- Poor hygiene
- Inadequate, dirty, torn or inappropriate clothing
- Untreated medical problems
- Poor nourishment/failure to thrive
- Emaciation
- Being left at home alone.

BEHAVIOURAL

- Tiredness/listlessness
- Low self-esteem
- Inability to concentrate or be involved
- Always hungry.

SIGNS AND INDICATORS OF SEXUAL ABUSE

PHYSICAL

- Bruises and scratches to genital area
- Soreness when walking, sitting, going to the toilet
- Pain or itching
- Sexually transmitted diseases
- Torn and stained underclothes
- Bedwetting, sleep disturbances
- Loss of appetite.

BEHAVIOURAL

* Hints of sexual activity through words, drawings or play
* Sexually precocious behaviour
* Use of sexually explicit language
* Preoccupation with sexual matter
* Informed knowledge of adult sexual behaviour
* Low self-esteem
* Withdrawn or isolated from other children.

It is important not to jump to conclusions: a burn may be caused by a genuine accident, a sudden change in behaviour could be because an elderly relative who requires a lot of care has moved in with the family; Mongolian blue spots, which resemble a series of bruises, appear naturally on the back and buttocks of some babies and are more common among babies of Asian, East Indian or African descent; circular bruising may be the result of 'cupping', a Chinese medical treatment.

Predisposing factors

Some factors have been found consistently (predictive indicators) in family characteristics and/or circumstances where abuse has occurred. However, the same factors can also be found in families where there is no abuse. Therefore, predictive indicators of child abuse must be used with **extreme caution**. Statistics of child abuse show that child abuse occurs in all social classes and in all types of family; they also show that the people most likely to abuse children are parents, partners of parents who are not the child's natural parent, relatives and neighbours, in that order.

Parental factors associated with risk of harm to children

PARENTS WHO WERE THEMSELVES ABUSED

A combination of factors are at work here, for example:

* Cultural – 'It didn't do me any harm, so it won't do my children any harm.'
* Past experience — Love and violence are confused because of the parent's own experiences of being abused by parents/carers.
* Poor role models for the parents — Parents do not know other ways of disciplining and controlling their children because this is how their parents did it.
* Low self-esteem — Parents may be emotionally damaged and inadequate.

VERY YOUNG PARENTS

* Emotionally immature parents may not be able to cope with the physical and emotional demands of a young baby.
* There may be conflict between their own needs and the needs of their child.
* There may be a lack of support, or negative reactions from their own parents.
* There may be an inability to recognise the needs of a baby/young child because of youth and inexperience.
* There may be resentment of a baby where there is a new and growing relationship between parents.
* The reality of caring for a baby does not fit in with the 'dream' that is reinforced by society, e.g. that babies bring happiness, smiles, fulfilment and that parents are never tired, frustrated or worn out with anxiety and worry.

PARENTS WHO EXPECT TOO MUCH OF THEIR CHILDREN

* Approval and love are conditional on good behaviour and positive achievements.
* Skills and behaviour are expected from a child that are way beyond the child's age and stage of development.
* A child who fails to match up to expectations is seen by parents as bold, lazy or resistant.

PARENTS WHO ABUSE SUBSTANCES

* Alcohol is often associated with violence; the adult may be predisposed to violent actions and reactions.
* Abuse of other substances is more often associated with neglect; money is spent on substances/drugs rather than on basic necessities such as food, clothing and heating.
* Abuse of substances may also lead to a general lack of responsiveness (inertia) on the part of the adult to the child and their needs.

PARENTS WHO ARE UNDER STRESS

Parents may be overwhelmed by any problem such as debt, grief, trauma or fear, with the result that the demands of a child may elicit an unreasonable response. Parents may blame the child partially or wholly for the stress. Parents may simply 'forget' to feed, clothe or show affection to the child, such is the level of their stress.

The reason for a person's stress may not be obvious to an outsider. It is important to remember that what is extremely stressful for one person may only constitute a minor problem for another. We must never judge the actions or reactions of another according to our own abilities to deal with stressful situations.

PARENTS WHO SUFFER FROM PSYCHIATRIC ILLNESS/MENTAL HEALTH PROBLEMS

Mood swings and unpredictable and bizarre behaviour patterns can be very distressing and traumatic for children. Depression in a parent can lead to the total neglect of a child and a total inability to respond to the child's needs. Post-natal depression can disrupt the bonding process and the mother's response to her baby in the early weeks and months.

Child factors associated with risk of harm

CHILDREN IN THE AGE RANGE OF 1–4 YEARS

It is during the period of 1–4 years that children are at their most demanding in terms of the individual attention they require. The novelty of a new baby wears off, and a child who has literally found its feet is much more demanding than one who has no option but to lie in the cot. At this period, the child is also beginning to assert their independence and individuality.

CHILDREN WHO ARE PERCEIVED AS BEING 'DIFFICULT'

In situations when there is disruption to the early bonding and attachment process between mother and infant, where the bonds of attachment have been weakened, the care of the child may be perceived as being very difficult. Similarly, children who are difficult to feed or comfort can be overwhelming for the parent. Children who are born prematurely may have a combination of these factors. Additionally, when children are difficult to feed or comfort, parents may feel a sense of failure.

CHILDREN WHO ARE 'DIFFERENT'

* A child who does not live up to the parents' expectations
* A child who is not the sex that the parents had hoped for
* A child who has a disability
* A child who is perceived by parents to be different without this being obvious to others.

The above factors may contribute to our understanding of child abuse and abusive situations but many people who lack resources and cope with highly stressful situations and/or extremely demanding children would never harm their child. On the other hand, abuse can and does occur in families and to individuals who would seem on the surface to have no difficulties at all.

Activity

Read this case study and answer the questions that follow.

CASE STUDY

Father	Octavio Perez	38 years	Unemployed
Mother	Catherine Donovan	32 years	Unemployed
Children	Louise Donovan	8 years	Local NS (2nd Class)
	Jack Donovan	6 years	Local NS (Senior Infants)
	Zoe Perez	4 years	ELC service
	Emma Perez	18 months	ELC service
Income	Jobseeker's Benefit		
Housing	Bed and breakfast (two rooms paid for by local authority)		
Telephone	087 1234 567		

Octavio and Catherine have just returned to Ireland from England where they had lived for a number of years. They had a business there which they were forced to close and, penniless, they returned 'home'. Neither of their respective families could help out by accommodating two adults and four children. In desperation, they approached the housing and social services and have been accommodated in a B&B until such time as they can be properly housed. They have been living there for four weeks now and it is far from ideal. It is in an old house and they have to share facilities with other residents who live on the same floor. The support services also secured a place for the two youngest children in the local ELC service. There is a long waiting time for houses in the area.

Catherine brings Zoe and Emma to the ELC service every morning and often they are neither fed nor dressed. She says that it is difficult to have access to the bathrooms in the mornings and there are no cooking facilities. The landlady has expressly said that they should not keep food in the room. On occasions you have noticed what appears to be slight bruising on Zoe's upper arms. Catherine has mentioned that Octavio does not know his own strength, that he used to be good with the children but now shouts at them all the time and has no patience whatsoever, but that he loves them and she will speak to him about his handling of the little girls. She tends to explain everything by pointing out that the situation in the B&B is impossible and that they will be moving soon.

During the past week, Emma has been out of sorts and extremely grumpy in the mornings. This morning she wandered around in a daze until nearly lunchtime. You were concerned that, despite having no temperature, she was coming down with something and the parents were phoned in the early afternoon. On arrival, Catherine gave a sort of laugh and said, 'Oh, we must have overdone the sleeping medicine last night'. When pressed for information, she explained that they have to keep the children quiet after 8.30 p.m.

She said a few drops of sleeping medicine is the lesser of two evils because it keeps the children calm, and therefore Octavio especially is calmer and not getting uptight and so sleeps better. She adds, 'Sure it is only for a few weeks until we get our new house'.

Identify all the factors outlined in the above case study which would:

1. constitute 'predisposing factors'
2. be considered signs and symptoms of child abuse.

Duties and roles in relation to child protection

ROLE OF THE ELC PRACTITIONER

* To provide care and stimulation to each child according to each child's needs
* To monitor the overall progress of each child
* To maintain regular, accurate, impartial, dated and signed records of each child's progress. Observations are particularly useful in this area
* To maintain a close but professional relationship with parents/carers
* To be aware of signs and symptoms of abuse in all its forms
* To keep the best interests of the child in mind at all times
* In times of doubt, to be prepared to err on the side of caution.

ROLE OF THE ELC PROFESSIONAL WHERE THERE IS A CONCERN OF HARM TO A CHILD

All services must have a Safeguarding Statement, which will include policy and procedure where a concern is raised in relation to child protection. It is necessary for all those involved in an ELC service to familiarise themselves with these and to follow best practice at all times.

GUIDELINES FOR BEST PRACTICE

* Keep meticulous records at all times; these records must be dated and signed.
* Record only facts and direct observations; hearsay and hunches are not evidence.
* Discuss concerns with the Designated Child Protection Officer/Liaison Person or mandated person as appropriate (see below, 'Role of designated child protection officer' and 'Mandated persons').
* In most cases, the Designated Liaison Person will take over at this point and may discuss concerns with the parents or guardians and will then decide whether or not to report to the local Tusla social work team.

- If, for some reason, appropriate action is not taken and you still have concerns about the child, you can discuss these with the Tusla social worker yourself.

If there is direct evidence of abuse, or if a child or someone else discloses facts of abuse to the ELC practitioner:

- Don't panic; remain calm.
- Reassure the child/person that he/she was right to tell.
- Give the child time and opportunity to say what he/she has to say. He/she may not do this all at once.
- Avoid shock/horror responses.
- Explain to the child what action will be taken — keep it simple.

ROLE OF THE MANAGER/DIRECTOR OF THE ELC SERVICE

- To ensure that professional standards are maintained
- To ensure that records of all notes, logs and correspondence are dated, signed and maintained
- To be aware of procedures to be followed in the case of suspected abuse
- To liaise with Tusla and any other relevant personnel
- To use the Standard Reporting Form if a report is being made
- To ensure that all staff/volunteers/students are Garda-vetted prior to becoming involved with the service
- To provide support and in-service training for staff
- To be prepared to take action in the case of suspected abuse
- To provide direct support and counselling for any staff member involved in an ongoing case.

Furthermore, the Children First Act 2015

> places specific obligations on organisations which provide services to children and young people, including the requirement to:
>
> - keep children safe from harm while they are using your service
> - carry out a risk assessment to identify whether a child or young person could be harmed while receiving your services
> - develop a Child Safeguarding Statement that outlines the policies and procedures which are in place to manage the risks that have been identified. (*See appendix 2 for a sample template of the safeguarding statement.*)
> - appoint a relevant person to be the first point of contact in respect of the organisation's Child Safeguarding Statement.
>
> (*Children First*, 2017, p. 30)

ROLE OF DESIGNATED CHILD PROTECTION OFFICER

The relevant person to be the first point of contact is often known as a Designated Child Protection Officer or Designated Liaison Person (DLP). Their role includes the following:

* Advise managers, supervisors and colleagues within a service about concerns regarding individual children (as appropriate)
* Advise on best practice and ensure that the service's child safeguarding policies and procedures are followed
* Organise and/or facilitate training and workshops for all staff in relation to child protection
* Report concerns, suspicions and allegations of child abuse to Tusla
* Create and maintain links with Tusla social workers and other relevant agencies and resource personnel
* Consult informally with a Tusla Duty Social Worker through the Dedicated Contact Point, if necessary
* Facilitate follow-up action
* Maintain records of all referrals in a secure and confidential manner
* Keep up to date on current developments regarding provision, practice, legal obligations and policies
* Ensure that the service's policies are brought to the attention of all employees and volunteers, including students on work practice placements
* Facilitate an annual review of child protection procedures and policies.

THE CHILD SAFEGUARDING STATEMENT

The Children First Act 2015 requires organisations that are providers of relevant services to prepare a child safeguarding statement. This is a written statement that specifies the service being provided and the principles and procedures to be observed in order to ensure, as far as practicable, that a child availing of the service is safe from harm. The service should ensure that the child safeguarding statement has due regard to the National Guidance and any other child protection guidelines issued by Tusla concerning child safeguarding statements under section 11(4) of the Children First Act 2015 (adapted from *Children First*, 2017, p. 34).

Templates are available on the Tusla website to assist services in carrying out a risk assessment and in drawing up their safety statement.

Tusla, *Child Safeguarding: A Guide for Policy Procedure and Practice* (2nd edition. Dublin: Government Publications, 2019)
https://www.tusla.ie/uploads/content/Tusla_-_Child_Safeguarding_-_A_Guide_for_Policy,_Procedure_and_Practice.pdf

Mandated persons

The Children First Act 2015 places a legal obligation on certain people, including ELC professionals, to report child protection concerns at or above a defined threshold, to Tusla. These mandated persons must also assist Tusla, on request, in its assessment of child protection concerns about children who have been the subject of a mandated report. The mandated person, under the legislation, is required to report any knowledge, belief or reasonable suspicion that a child has 'been harmed, is being harmed, or is at risk of being harmed'.

If there is doubt about whether the concern reaches the legal definition of harm for making a mandated report, Tusla can provide advice in this regard. If the concern does not reach the threshold for mandated reporting, but there is a reasonable concern about the welfare or protection of a child, a report should be made to Tusla anyway (adapted from *Children First*, 2017, pp. 19–20).

The mandated person may or may not also be the Designated Liaison Person.

Think about

In relation to the case study on p. 100:

1. What actions should the ELC practitioner take in the short term in this situation?
2. What other persons in the service might get involved and what actions should they take?
3. In the long term, are there any actions that should be taken by the manager and the staff in general?
4. Complete the Tusla Child Protection and Welfare Reporting Form on the following pages.

Child Protection and Welfare Report Form

MANDATED PERSONS AND NON MANDATED PERSONS
(Children First Act 2015 & Children First National Guidance)

Use block letters when filling out this form.
Fields marked with an * are mandatory.

1. Tusla Area (this is where the child resides)*	

2. Date of Report*	

3. Details of Child

First Name*		Surname*	
Male*	☐	Female*	☐
Address*		Date of Birth*	
		Estimated Age*	
		School Name	
		School Address	
Eircode			

4. Details of Concerns*

Please complete the following section with as much detail about the specific child protection or welfare concern or allegation as possible. Include dates, times, incident details and names of anyone who observed any incident. Please include the parents and child's view, if known. Please attach additional sheets, if necessary

Please see *'Tusla Children First – A Guide for the Reporting of Child Protection and Welfare Concerns'* for additional assistance on the steps to consider in making a report to Tusla

5. Type of Concern

Child Welfare Concern	☐		
Emotional Abuse	☐	Physical Abuse	☐
Neglect	☐	Sexual Abuse	☐

6. Details of Reporter

First Name		Surname	
Address If reporting in a professional capacity, please use your professional address		Organisation	
		Position Held	
		Mobile No.	
		Telephone No.	
Eircode		Email Address	

Child Protection and Welfare Report Form

MANDATED PERSONS AND NON MANDATED PERSONS
(Children First Act 2015 & Children First National Guidance)

Is this a Mandated Report made under Sec 14, Children First Act 2015?*	Yes	☐	No	☐
Mandated Person's Type				

7. Details of Other Persons Where a Joint Report is Being Made

First Name		Surname	
Address If reporting in a professional capacity, please use your professional address		**Organisation**	
		Position Held	
		Mobile No.	
		Telephone No.	
Eircode		**Email Address**	

First Name		Surname	
Address If reporting in a professional capacity, please use your professional address		**Organisation**	
		Position Held	
		Mobile No.	
		Telephone No.	
Eircode		**Email Address**	

8. Parents Aware of Report

Are the child's parents/carers aware that this concern is being reported to Tusla?*	Yes	☐	No	☐
If the parent/carer does not know, please indicate reasons:				

9. Relationships

Details of Mother

First Name		Surname	
Address		**Mobile No.**	
		Telephone No.	
		Email Address	
Eircode			

Is the Mother a Legal Guardian?*	Yes	☐	No	☐

Details of Father

First Name		Surname	
Address		**Mobile No.**	
		Telephone No.	
		Email Address	
Eircode			

Child Protection and Welfare Report Form

MANDATED PERSONS AND NON MANDATED PERSONS
(Children First Act 2015 & Children First National Guidance)

Is the Father a Legal Guardian?*		Yes	☐	No	☐

10. Household Composition

First Name	Surname	Relationship	Date of Birth	Estimated Age	Additional Information e.g. school, occupation, other

11. Details of Person(s) Allegedly Causing Harm

First Name*		Surname*	
Male*	☐	Female*	☐
Address		Date of Birth	
		Estimated Age	
		Mobile No.	
		Telephone No.	
Eircode		Email Address	
Occupation		Organisation	
Position Held			

Relationship to Child	
Address at time of alleged incident	
If name unknown please indicate reason	

First Name*		Surname*	
Male*	☐	Female*	☐
Address		Date of Birth	
		Estimated Age	
		Mobile No.	
		Telephone No.	
Eircode		Email Address	
Occupation		Organisation	
Position Held			

Relationship to Child	
Address at time of alleged incident	
If name unknown please indicate reason	

Child Protection and Welfare Report Form

MANDATED PERSONS AND NON MANDATED PERSONS
(Children First Act 2015 & Children First National Guidance)

12. Name and Address of Other Organisations, Personnel or Agencies Known to be Involved Currently or Previously with the Family

Profession	First Name	Surname	Address	Contact Number	Recent Contact e.g. 3/6/9 months ago
Social Worker					
Public Health Nurse					
GP					
Hospital					
School					
Gardaí					
Pre-school/ crèche					
Other					

13. Any Other Relevant Information, Including any Previous Contact with the Child or Family

Please ensure you have indicated if this is a mandated report in section 6.
Thank you for completing the report form.

In completing this report form you are providing details on yourself and on others. Details such as name, address and date of birth fall under the definition of 'Personal Data' in the Data Protection Acts, 1988 & 2003. Tusla has a responsibility under these Acts in its capacity as a Data Controller to, amongst other things, obtain and process this data fairly; keep it safe and secure; and to keep it for a specified lawful purpose. That purpose is to fulfil our statutory responsibility under the Child Care Act 1991 to promote the protection and welfare of children. Tusla may, during the course of the assessment of this report disclose such Personal Data to other agencies including An Garda Síochána. Further details about Tusla's responsibilities as a Data Controller and your rights as a Data Subject can be found on our website, www.tusla.ie. As you are providing Personal Data on others, you are a Data Processor. We ask that you only provide those details that are necessary for the report and that you keep this report and the Personal Data contained in it secure from unauthorised access, disclosure, destruction or accidental loss.

14. For Completion by Tusla Authorised Person on Receipt of Report

Report Received by				
First Name		Surname		Date

Mandated Report Acknowledgement by

Child Protection and Welfare Report Form

MANDATED PERSONS AND NON MANDATED PERSONS
(Children First Act 2015 & Children First National Guidance)

First Name		Surname		Date Sent	

Authorised Person Signature*	
Date*	

Child Previously Known		Yes	☐	No	☐
Allocated Case No					

This form can be found at *https://www.tusla.ie/uploads/content/Child_Protection_and_Welfare_Report_Form_FINAL.pdf*

OTHER RELEVANT OR SUPPORTING LEGISLATION

* **Child Care Act 1991:** This is the key piece of legislation which regulates childcare policy in Ireland. It is the basis for the Pre-School Regulations 2016 and for *Children First: National Guidance for the Protection and Welfare of Children* (2017).

* **Protections for Persons Reporting Child Abuse Act 1998:** This legislation provides protection from prosecution or liability if a person reports child protection concerns to Tusla in good faith and in a child's best interests.

* **Criminal Justice Act 2006:** This Act makes it an offence for a person who is in a position of responsibility for a child to fail to protect that child from harm or to recklessly endanger the child in some way.

* **Criminal Justice (Withholding of Information on Offences against Children and Vulnerable Persons) Act 2012:** Under this Act, it is a criminal offence to withhold information about a serious offence against a child or a vulnerable person.

* **National Vetting Bureau (Children and Vulnerable Persons) Acts 2012–2016; Children First Act 2015:** This legislation places statutory obligations on employers in relation to Garda vetting requirements regarding anyone working with children and vulnerable adults.

* **Criminal Law (Sexual Offences) Act 2017:** This legislation addresses the sexual exploitation of children and makes it an offence to obtain or provide any child for the purposes of sexual exploitation. It includes as offences the grooming of children for the purpose of exploitation and the use of modern technology to prey on children.

* **Domestic Violence Act 2018:** This legislation recognises the harm that domestic violence, including coercive control, can do to children and makes provision to take account of this.

Supporting the ELC professional

Only about a third of reported cases result in court cases and care proceedings. For the most part, children who are at risk continue to attend their local schools and ELC services. On the surface, it may seem that very few changes occur as a result of making a report, but the practitioner must continue to work with the child and family. If professionalism and impartiality are maintained at all times and the best interests of the child are always kept in mind, then it will be possible to re-establish working relationships with the parent, which may have suffered because of the abuse allegations made by the ELC service. For the person working directly with children and parents, the stress and anxiety provoked in situations where abuse occurs cannot and should not be underestimated. If this person does not take action, a child may suffer further abuse, and if he or she does take action, he or she should receive adequate support from colleagues, management and other professionals.

ALLEGATIONS OF ABUSE AGAINST ELC STAFF

When allegations of abuse are made against staff, it can be a very traumatic time for all those involved. Nevertheless, it is equally important that the procedures in place for dealing with allegations of abuse by any adult are also adhered to in relation to allegations against staff. If the allegations are serious, then the staff member will be suspended pending investigation.

In the case of an allegation against a staff member, there is even more need for support for the staff of the setting, reasons for which include the following:

* When abuse involves an outsider, there will probably be one or maybe two children involved; if abuse occurs within the setting there may be several children involved.
* The staff member involved may be well known or may even be a friend.
* Feelings of guilt and/or anger may be very strong.

Because of the increased awareness of child abuse generally, people who work with young children are often fearful that they will be wrongly accused. There is a great fear of the irreparable damage that is done to reputation after an untrue or inaccurate allegation has been made. If practitioners adhere strictly to principles of good practice, then this is most unlikely to happen and the staff member, if accused, will have the confidence that he/she has done nothing wrong. Poor professional practices such as shouting at children, ridiculing them or imposing extreme 'time out' should be dealt with through supervision, and the member of staff should be helped through extra training and support to enable him or her to develop appropriate practices. Bad practice should never be condoned for any reason.

Empowering children

The encouragement and promotion of healthy social and emotional development is vital for the wellbeing of all children whatever their circumstances. Promoting confidence, independence and a sense of self-worth in children may help them to tell about an abusive situation or to avoid it altogether. Being skilled in any, or all, of the following areas gives children a greater feeling of control and perhaps assertiveness. Their ability to cope in different situations is greatly enhanced if they have been helped to:

* increase their self-awareness
* build up self-esteem
* develop an ability to express themselves (language skills)
* take control where it is age and stage appropriate
* cope with the unexpected
* identify their champions/people who will stand up for them
* develop problem-solving skills.

Although it is essential that children learn some skills of self-protection, it is important to keep in mind that this in no way exonerates the adult from the responsibility of protecting them. Children cannot be expected to protect themselves and there is no conclusive research showing that children who have avoided abuse did so because they had any particular skills.

Activity

In small groups, work together to identify ways in which the ELC practitioner can help to empower children.

* Review the role of the practitioner in promoting all-round, healthy, social and emotional development.
* Plan a range of activities for children of different ages that would help them to master some of the skills listed above. Different groups could focus on different age groups. When you have finished, feedback to the whole group.

For example: 'What if' games — 'What if you fell and hurt your knee?' This type of activity will help children to learn problem-solving skills and to cope with the unexpected.

When working with children, do not focus on abusive or dangerous situations, since children will learn more easily from situations that are familiar to them.

In any activity cited, include some that cover the fact that children need to know how:

to be safe	to protect their own bodies
to say 'no'	to get help
to tell	to be believed
not to keep secrets	to refuse touches
to cope with strangers	to break rules.

RECAP QUESTIONS

1. What are the four categories of child abuse?
2. What is the role of the ELC practitioner in relation to all children?
3. List three things you should do immediately if you are concerned about a child.
4. Is there a difference between a 'mandated person' and a 'designated liaison person'?

9

Síolta: The National Quality Framework for Early Childhood Education (2006)

Introduction

Síolta (the Irish word for 'seeds') is the national quality framework for the early childhood sector. It establishes the quality standards to which all services should aspire. It is designed to support practitioners in the development and delivery of high-quality care and education services for children aged from birth to six years.

Síolta can be used no matter what kind of curriculum is followed, for example a play-based curriculum, Montessori, HighScope or primary school. However, in the current development of ELC services it is often twinned with Aistear (the national curriculum framework).

Síolta is designed to define, assess and support the improvement of quality across all aspects of practice in early learning and care settings where children aged birth to six years are present. These settings include:

* Full- and part-time day care
* Childminding
* Sessional services
* Infant classes in primary schools.

Early learning and care services participating in the free pre-school (ECCE) year must agree to provide an appropriate educational programme for children that adheres to the principles of *Síolta*.

Services are supported in meeting this requirement through the assistance of *Síolta* coordinators, their local City and County Childcare Committee (CCC) and *Better Start* mentors.

The Early Years Education Policy Unit within the Department of Education and Skills manages the *Síolta* programme and provides a leadership and supportive role. The National *Síolta Aistear* Initiative (NSAI) was established in 2016 to support the coordinated rollout of *Síolta: The National Quality Framework* and *Aistear: The Early Childhood Curriculum Framework* (see Chapter 10).

The 12 *Síolta* principles and 16 *Síolta* standards

Síolta is underpinned by 12 guiding principles of best practice. The 12 principles underpin 16 stated standards, which ELC services work towards achieving. Services describe their own practice in each standard, make plans for improving their practice and collect a portfolio of evidence to demonstrate the progress they have made. The model then offers signposts for reflection, affording practitioners the opportunity to examine how they are meeting these standards.

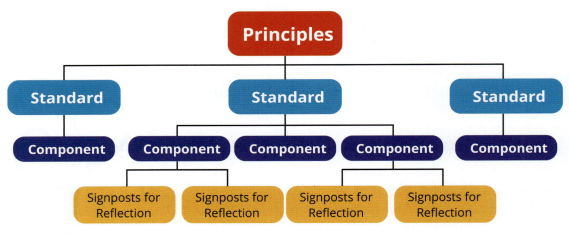

THE 12 PRINCIPLES

1. Childhood is a significant and distinct time in life that must be nurtured, respected, valued and supported in its own right.
2. The child's individuality, strengths, rights and needs are central in the provision of quality early childhood experiences.
3. Parents are the primary educators of the child and have a pre-eminent role in promoting his/her wellbeing, learning and development.
4. Responsive, sensitive and reciprocal relationships, which are consistent over time, are essential to the wellbeing, learning and development of the young child.

5. Equality is an essential characteristic of quality early childhood care and education.

6. Quality early childhood settings acknowledge and respect diversity and ensure that all children and families have their individual, personal, cultural and linguistic identity validated.

7. The physical environment of the young child has a direct impact on his/her wellbeing, learning and development.

8. The safety, welfare and wellbeing of all children must be protected and promoted in all early childhood environments.

9. The role of the adult in providing quality early childhood experiences requires cooperation, communication and mutual respect.

10. The provision of quality early childhood experiences requires cooperation, communication and mutual respect.

11. Pedagogy in early childhood is expressed by curricula or programmes of activities which take a holistic approach to the development and learning of the child and reflect the inseparable nature of care and education.

12. Play is central to the wellbeing, development and learning of the young child.

Activity

Describe ways in which an ELC service can demonstrate commitment to the principles of *Síolta* in the following areas:

* Provision of play
* Communication with families
* Physical care of the child
* Selection of resources for the service
* Other elements of the service.

THE 16 STANDARDS

Standard 1 Rights of the child: This means that the child is enabled to exercise choice and to use initiative as an active participant and partner in their own development and learning.

Standard 2 Environments: Enriching environments, both indoor and outdoor (including materials and equipment), are well maintained, safe, available, accessible and adaptable. Children have a right to quality services that are developmentally appropriate and offer a variety of challenging and stimulating experiences.

Standard 3 Parents and families: Valuing and involving parents and families requires a proactive partnership approach evidenced by a range of clearly stated, accessible and implemented processes, policies and procedures.

Standard 4 Consultation: Ensuring inclusive decision-making requires consultation that promotes participation and seeks out, listens to and acts upon the views and opinions of children, parents and staff and other stakeholders, as appropriate.

Standard 5 Interactions: Fostering constructive interactions (child/child, child/adult and adult/adult) requires explicit policies, procedures and practice that emphasise the value of process and are based on mutual respect, equal partnership and sensitivity.

Standard 6 Play: Promoting play requires that each child has ample time to engage in freely available and accessible, developmentally appropriate and well-resourced opportunities for exploration, creativity and 'meaning making' in the company of other children, with participating and supportive adults and alone, where appropriate.

Standard 7 Curriculum: Encouraging each child's holistic development and learning requires the implementation of a verifiable, broad-based, documented and flexible curriculum or programme.

Standard 8 Planning and evaluation: Enriching and informing all aspects of practice within the setting requires cycles of observation, planning, action and evaluation, undertaken on a regular basis.

Standard 9 Health and welfare: Promoting the health and welfare of the child requires protection from harm, provision of nutritious food, appropriate opportunities for rest and secure relationships characterised by trust and respect.

Standard 10 Organisation: Organising and managing resources effectively requires an agreed written philosophy, supported by clearly communicated policies and procedures to guide and determine practice.

Standard 11 Professional practice: Practising in a professional manner requires that individuals have skills, knowledge, values and attitudes appropriate to their role and responsibility within the setting. In addition, it requires regular reflection upon practice and engagement in supported, ongoing professional development. (Components relevant to this standard are further explored below.)

Standard 12 Communication: Communicating effectively in the best interests of the child requires policies, procedures and actions that promote the proactive sharing of knowledge and information among appropriate stakeholders with respect and confidentiality.

Standard 13 Transitions: Ensuring continuity of experiences for children requires policies, procedures and practice that promote sensitive management of transitions, consistency in key relationships, liaison within and between settings, the keeping and transfer of relevant information (with parental consent) and the close involvement of parents and, where appropriate, relevant professionals.

Standard 14 Identity and belonging: Promoting positive identities and a strong sense of belonging requires clearly defined policies, procedures and practices that empower every child and adult to develop a confident self and group identity, and to have a positive understanding and regard for the identity and rights of others.

Standard 15 Legislation and regulation: Being compliant requires that all relevant regulations and legislative requirements are met or exceeded.

Standard 16 Community involvement: Promoting community involvement requires the establishment of networks and connections evidenced by policies, procedures and actions that extend and support all adults' and children's engagement with the wider community.

COMPONENTS

There are 75 components related to the standards which allow for the practical application of the standards. Components of Quality are also explained by a set of signposts in the *Síolta* manual.

Example of a component

Standard 11 Professional Practice has five components: 11.1, 11.2, 11.3, 11.4 and 11.5. Component 11.3 states that: 'The setting supports and promotes regular opportunity for practitioners to reflect upon and review their practice and contribute positively to the development of quality practice in the setting.' Signposts for Reflection for Component 11.3 are:

11.3.1	What processes are in place to allow practitioners time to reflect on their own practice, in order to identify areas where obtaining additional knowledge or changing approaches is necessary?
11.3.2	How often is time scheduled in your setting for group reflection and discussion about practice?
11.3.3	How are practitioners encouraged to share their experience and ideas regarding practice in the setting?

(*Síolta User Manual*, 2017, p. 84)

Activity

Access the *Síolta User Manual* and, choosing two standards, find the components and signposts for reflection.

https://www.siolta.ie/media/pdfs/siolta-manual-2017.pdf

PRACTICAL APPLICATION OF *SÍOLTA* STANDARDS

EXAMPLE: STANDARD 11: PROFESSIONAL PRACTICE

Practising in a professional manner requires that individuals have skills, knowledge, values and attitudes appropriate to their role and responsibility within the setting. In addition, it requires regular reflection upon practice and engagement in supported, ongoing professional development.

This standard can be practised and applied using the following components:

Component 11.1 All adults working within the setting can provide evidence that they have achieved levels of skills and knowledge appropriate to their role and responsibilities.

Component 11.2 All adults subscribe to a set of core principles, which inform all aspects of their practice in early childhood care and education settings.

Component 11.3 The setting supports and promotes regular opportunity for practitioners to reflect upon and review their practice and contribute positively to the development of quality practice in the setting.

Component 11.4 Adults within the setting are encouraged and appropriately resourced to engage in a wide variety of regular and ongoing professional development.

Component 11.5 Adults demonstrate sensitivity, warmth and positive regard for children and their families.

Using component 11.1, we can apply the following signposts for reflection:

11.1.1 What levels of qualifications have been attained by adults working in the setting?

Think about, for example, National Framework for Qualifications level indicators; professional qualification requirements

11.1.2 Can adults working directly with children in the setting demonstrate that they have skills and knowledge in core areas appropriate to their role and responsibilities?

Think about: in a practical setting, children with additional needs

11.1.3 Are those in managerial roles qualified to at least Bachelor degree level or equivalent?

11.1.4 Are adults working in autonomous or supervisory positions qualified to at least QQI Level 6 or equivalent?

11.1.5 Are all adults included for the purposes of calculating ratios of adults to children in the setting qualified to QQI Level 5 or equivalent?

11.1.6 Are all other adults who are unqualified, or in the process of acquiring training and qualifications, treated as supernumerary in the setting?

11.1.7 Are adults working in support positions appropriately qualified?

11.1.8 What evidence can adults provide to demonstrate the levels of skills and knowledge they have achieved?

Think about, for example, formal learning (e.g. qualifications, certified learning, etc.); informal learning (e.g. portfolios of learning, experience, etc.).

Activity

Over a period of several days, carry out three observations of a child in your placement as follows:

* Observation 1: Observe the child during an adult-led large group activity such as circle time or lunchtime.
* Observation 2: Observe the same child during a small-group activity with their peers, such as a cooperative play situation in which an adult is either not involved or only involved periodically.
* Observation 3: Observe the child during a one-to-one interaction with an adult.

In each of the observations:

* Note the child's interactions with the adult. In your evaluations, comment on the quality and value of the different types of interactions for the child's language, emotional and social development.
* Draw some conclusions based on the above.
* Note how the findings from your observations inform your professional practice with the children.

QUALITY INDICATORS

It is neither possible nor appropriate to set down exact and unchanging quality standards to be applied across the board in ELC services. Each centre must formulate its own definition of quality, one which meets all the needs of the children and adults involved. Such a definition must take account of agreed quality indicators such as those set out in the *Síolta* NQF and must be arrived at through discussion and agreement with all the parties. This means that defining quality is a process rather than an end, a process which is ongoing and which involves continuous self-evaluation.

PROFESSIONAL PRACTICE IN ELC

High quality in an ELC service is evident in:

* the ethos, or underpinning values
* the adults and the relationships involved.

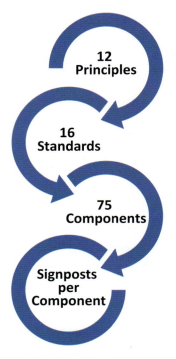

Activity

Identify the underpinning values evident in this mission statement.

LITTLE TREASURES CRÈCHE ETHOS:

The ethos of the centre is to treat each child with the utmost respect. Each child is valued as an individual and is encouraged to reach his/her own maximum potential at his/her own pace.

Mission Statement:

At Little Treasures Crèche we are committed to:

- Providing the highest quality childcare for all our families.
- Continually striving to help nurture, challenge and foster independence in all the children in our care.
- Providing a safe, warm, stimulating age-appropriate environment, where all children are encouraged to learn, grow and actively explore.
- Developing strong partnerships with our parents, committing to working together to build a foundation that nurtures each child's self-esteem and confidence.

Centre Policies & Curriculum:

Each child is consistently encouraged to develop naturally at his/her own pace. This growth is documented in each child's own individual developmental folder which parents are encouraged to browse. A nursery booklet is available with an overview of centre policies for parents and families.

Aistear: The Early Childhood Curriculum Framework (2009)

Introduction

Aistear (NCCA, 2009), the Irish word for 'journey', is the National Early Childhood Curriculum Framework for all children from birth to six years. It provides information, ideas and suggestions to help support children's learning and development during this important stage of their lives. The main aim of Aistear is that all children can grow and develop as competent and confident learners. Aistear includes principles, themes and guidelines for good practice. It is not a prescriptive programme that sets out activities and worksheets for babies, toddlers and young children but one which leaves plenty of room for individuals and services to use it as a framework to develop a curriculum suited to their particular demographic of children or as a framework for an existing curriculum in the ELC service.

Aistear

* is a set of shared principles and themes that underpin quality early childhood provision (see *Síolta*, 2006) and support children's learning and development through the provision of age-appropriate play and learning opportunities
* is taking place where there are caring, supportive relationships with adults and other children

- is designed for use in all ELC settings including the home, crèche, nursery, pre-schools, Naíonraí and also includes junior and senior infant classes in primary schools
- recognises and celebrates early childhood as a unique period in life, when children enjoy and learn through experience
- helps adults to plan learning experiences that enable children to grow and develop as competent and confident learners, within nurturing relationships with others
- describes the types of learning (disposition, values and attitudes, skills, knowledge and understanding) that are important for children in the early years
- offers ideas and suggestions on how this learning might be fostered
- provides guidelines on supporting children through partnership with parents, nurturing interactions, play and assessment.

Principles of early learning and development

Aistear is based on 12 principles, presented in three groups, which are deemed as being crucial to and underpinning early learning and development.

Children and their lives in early childhood	Children's connections with others	How children learn and develop
1. The child's uniqueness	4. Relationships	7. Holistic learning and development
2. Equality and diversity	5. The adult's role	8. Active learning
3. Children as citizens	6. Parents and family and community	9. Play and hands-on experiences
		10. Relevant and meaningful experiences
		11. Communication and language
		12. The learning environment

Each principle is presented using a short statement followed by an explanation of the principle from the child's perspective. This highlights the adult's role in supporting children's learning.

Aistear themes

Early learning and development is presented in four interconnected themes in Aistear.

1. **Wellbeing**
   Wellbeing focuses on developing as a person. It has two main elements: psychological wellbeing (including feeling and thinking) and physical wellbeing.

2. **Identity and Belonging**
   Identity and belonging is about children developing a positive sense of who they are, and feeling that they are valued and respected as part of a family and community.

3. **Communicating**
   The theme of communicating is about children sharing their experiences, thoughts, ideas and feelings with others with growing confidence and competence in a variety of ways and for a variety of purposes.

4. **Exploring and Thinking**
   The theme of exploring and thinking is about children making sense of the things, places and people in their world by interacting with others, playing, investigating, questioning, and forming, testing and refining ideas.

The themes are used to describe how children learn. Each theme is presented using four aims, which in turn are divided into six learning goals. Each theme offers ideas and suggestions for learning opportunities and experiences which adults could provide for children in working towards the aims and goals of each theme. These 'Sample Learning Opportunities' can be adapted and developed for different situations across the different age groups (babies, toddlers and young children).

Guidelines for good practice

Good quality early years practice relies less on a content-led curriculum and direct instruction and more on early years frameworks of values and principles, respecting the process underpinning an emergent or enquiry-based curriculum. (Hayes *et al.*, 2017, p. 142)

The guidelines for good practice are listed under four headings:

1. Building partnerships between parents and practitioners
2. Learning and developing through interactions
3. Learning and developing through play
4. Supporting learning and development through assessment

These guidelines describe how the adult can support early learning and development across the themes and outline a wide variety of sample learning experiences. The first two guidelines are covered elsewhere in this book, in particular in Chapters 4, 17 and 18. 'Learning and developing through play' is explored in other modules, particularly 'Curriculum, Play and Creative Studies'. What follows is a brief exploration of Aistear guidelines on the use of assessment in supporting learning.

Guidelines on assessment

Assessment is sometimes seen as a negative element of a process; however, it is an essential tool in discovering what one knows and does not know in a given subject area. We make assessments and judgements all the time about our own learning and development and that of others. As adults working with children, we make judgements on a daily basis about a child's abilities, their progress and how we can facilitate a more enriched learning experience for them. According to Aistear:

> **Assessment is the ongoing process of collecting, documenting, reflecting on and using information to develop rich portraits of children as learners in order to support and enhance their future learning. (NCCA, 2009, p. 72)**

Sometimes, assessing children using the four actions listed above happens in a matter of minutes, but mostly assessment is planned and takes place over a period of time, usually focusing on certain aspects of development and learning.

In the early years, babies, toddlers and young children are growing at a rapid pace; their brain is developing faster in the first five years of their life than it will ever grow again. Therefore, the provision of stimulating environments filled with social interactions is brain food for the healthy development of the child. In order to provide children with the optimum levels of opportunities to fulfil their development and learning needs, we need to adopt two approaches to assessment. One is assessment **for** learning and the other is assessment **of** learning.

> ## DEFINITIONS
>
> **Assessment for learning** focuses on using assessment information to help children with the next steps in their learning and development. For example, if you have observed a child is completing an 8-piece jigsaw without any help, you may suggest they try a 10-piece jigsaw.
>
> **Assessment of learning** is to inform others such as parents and other professionals about the child's progress. Parents are invariably delighted to know and have evidence of their child's learning and developmental progress, but assessment is also helpful in identifying any issues. For example, if a child was getting very frustrated using peg boards or threading spools, there may need to be further assessments of the child's learning to ensure there are no underlying issues.
>
> It is important to remember that ELC practitioners are not diagnosticians although they may often be the ones to notice early signs of potential difficulties.

The adult should consider the following questions when thinking about assessment.

Making a judgement

1. What aspects of children's learning and development do I want to focus on in my assessment?
2. Who will make the judgement – me, the child, or both of us?

Recording

1. How will I record the judgement—as a mental note, as a written note, as a comment or story, as a drawing, as a photograph or video recording, on a checklist?
2. How will I ensure that, over time, I am building up rich portraits of children's learning and development?
3. Will I give children opportunities to record their own judgements? How?

Sharing

1. What do I want to say to children about their learning and development?
2. What do I want to share with children's parents?
3. How will I share the assessment information? (NCCA, 2009, p. 72)

When adults are assessing children's progress in ELC, Aistear recommends they should look for evidence of the child's progress in the following areas:

* Dispositions: for example, curiosity, concentration, resilience and perseverance
* Skills: for example, walking, cutting, writing and problem solving

* Attitudes and values: for example, respect for themselves and others, care for the environment and positive attitudes to learning and to life
* Knowledge and understanding: for example, classifying objects using colour and size, learning 'rules' for interacting with others, finding out about people in their community, and understanding that words have meaning (NCCA, 2009, p. 74).

ASSESSMENT METHODS

There are five assessment methods:

1. Self-assessment
2. Conversation
3. Observation
4. Setting tasks
5. Testing

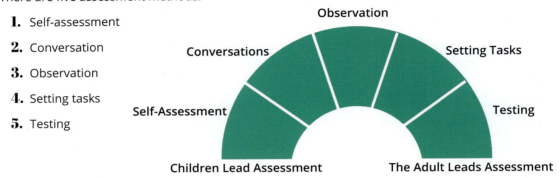

1. SELF-ASSESSMENT

Self-assessment involves children thinking about their own learning and development. Children do this as part of how they learn, and often they are the best assessors of what they have done and achieved. Over time, they are better able to think about what they did, said or made, and to make decisions about how they might do better next time. This helps them to set personal goals and to work towards these goals together as a group or individually (NCCA, 2009, p. 81).

2. CONVERSATION

Conversation is a method whereby children take the lead in making judgements about their own progress as learners. Adults and children, and children and children, talk to each other about what they are doing and thinking. These conversations complement all other assessment methods. For example, observations can alert the adult to a particular aspect of children's learning and development while follow-on conversations can give the adult a better understanding of what children can do or understand. Most conversations just happen, while some are planned (NCCA, 2009, p. 84).

3. OBSERVATION

Observation involves watching and listening to children and using the information gathered through this to enhance their learning and development. The adult may use different types of observations depending on what he/she wants to find out. Like conversations, observations can be planned or spontaneous and are best carried out by an adult who knows the child well (NCCA, 2009, p. 87).

4. SETTING TASKS

Setting tasks for assessment purposes involves the adult designing activities to gather information on a specific aspect of learning and development. Sometimes the adult might set tasks at the end of a particular period of time or after a piece of work or project on a topic has been done (NCCA, 2009, p. 93).

5. TESTING

Testing involves the adult leading the assessment. Ongoing observations and conversations with children provide the adult with rich information on children's progress and achievements as young learners. Testing in early childhood usually involves using a commercially produced set of tasks and/or questions to collect information about specific aspects of a child's learning and development, such as motor and social skills, behaviour, oral language and understanding. Some of the tests are known as standardised tests and are usually used in primary schools or for children with special educational needs. These tests are used, scored and interpreted in the same way across all settings which use them. The test scores compare a child's learning and development with that of other children of the same age. It is important to remember that test scores for young children can be unreliable. It is also important to remember that, as tests are standardised for particular populations of children, the results for a child who may have a different first language, for example, should be interpreted and used with care.

Together with information from other assessment methods, test scores can help identify children who might experience learning difficulties now or in the future. This is called screening. Other tests, known as diagnostic tests, may be used with individual children (with parental permission) to help identify a specific difficulty and to provide supports and resources to minimise the potential impact of this on their learning and development (NCCA, 2009, pp. 98–99).

While these guidelines present the methods individually, each method often involves using other methods in addition. A combination of methods helps the adult build richer and more authentic portraits of children as learners.

Assessment Challenges and Strengths

Method	Challenges	Strengths
Self-assessment	Can place too much emphasis on what children make or do without looking at why. Children need time to develop skills to think about their learning.	Helps children develop an understanding of themselves as learners. Encourages children to feel a sense of pride and achievement in themselves. Enables children to take greater responsibility for their learning. Makes learning more enjoyable and motivating.

Method	Challenges	Strengths
Conversation	Children's developing ability to communicate influences what information they can share and how. The adult needs to listen carefully to how and what children communicate. The adult requires time to develop skills to encourage and enable children to share insights on their learning and development through talking. Can be time-consuming. Can be difficult to do with a large group.	Gives children opportunities to talk about their work, experiences, family, likes and dislikes. Provides information about why children reacted in a particular way about what they did or said, or how they made things.
Observation	Planned observations and, especially, target child observations require time. The adult requires time to develop skills in recording key pieces of information. The adult needs to be aware of what information he/she is looking for, and to be mindful of how that influences the observations.	Can be spontaneous or planned, and can be carried out in a few seconds or minutes. Provides information about the context in which children's learning and development takes place. Gives immediate information about how and what children are learning and experiencing.
Setting tasks	Often requires particular resources. The adult needs time to observe children taking part in the tasks, and, where helpful, to talk to them.	Can provide samples of children's work as evidence of their learning and development. Provides information about children's learning in activities which interest them.
Testing	Test scores can be unreliable. Tasks and questions can lack meaning and relevance for children and may be culturally inappropriate. Can be time-consuming.	Helps to identify children who may have learning difficulties. Indicates specific learning difficulties.

Documentation

It is important to document any assessment of babies, toddlers and young children. This record helps to tell a story about children's journey through the early years. It can be very helpful when sharing information with parents and other professionals and constitutes a very effective tool when building partnerships with families. Documentation is also crucial to furthering our knowledge of children and can be used for research purposes.

Effective assessments and documents should enable ELC practitioners to be informed about what children understand, what they can do and how they approach learning. When we know what excites children and stimulates their brain, we can make learning more fun and enjoyable. Tapping into their unique interests and exploring it with them is essential on their journey as capable, competent learners.

There are seven types of documentation that ELC services can use to store the assessments of children. Some of these are informal, yet capture an enormous amount of information about a child's learning and development, for example a Post-it or a photograph.

SEVEN TYPES OF DOCUMENTATION

1. SAMPLES OF CHILDREN'S WORK

Resources: Children's work

Method: The adult stores samples of children's work. Sometimes the children choose the samples, sometimes the adult decides what is chosen, and at other times the children and adult choose together.

Age group: Six months to six years

2. NOTES

Resources: Notebook, Post-its, computer with word processing package

Method: The adult makes brief notes, often consisting of just key words, about a particular event, activity or task. Sometimes the notes may be longer, giving details about a particular aspect of the child's learning. The notes may focus on an individual child or a group of children. Over time, the notes tell a story of what the children do, say and understand.

Age group: Birth to six years

3. ICT (PHOTOGRAPHS AND VIDEO OR AUDIO RECORDS)

Resources: Camera, video recorder, audio recorder, tapes

Method: The adult uses the camera or video or audio recorder to capture moments in children's learning and development. Each photograph and video or audio clip helps tell a story. A collection created over time can show the child's progress and achievements. A series of photographs can be taken on one day to show the child's progress in a particular activity.

Age group: Birth to six years (with written prior parental consent)

4. STORIES

Resources: Notebook, Post-its, computer with word processing package

Method: The adult makes brief notes about children's involvement in a particular event, activity or task. The notes may focus on an individual child's contribution or the contributions of a group of children. In contrast to notes, this type of documentation gives more detailed information about a particular child's interactions with others, as well as the relevant objects and places, in sequence. These stories help the adult to see and understand better the progress children are making in relation to Aistear's dispositions, skills, attitudes and values, knowledge, and understanding. Samples of children's work and photographs can enrich the stories.

Age group: Birth to six years

5. DAILY DIARIES OR RECORDS OF CARE

Resources: Notebook, folder, computer with word processing package

Method: The adult (often the key worker) makes brief notes each day about a child's routines and responses, for example what the child ate, how much he/she slept, his/her nappy changes and different interactions and activities. Based on behaviour, body language and verbal feedback from children, the adult may also note particular things the child likes, prefers and achieves. The diary or record is shared with parents by sending it home. Parents can be invited to comment and provide information on things that their children enjoy as well as things they find difficult.

Age group: Birth to three years, and up to six years for children with special educational needs

6. CHECKLISTS

Resources: Pre-prepared checklists

Method: The adult uses checklists to record information about particular aspects of children's learning, usually at the end of a given period of time. The adult makes judgements against predetermined descriptions. These might focus, for example, on physical interaction or early literacy skills. The adult usually ticks a heading which best describes the children's progress to date.

Age group: Birth to six years

7. REPORTS

Resources: Templates for reports

Method: The adult uses information from a range of assessment methods and documentation to develop reports on children's learning and development. He/she shares these reports with parents. As the reports focus on a summary of children's progress and achievement, they are developed at particular times in the year, for example in the summer when the child has completed a year in the setting. In the case of some children, the ELC service may receive a report from another professional, such as a psychologist, a speech and language therapist, a play therapist or a physiotherapist. These reports may then be used to further inform work with these children.

Age group: Birth to six years

Reports are usually used for children with additional educational needs and for children at primary school (NCCA, 2009, pp. 75–76).

Finally, it is important to note that assessment and documentation is an essential element of work in an ELC setting. Critical information about a child's physical, intellectual, language, emotional and social developmental needs can be revealed in this way. However, ELC practitioners are not diagnosticians and decisions about a child's need, for example, for further assessment should be made by parents based on open communication between them and the ELC service.

ETHICAL CONSIDERATIONS

It is important when engaging in assessment that practitioners remember that children come from diverse backgrounds and have varying abilities and this in turn shapes how children learn and think. It is imperative that time is given in assessment to 'capture the depth and breadth' of a child's learning (NCCA, 2009, p. 80). It is also essential that information is shared with parents and equally that parents have opportunities to share with practitioners so that any assessment reflects the whole child, their strengths, interests and needs. This is a matter of both ethics and professionalism.

The *Aistear Síolta Practice Guide* (2015)

The *Aistear Síolta Practice Guide* has been developed to support practitioners in using *Aistear: The Early Childhood Curriculum Framework* (2009) and *Síolta: The National Quality Framework for Early Childhood Education* (2006) together and help them to develop the quality of their curriculum in order to better support children's learning and development.

The guide contains many valuable resources, including videos, which support practitioners in

- critically reflecting on curriculum and identifying the positives
- identifying what needs to be prioritised for development
- planning actions for change in ELC settings.

The practice guide includes four 'Curriculum Foundations' and six interconnected 'Curriculum Pillars'.

Four Curriculum Foundations

CURRICULUM FOUNDATIONS	
Elements	**Purpose**
Overview	The overview makes connections between the two frameworks and lists the different resources that are available in Curriculum Foundations.
Element 1: Developing your Curriculum and Curriculum Statement	This element helps practitioners review their current curriculum and develop a more emergent and inquiry-based one.
Element 2: Principles including Rights of the Child and Practitioner Image of the Child	This element looks at the principles of *Aistear* and *Síolta* and focuses in particular on the rights of the child and the practitioner's image of the child. It provides activities to help practitioners embed the principles in their work.

CURRICULUM FOUNDATIONS	
Elements	**Purpose**
Element 3: Themes of Aistear	This element helps practitioners to become familiar with Aistear's themes so that they can use them to support their work with children.
Element 4: Professional Practice	This element looks at the professional role of the practitioner, reflective practice and the concept of pedagogical leadership.

Each Curriculum Pillar includes an overview and five categories of resources which are summarised in this table. It is important that practitioners work on the four elements of Curriculum Foundations before undertaking work on Curriculum Pillars.

Six Curriculum Pillars

CURRICULUM PILLARS	
Category of resource	**Purpose**
Overview	This provides an outline of the Curriculum Pillar, makes connections with Aistear and Síolta and lists the resources available in this part of the practice guide.
Self-evaluation tools	These tools provide prompts to help practitioners reflect on their work in order to identify successes and challenges and to note changes they would like to make.
Examples and ideas for practice	These resources show examples of curriculum from different early childhood settings.
Resources for sharing	These resources include tip sheets, posters, presentation materials and questionnaires.
Action-planning tools	Templates are provided to help practitioners plan for changes in a particular area of their work.
Gallery	Photos from a range of early childhood settings offer additional ideas about aspects of curriculum.

(https://www.aistearsiolta.ie/en/introduction/overview/aistear-siolta-practice-guide-introduction.pdf)

The purpose of the following two activities is to familiarise you with the *Aistear Síolta Practice Guide*, which will help you gain access to the wealth of resources available to you as a learner now and as an ELC practitioner later on.

Activity 1

 Go to **http://www.aistearsiolta.ie/en/cpd/introduction-aspg-birth-6.pdf** and watch the short videos. Spend some time exploring the resources available on the site.

Next go to **http://www.aistearsiolta.ie/en/cpd/**. Pick an age group, then pick one of the topics. Look at the videos and discussion and fill in your reflections on what you have learned.

Complete an action plan and think about how you might incorporate one of the ideas into activities while on your professional practice placement.

Activity 2

Go to **https://www.aistearsiolta.ie/en/play/examples-and-ideas-for-practice/**. Choose 'Using books in pre-school settings to think and talk about measure'. Reflect on what you learned from the video and how you could use it in your placement. As a group, pick different topics and share the insights and information that you have learned.

As you will have learned from these activities, there are resources and suggestions to help develop all areas of your practice and to reflect on your learning and development as you progress. The *Aistear Síolta Practice Guide* is an invaluable resource, and it is a good idea to explore it as a starting point when you are planning activities in your professional practice placement or for purposes of assessment and assignments.

Section 3

Professional Practice Placement

Preparation for placement

12

> **This chapter will explore:**
> * provision of ELC services in Ireland
> * potential professional practice placements.

Introduction

Ireland signed the UN Convention on the Rights of the Child in 1989 and the Pre-school Regulations were first introduced in 1996. Since then, there has been a seismic shift in the progress that has taken place in the regulation, standardisation and development of ELC services. Prior to this, services had developed in an ad hoc manner largely in response to the economic needs of the country as opposed to the developmental needs of children. As a result, Ireland provided and continues to provide a relatively low level of state support for ELC services, in comparison to many of our European neighbours.

Core developments in relation to children 1989–2021

1989	UN Convention on the Rights of the Child
1991	Child Care Act
1992	UN Convention ratified in Ireland
1996	Pre-school Regulations
2000	National Children's Office
2002	Centre for Early Childhood Development and Education (CECDE)
2003	Children's Ombudsman
2005	Establishment of the Office of the Minister for Children (OMC)

2006	*Síolta: The National Quality Framework for Early Childhood Education*
	Pre-school Regulations updated
	Diversity and Equality guidelines launched
2009	*Aistear: The Early Childhood Curriculum Framework*
2010	Free Pre-school Year in Early Childhood Care and Education (ECCE) Scheme – the first universal state-funded provision of early years education
	Introduction of the Community Childcare Subvention (CCS)
	Childcare Employment and Training Support Scheme (CETS)
	Workforce Development Plan
2011	Establishment of the Department of Children and Youth Affairs
2014	*Better Start*: The Quality Development (mentoring) Service
2015	National Early Years Inspectorate established
	Child Care Act
2016	Introduction of second free pre-school year
	Introduction of AIM – the access and inclusion programme
	Pre-school Regulations updated
	Diversity and Inclusion Guidelines updated
2017	*Children First: National Guidance for the Protection and Welfare of Children*
2018	*First 5: A Government Strategy for Babies and Young Children* published
	Tusla Early Years Quality and Regulatory Framework launched
2021	New Level 5 and 6 ELC Awards Programme published by QQI

This chapter outlines the range of ELC services currently available in Ireland. The term 'ELC service' is used here to denote only those services concerned with early learning and care designed for children aged 0–6 years. Ireland has a limited state-supported mainstream ELC system and does provide a limited ECCE service for the children of working parents, with the result that many parents turn to the private sector to meet their full-time childcare needs. Altogether, a high percentage of children under six years attend some form of ELC service, whether full time, part time, publicly or privately funded.

ELC services

ELC services fall broadly into two categories:

1. Services aiming to meet children's developmental needs — playgroups, naíonraí, parent and toddler groups, Montessori pre-schools. These are known as 'sessional' or part-time services.

2. Services aiming to meet the needs of parents who are employed, or who are in full-time education or training — private crèches and family day care (childminding) including au pair services and nannies. These services are 'full-time' and are also aimed at meeting the developmental needs of children.

Seven national voluntary childcare organisations currently receive funding from the Department of Children, Equality, Disability, Integration and Youth (DCEDIY) to promote quality ELC services. They are:

1. Early Childhood Ireland (www.earlychildhoodireland.ie)
2. Barnardos (www.barnardos.ie)
3. Childminding Ireland (www.childminding.ie)
4. Irish Steiner Waldorf Early Childhood Association (https://iaswece.org/europe/ireland/)
5. National Childhood Network (www.ncn.ie)
6. National Parents Council (www.npc.ie)
7. St Nicholas Montessori Teachers' Association (www.montessoriireland.ie)
8. Gaelscoileanna Teo (www.gaelscoileanna.ie).

These organisations (or their predecessors) have played a proactive and supportive role in the development of quality ELC services for many years.

ELC services fall into three main types:

1. Statutory services
2. Voluntary services
3. Private services.

> **Statutory services** are provided by the State and are prescribed by state law. The State is responsible for funding such services although that does not necessarily mean that they are free to everyone; some are public, and some are private. This is referred to as a two-tiered system.

State provision for children aged 0–6 years is provided within the national school system as children can enrol in primary school from the age of four upwards.

Additionally, the Early Start Programme aims to tackle educational disadvantage by targeting children who are at risk of not reaching their potential within the education system. It is a one-year preventive intervention scheme offered to pre-school children (3–4 years) in some primary schools in designated disadvantaged areas, often referred to as DEIS schools (Delivering Equality of Opportunity in Schools).

There is a Visiting Teacher Service provided by the DES for young children with visual and/or hearing impairment, from the age of two years. Also, there is a growing number of special pre-school class units attached to primary schools for children with autistic spectrum disorders.

Outside of these services provided within the primary school system, all other services are provided by community, voluntary and (predominantly) private operators.

> A service is described as **voluntary** when it has been set up by people who identify a need and who organise the resources to meet that need without being required to do so by law. Voluntary agencies or groups may receive government grants but usually that falls far short of their full financial requirements, so a lot of fundraising and voluntary work is often involved. It is incorrect to assume that all those working for voluntary organisations are volunteers and unpaid. Most established voluntary organisations have permanent employees and are subject to standard labour laws and rates of pay.

Within pre-school provision, Barnardos is a voluntary organisation which in addition to the provision of pre-school services also mentors others who are setting up or running ELC services.

The St Vincent De Paul Society is another voluntary organisation that provides some ELC services within six resource centres throughout the country. The society is also very active in campaigning for change, especially for disadvantaged families.

The Community Childcare Subvention (CCS) Programme subsidises childcare for disadvantaged families provided that they use community-based not-for-profit ELC facilities. Under the programme, ELC services are subsidised to enable reduced fees to be charged to certain groups of parents. All fees received under the subvention scheme go directly to the ELC service.

> A **community ELC service** is managed by a voluntary management committee. There are fees but the services are run on a not-for-profit basis. The fees are worked out on a sliding scale according to family income. Community pre-schools are subsidised by Pobal and give preference to families on lower incomes, and to those parents returning to work or education.

> Pobal works on behalf of the government and in conjunction with communities and local agencies to support social inclusion and local and community development. This is done by managing funding and providing support for programmes in the areas of Early Learning and Care, Social Inclusion and Equality and Inclusive Employment and Enterprise.

A majority of ELC services in Ireland are private services. However, they must register with Tusla and adhere to the Pre-school Regulations 2016 as well as to the Síolta and Aistear initiatives, especially if they are offering places to children under the ECCE scheme.

> **Private services** are primarily set up to make a profit while meeting an identified need.

The Early Childhood Care and Education (ECCE) Programme (ECCE Scheme) provides two free years of early childhood care and education for all children of pre-school age. In general, children can start ECCE when they are two years eight months old and continue until they transfer to primary school. The State pays a capitation fee to participating services. In return, they provide a pre-school service free of charge to all children within the qualifying age range for a set number of hours over a set period of weeks (DCEDIY, 2020).

Whether private, voluntary or community, the following types of services are available to children aged 0–6 years in Ireland and are divided into sessional and full-time provision.

Sessional Services

PLAYGROUPS

Playgroups usually operate for up to three and a half hours per day, cater for children aged between two and a half years up to school-going age and are eligible to provide the ECCE scheme. Playgroups aim to promote the educational and social development of children through play and the involvement of parents/family. Funded places may also be available in community playgroups, which are usually managed by local committees. Many operate out of community centres, halls or school premises, and receive grant aid from local authorities or government departments to cover costs of equipment and/or premises, in addition to their own fundraising.

NAÍONRAÍ

These are playgroups that operate through the medium of Irish. Naíonraí are supported by Gaelscoileanna Teo (a national support organisation in the pre-school, primary and post-primary Irish-medium education sector) and are eligible to provide the ECCE scheme.

PARENT AND TODDLER GROUPS

These are aimed at providing play and socialisation opportunities to babies and toddlers within the safe and secure environment of their parent's presence. They are mostly informal, often meeting in the houses of the parents involved or in local community facilities.

MONTESSORI PRE-SCHOOLS

These pre-schools are run according to the principles and methods devised by Dr Maria Montessori. Most operate on an academic year basis, and while the Montessori method is designed to offer a complete educational programme for the child up to 12 years, in practice in Ireland Montessori schools mainly cater for the three to six-year age group.

THE EARLY START PRE-SCHOOL PROGRAMME

This is defined as a compensatory/intervention programme designed to alleviate educational disadvantage, and to provide more widespread access to early childhood services in economically and socially deprived areas. The programmes are based within primary schools, and avail of special grants to cover start-up and running costs, as well as to develop parental involvement, thus making them 100 per cent funded by the Department of Education and Skills.

ELC SERVICES FOR CHILDREN WITH ADDITIONAL NEEDS

These services are mainly provided by voluntary organisations, as part of their special school provision, and are funded by the Departments of Health and the Department of Education and Skills under the National Development Plan. They are linked to special education primary schools or specialist services such as Cerebral Palsy Ireland and St Michael's House services.

A new Access and Inclusion Model (AIM) was introduced in June 2016 for children starting ECCE in September 2016. AIM supports a child-centred model, involving seven levels of progressive support, moving from universal to targeted support, based on the needs of the child and the pre-school provider.

Universal supports are designed to promote and support an inclusive culture within ELC settings by means of a variety of educational and capacity-building initiatives such as:

* the development of an inclusion charter and guidelines
* a new higher education programme leading to a Leadership for Inclusion in the Early Years (LINC) certificate
* a broad-funded multi-annual programme of formal and informal training for ELC staff in relation to disability and inclusion.

Targeted support can be in the form of

* expert advice and mentoring
* therapy services
* provision of grants for specialised equipment and minor alterations.

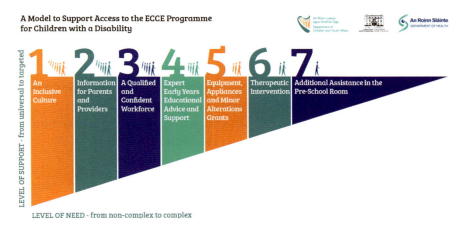

FULL-TIME SERVICES – CRÈCHES, PRE-SCHOOLS, DAY CARE CENTRES

Since these terms are often used interchangeably with, in fact, no actual difference between them, it is convenient to deal with them all under one heading: early learning and care (ELC) services. These offer full-time care and education for children from about 12 weeks old to school-going age. Most ELC services have now adopted the standardised Aistear curriculum framework for the children using their service.

An increasing number are responding to the demand for after-school collection and care, which means in effect that an ELC service can accommodate age groups as diverse as 12 weeks old up to 12 years. Many provide hot meals and snacks throughout the day for the children; in a minority of cases this is provided by the parents. ELC services may be privately or publicly financed. They are usually open for a minimum of eight hours per day and aim to meet the needs of parents who are in paid employment or in education.

FAMILY DAY CARE – CHILDMINDING IN YOUR OWN HOME

This is where children are looked after in someone else's home or in your own home, including nannies, au pairs and paid relatives of the child. Full- and part-time care is offered to a range of age groups, and hours are usually by negotiation. According to Census 2016, it is by far the most commonly used form of childcare for very young children. It is equally accessible to both rural and urban families and is considered to offer the nearest thing to a home environment for a child, where they can develop a one-to-one relationship with a single adult.

The National Childminding Initiative provides support for childminders and for people interested in becoming childminders. It is administered in local areas by the City and County Childcare Committees (CCCs), which offer initial training and support in accessing a start-up grant (Childminder Development Grant Scheme) that can be used to establish the service, buy safety equipment and toys or to make minor adjustments to the physical environment.

> Childminders minding more than three children in their own home must notify Tusla. A childminder should look after no more than five pre-school children including their own pre-school child. No more than two of these children should be less than 15 months old. Exceptions to this can only occur in the case of siblings or multiple births. Childminders catering for three or less children can voluntarily notify their childminding service. However, they are under no legal obligation to do so.
>
> (Early Childhood Ireland)

Childminding Ireland offers support and advice, and their website contains information on:

* nationally agreed guidelines for good childminding practice
* registration and notification to Tusla
* support services provided to childminders by the CCCs, the Childminder Advisory Officers and Childminding Ireland.

CITY AND COUNTY CHILDCARE COMMITTEES (CCCs)

Thirty-three CCCs representing a wide variety of local childcare and education interests were established in 2001 to encourage the development of childcare locally. They offer a wide variety of services, including:

* advice on setting up a childcare business
* childcare information sessions
* training courses, advice and support on participating in any of the schemes being rolled out
* services to parents, such as providing information on local childcare facilities and information on parent networks.

ELC SERVICE IN A DROP-IN CENTRE

This refers to a service where a pre-school child is cared for over a period of not more than two hours while the parent or guardian is availing of a service or attending an event. Such services are mainly located in shopping centres, leisure centres or other establishments as part of customer/client service.

TEMPORARY ELC SERVICE

This refers to a service where a pre-school child is cared for while the parent or guardian is attending a once-off event such as a conference or a sports event.

OVERNIGHT SERVICES

This refers to a service in which pre-school children are taken care of for a total of more than two hours between the hours of 7 p.m. and 6 a.m. except where exemptions in relation to childminders apply (see Part 12 [58L] of the Child and Family Agency Act 2013).

Activity

Read this scenario and answer the questions that follow.

> The Holden family have a three-year-old son and triplets aged 15 months. Their neighbour, Ms McKenzie, has three children – a four-year-old and twins aged two and a half. Ms McKenzie also minds her niece, aged four and a half years. She now plans to mind the Holden children for four hours every morning.

1. Do the exemptions in Part 12 of the Child and Family Agency Act 2013 apply to this childminder?
2. Does Ms McKenzie need to notify Tusla of her intentions to become a childminder?
3. Where can Ms McKenzie go for advice and support?
4. Can Ms McKenzie avail of any grants or other practical support, e.g. training?

SCHOOL-AGE CHILDCARE

Many ELCs – statutory, voluntary or private – offer services to provide care for children after school up to the age of 12 although not all will go up to this age. Stand-alone school-age services (i.e. no ELC offered) must notify and register with Tusla under the Pre-school Regulations 2016. Barnardos and a number of CCCs have produced guidelines for a model of good practice for school-aged childcare services.

The National Childcare Scheme (NCS) is a new scheme that provides financial support to help parents to meet the costs of childcare. It provides two types of childcare subsidy for children over six months of age:

* A universal subsidy for children under three. Children over three who have not yet qualified for the ECCE are also eligible. It is not means-tested.
* An income-assessed subsidy for children up to 15. It is means-tested and replaces the After School Childcare Scheme.

If one qualifies for this subsidy, after-school childcare for up to five days per week at a daily rate of €3 (in 2021) per day/per child (€15 per week/per child) is covered. Pick-up options are also available.

The scheme also provides full-day childcare during school holidays at no additional cost to the parent. However, in order to avail of childcare during the school holidays the child must have been enrolled in ongoing after-school childcare during the school year.

Activity

Investigate three (different and local) potential professional practice placements under the following headings:

* Location
* Type of service
* Opening hours
* Number of children
* Age of children
* Number of staff
* Fees and schemes that may be accessed by parents.

RECAP QUESTIONS

1. What type of ELC services are available in Ireland?
2. What schemes are available to financially support families in accessing a service?

Knowledge, skills and competences

13

This chapter will explore:
- writing an effective CV and application letter
- preparing for an interview
- knowledge and skills relating to job applications
- digital skills
- interview skills.

Writing a Curriculum Vitae

Commonly referred to by the initials CV (and sometimes called a resumé), a curriculum vitae provides a summary of a person's qualifications, skills and work experience. Apart from name, address and contact details, there is no need to add any other personal information (for example age or gender). A curriculum vitae should be free of all spelling mistakes and typos.

When writing a CV, consider it an advertisement of yourself, in which there is only limited space to talk about yourself. Often employers receive a lot of CVs from job applicants, and therefore they want to see the relevant details at a glance. Information should be organised as follows:

- Name and contact details
- Personal profile
- Education and qualifications
- Work experience
- Skills and personal qualities relevant to the position advertised
- Interests and hobbies
- Referees.

NAME AND CONTACT DETAILS

A full name and address including postcode should be given. Regarding email addresses, ensure that a relatively formal email address is given; jokey or rude email addresses are inappropriate and unprofessional, and therefore, if necessary, a new email address should be created for the purposes of application.

> **Discuss**
>
> Why is it unnecessary to give personal details such as age, gender, marital status, religion, etc.?

PERSONAL PROFILE

A personal profile gives the opportunity to relay information regarding skills and qualities. If you are at the beginning of your career, it can be at least as important as the rest of your CV. It should be concise and to the point, with statements backed up with evidence. For example:

* If you say that you are a team player, you might back this up by noting that you have played basketball with your local club for the past five years.
* If you say that you have good communication skills, you might back this up by noting that you represented your school at national level in debating competitions.
* If you say that you can be depended upon to remain calm in the face of a crisis, you might back this up by noting that you have been a member of the Red Cross for the past three years.

A personal profile can make you stand out from the crowd, but it should not be very long or rambling. Your personal profile could include your unique selling proposition/point (USP).

> **DEFINITION**
>
> **Unique selling proposition or point (USP)**, a term more often used in relation to goods, refers to what makes a product unique or special. In ELC services, you will be competing with similarly trained persons, many of whom may have more experience than you. Therefore, you need to analyse your skills and experiences and identify those that help you stand out from the crowd.

EDUCATION AND QUALIFICATIONS

A CV is usually organised chronologically (with your most recent qualification listed first) but if there is a specific qualification required for the position advertised, this might be put first. If you are at the beginning of your career, full Leaving Certificate (or equivalent) results can be listed, but it is not necessary to list Junior Certificate (or equivalent) results.

WORK EXPERIENCE

Work experience should also be listed chronologically, with most recent positions listed first. If you are at the beginning of your career, you might list work experience placements and/or holiday employment. However, if you have been employed in the sector for the past 10 years, this detail is likely irrelevant unless there is a specific placement or work experience that would highlight your suitability for the position being advertised.

Do not leave gaps in your CV as this will most certainly be picked up at interview. If a gap is due to taking a year out to travel, etc., then indicate this clearly. If it was because you had been unable to find work, then you need to consider how you will explain this.

SKILLS AND PERSONAL QUALITIES

In Chapter 5 you completed a skills audit. When applying for a position, identify the skills and personal qualities most suitable to the position. You should be able to produce evidence that demonstrates that you possess these qualities and skills. Remember that you may be asked at interview to elaborate on any information listed in your CV.

INTERESTS AND HOBBIES

While being honest, try to include something that is not too generic, or at least try to be specific about any generic hobbies. Most people enjoy meeting friends and listening to music; perhaps you meet friends to go for walks or keep fit, or you listen to a specific genre of music.

REFEREES

Include the names, addresses and contact details of two people who can corroborate what you have said. Make sure that you have their permission to be listed as referees. Referees are usually known to you from previous employment or can be teachers from your school or college, but they are not family or friends.

There are many websites offering free CV templates and many more offering advice on how to write a CV. It is generally accepted that your CV should be two pages at most. However, if you can fit the relevant information on one page without it looking cluttered, the prospective employer can see all your relevant information at a glance.

It is vitally important that you get someone, maybe even two people, to proofread your CV to check for spelling mistakes, clarity and use of language. Even with the best qualifications and work experience, if you submit a sloppy CV you may not even get to the interview stage.

Some employers require the completion of an application form instead of the submission of a CV. The same advice applies regarding spelling or language in this instance.

CV EXAMPLE 1

Curriculum Vitae

Maria Johnson
1 Cedar Wood
Co. X A24 BC34
Phone: 086 203 3255
Email: mjohnson@email.com

Professional Profile

An experienced and caring Childcare Assistant who has worked in a large early years service to date for the past two years. Enjoys the challenge of a hectic workplace and excels in offering children holistic care regardless of their abilities or circumstances. Has particularly enjoyed working in partnership with parents of children who have additional needs.

Key Skills

- Team working
- Communication and interpersonal skills
- Empathy
- Child safeguarding
- Monitoring and recording necessary observations
- Hygiene
- Providing care in a fun and enjoyable manner

Work Experience

ABC Early Years Service
Childcare Assistant (October 2019–May 2021)

Worked under the supervision of qualified childcare staff to provide high-quality care to children. Was key worker to two children who had additional needs.

Duties

- Provided holistic care under supervision
- Answered queries from parents and guardians
- Observed children and planned age and stage appropriate activities
- Helped children gain independence with activities of daily living
- Reported concerns

- Recorded all relevant aspects of children's daily experiences and completed necessary paperwork
- Attended staff meetings
- Respected confidentiality at all times
- Showed empathy and compassion for all

Qualifications and Achievements

Level 5 QQI Award – Early Childhood Care and Education (2018–2019) with distinctions in all modules

Additional Certificates

Paediatric First Aid

Irish Sign Language

Child Protection

Manual Handling

Education

St Anne's Community College (2012–2017)

Leaving Certificate – Four higher level subjects taken

- Home Economics
- English
- Biology
- Spanish

Hobbies and Interests

Swimming competitively

Craft activities (puppet making and paper craft)

Cooking

Referees

Ms A Ortez,
Pastoral Care and Guidance teacher,
St Anne's Community College,
Plunkett Street
Co. X B65 GH67
Aoortez1@gmail.com
Tel: 01 2556444

Ms Flora Joyce,
Manager,
ABC Early Years Service,
Pearse Street,
Co. X H19 KL54
fjoyce@abcservices.com
Tel: 01 123 3456

CV EXAMPLE 2

Curriculum Vitae

Jeannie Wells
1 Ashfield Grove
County Y A54 BR62
Phone: 087 444 2323
Email: jenandtonic@gmail.com

Professional Profile
I'm an hard working individual who loves working. Partictclary, I enjoy playing outdoors with the children as I am very good at all sports. I have two years experience working in childcare and that is why I would be a great asset to your service.

Key Skills
- Communication
- Energy
- Enthusiasm
- Computer skills

Work Experience
Sunny Early Years Service
Childcare Assistant (October 2019–May 2021)
Worked wtih qualified childcare staff to provide high-quality care to children.
Duties
- Provide everyday care
- Dealt with parents, mostly mothers
- Helped children with skills like eating and dressing
- Changing nappies, feeding and general care
- Kept records and parperwrk
- Attended staff meetings
- Respected confidentiality

Qualifications and Achievements
Level 5 QQI Award – Early Childhood Care and Education (2018–2019)
Additional Certificates
First Aid
Irish Sign Language
Tuslas child protection training
Manual Handling

Education
St Finbarrs Community College (2012–2017)
Leaving Certificate passed all subjects with some honours.

Hobbies and Interests
- Hanging out with friends
- Music
- Social media

Mr O'Sullivan
Pastoral Care and Guidance teacher,
St Gabriel's Community College,
Castle Street
Co. Y
gosullivan@gmail.com
Tel: 021 4667888

Referees
Mrs J. Wells
1 Ashfield Grove,
Co. Y A54 BR62
jrwells@gmail.com
Tel: 01 4667888

> ### Activity
>
> You are a prospective employer. Examine both CVs and identify the positive and negative points in both. Which applicant would you call to interview and why? Write your own personal CV.

Letter of application

An application or covering letter is usually required to accompany a CV or application form. If appropriate, the letter should be addressed by name to the person who will be considering the application. If there is no named person on the advertisement, then you can telephone the organisation and ask to whom the applications should be addressed. This may or may not be possible if application has to be made online.

A good letter will be three or four paragraphs long, succinct and to the point. The opening paragraph should state the position for which you are applying and briefly outline why you are applying.

The second paragraph might outline why you would be particularly suited to the role for which you are applying. This can be where you marry the needs of the company or organisation (demonstrating that you have done research) to two or three skills, qualities or qualifications that are mentioned in your CV. Without being arrogant, show that you are confident that you are competent to fulfil the position as required.

The last paragraph should thank the reader for their attention and that you would welcome the opportunity for further discussion.

If the letter is addressed to a named person, the sign-off 'Yours sincerely' is used. If a person has not been named in the greeting, the sign-off 'Yours faithfully' is used.

As the application letter is the first thing the employer will see, it is vital to have it proofread by someone else to ensure that there are no mistakes in it.

There are many examples online to help you compose a good covering letter. A word of warning, however: do not be tempted to copy one word for word. This will be obvious to the reader as it will be too general and vague. You need to make it personal.

APPLICATION LETTER EXAMPLE 1

1 Cedar Wood
County X
A24 BC34

28th May 2021

Ms Julia Sanchez,
Manager,
Early Years Service,
Manor Road,
Co. Z L21 DF32

Dear Ms Sanchez,

I am writing in response to your advertisement (Early Childhood Ireland 4.5.2021) for a childcare assistant in your Early Years service.

I am enthusiastic and energetic, which I believe are essential qualities when working with children. I possess excellent communication and interpersonal skills and I am passionate about helping children to reach their potential whatever their backgrounds or ability.

I would be very interested in joining your team as my research shows that your service is vibrant and forward-looking with a clearly stated commitment to equality and diversity. I also note that your staff are encouraged to become involved in continuous professional development and I would love to enhance my skills with further training if deemed appropriate.

My attached CV outlines my training and experience to date, and I would be very happy to meet with you at your convenience to discuss further any aspects of my application.

Looking forward to hearing from you.

Yours sincerely,

Maria Johnson

APPLICATION LETTER EXAMPLE 2

1 Ashfield Grove
County Y
A54 BR62

28th May 2021

Ms Julia Sanchez,

Early Years Service,

Manor Road,

Co. Z L21 DF32

Dear Julia,

I am writing to apply for the job that you recently advertised for a childcare worker.

I am really interested in applying for the job because I would like a change. I have been working in my present job for a long time.

I am hardworking, punctual, loyal and I love working with small children.

You can see my experience and all my training in my attached CV and I would love too speak more with you about what you can offer and to discuss wages.

Looking forward to hearing from you.

Yours sincerely,

Jeannie

Activity

For each letter, identify positive and negative points. How could you improve on both letters?

Find an advertisement for a post in an ELC service and compose your own letter of application for that post.

Preparing for a job interview

An interview means that the employer, having read your CV/application form, is sufficiently interested in you to explore further if you are suitable for the position advertised. However, the interview is a two-way process. You want to make a good impression, but you also want to find out more about the work and the organisation.

Preparation for the interview is of paramount importance.

- Research the organisation: what they do, their mission statement and values, size, departments.

- If it is an ELC service, establish the number of children enrolled and the age range; diversity within both the child and staff population; what curriculum or specific programmes they use; whether there are any career progression possibilities within the organisation. Information can be gleaned from:
    - the company website
    - any brochures or advertising material
    - the company's Facebook page, Instagram or Twitter account – this will give you an idea of the culture and atmosphere of the company
    - parents who have used/are using the service*
    - family, friends, people in the local community.

However, note that one's views are invariably biased depending on whether one has had a positive or negative experience with a service, so keep this in mind if you are speaking to people who have used the service.

- Contact the manager and ask if you can visit prior to the interview. It may not be allowed but it shows you are genuinely interested.

- Prepare answers to questions you may be asked:
    - Try to anticipate questions which will come directly from your CV.
    - Anticipate questions specific to the role for which you are interviewing, e.g. what would you do in a certain situation? If you can have an example of how you acted in a similar situation previously then that is a good way to answer, as it shows your experience and your ability to review your actions.

THE STAR METHOD OF RESPONSE TO INTERVIEW QUESTIONS

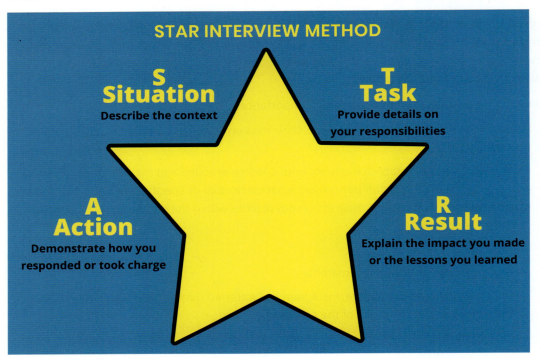

Situation: Set the scene of your example.

* What was the main issue?
* Who was involved?

Task: Describe your responsibility in the situation.

* What responsibility did you have?
* Did a boss assign the responsibility?
* Were you part of a team/group or taking sole responsibility?

Action: What happened?

* What did you do first?
* Did others react?
* What did you do next?

Result: Describe the outcome.

* Did you successfully handle the situation?
* Were people satisfied with the outcome?
* Were you satisfied with the outcome?
* What did you learn from the situation? (Doyle, 2021)

Activity

1. Describe a situation where you had to deal with an incident of difficult behaviour.
2. Working with another person, take turns to practise your answers to these two questions using the STAR model. Give each other feedback.
    * 'On your CV I see that you have had numerous work experience placements and part-time employment, so what kind of manager/boss do you prefer and why?'
    * 'How do you cope if you have several responsibilities?'

When applying for a position, you should carefully consider why you want the job and in what way your qualifications match the role that will be required of you. Consider your answers to these common interview questions:

* Why do you want to work here?
* What makes you a good fit for this position?
* What are your particular strengths?
* What about your weaknesses?
* Are there any questions you would like to ask?

If you are asked a question about something specific and you do not know the answer, it is better to be honest rather than to waffle and become confused.

If you are asked about previous employment or work experience, do not criticise your previous boss or colleagues.

Sometimes you may be asked scenario-based questions, for example 'What would you do if your fellow colleague was always coming in late or if a parent was always late picking up a child?'

Always have at least two questions ready to ask. These should obviously be relevant to the company who is interviewing you. These could be generic questions such as:

* What is the greatest challenge facing ELC staff in your service/pre-school today?
* What qualities do your most successful/happiest employees have?

Alternatively, they could be more specific:

* I note from research that I have done that the company has expanded greatly in the last 12 months. Are you going to be expanding further?
* I note that you use the XXX programme. Will there be opportunities for further training in this area?
* Online tools are changing very quickly in the sector. Will there be opportunities for training so that I can put them to optimum use?

If you can find information about the company online, it is likely that they will find information about you too. It's time to think about reviewing your public online persona and your digital footprint and cleaning both up if necessary!

DEFINITION

A **digital footprint** is the impression left behind by your online activity, whether it is the sites you have browsed, interactions with others, content that you have published such as posts on social media or blogs, pictures you have posted, information about where you have been, etc. Always be conscious of what you post and the digital footprint you are leaving behind.

Practise answering interview questions with a friend or in front of a mirror, but don't over-practise. You do not want to sound too rehearsed and you want to have flexible answers as you have no way of knowing exactly what questions will be asked. Voice record yourself using your phone and count how many times you hesitate or use filler words such as 'uh' or 'like'. Alternatively, video record yourself and pay attention to your body language, eye contact and demeanour – it should be confident without being brash or pushy.

Practical preparation

PERSONAL PRESENTATION

What you wear and how you present yourself is very important. Whatever your personal style, it is better to err on the side of caution and choose either formal business or smart casual attire. The result should be understated, logo-free, clean and neat. The objective is to present as a professional, capable person.

Do not wear any strong scents. People can be very sensitive to smells.

Accessories should be understated and conservative.

ARRIVING ON TIME

Whatever way you travel, be sure to get there on time, or better still, 15 minutes early. It is better not to have any arrangements made for after the interview as you may start to feel stressed if the interview is delayed or running long.

AFTER THE INTERVIEW

After the interview, write a letter (soft or hard copy) thanking your interviewer for their time, reiterating why you would like to work in their service and stating that you are looking forward to hearing from them. If you are unsuccessful in the interview, you may ask for feedback or a review of the interview, which might be helpful in preparing for your next application.

RECAP QUESTIONS
1. What is a personal profile?
2. What is a USP?
3. How would you prepare for an interview?

14

Professional practice placement

> **This chapter will explore:**
> * preparation for professional practice placement
> * induction in ELC.

Introduction

Professional practice placement is also known as work experience and is an important part of any course of study. In fact, it is integral to all learning and development; it is sometimes referred to as the spine of a course. It gives relevance to all subject areas including psychology, curriculum, social policy and inclusion. The professional practice placement gives you the opportunity to apply theory to practice in a real-life situation, for example carrying out a child observation and planning a child-centred activity.

> Evidence shows that the most effective early childhood practice is that which has a sound theoretical base. We know that the adult and their style of engagement has a profound impact on the learning experiences of children and sets the scene for their sense of engagement with the world. (Mhic Mhathúna & Taylor, 2012, p.xii)

The placement should also enable you to experience support and supervision, apply practical skills, use inter- and intrapersonal skills, develop techniques in reflective practice and begin to form a sense of your own professional identity.

Preparation for professional practice placement

When thinking about the professional practice placement, a good way to look at it is through three lenses: the **before**, the **during**, and the **after**. In this way, you can identify your role in each scenario.

* How should I prepare for professional practice placement?
* How should I conduct myself on professional practice placement?
* What/How will I learn from my experience on professional practice placement?

HOW SHOULD I PREPARE FOR MY PROFESSIONAL PRACTICE PLACEMENT?

1. Do some research on the ELC service to find out its exact location, the type of service, the opening hours, the facilities, etc.
2. Do an audit of the personal and vocational skills that you need to work in a professional practice placement in ELC.
3. Set some SMART goals (see Chapter 6, page 67) for yourself in order to gain the best outcome from your professional practice placement.
4. Be familiar with the expectations the professional practice placement has of your competency to work in an ELC setting.

Starting a professional practice placement is both an exciting and nervous time for you, filled with opportunities and challenges.

Activity

1. Think about the challenges you have faced in your life.
   * How did you deal with these challenges?
   * What resources did you use to meet those challenges? (Resources can be internal and external.)
   * Which resources worked and why?

2. Make a list of the possible challenges and opportunities you may face during your professional practice placement.

Opportunities	Challenges
1. offered a part-time job	1. getting to work on time
2.	2.
3.	3.
4.	4.

   * How will you deal with these opportunities and challenges?
   * What resources will you need to manage these challenges?

3. Design a tool kit for yourself. In this kit you should have tools to help you get through the challenges you are facing; for example:
   * Prepare yourself (self-care, clothes, snacks, drink, paperwork, travel arrangements, etc.)
   * Arrive at the ELC service 15 to 20 minutes early
   * Focus on what you are being asked to do (listening skills)

- Walk daily (minimum 20 mins)
- Keep a reflective journal (this can be short snippets of how you feel daily, a 'check-in' space)
- Use some mindfulness techniques (for example, see the HSE (2018) document, Mindfulness)
- Discuss any issues with the supervisor (the sooner the better).

PREPARING FOR YOUR FIRST VISIT TO YOUR PPP

Make a phone call to the ELC service and request a suitable date and time to visit in advance of your start date. Ideally, you should be meeting with the professional practice placement supervisor; if this is not the case, the person assigned to meet you will be furnished with all the relevant information needed for your induction. You should have the following documents with you:

1. A copy of your Garda vetting clearance
2. Your CV
3. Two references
4. *Children First* e-Learning Certificate
5. All the relevant documents from the provider, namely:
   - Public liability insurance
   - Work-based assessment competency report form
   - Mandatory activities verification form
   - Code of practice
   - Attendance sheet.

The placement will keep all the documents but please ensure they take a copy of your Garda vetting clearance form. You should retain the original document.

The induction

An induction is a process of integration into a new work environment. It is imperative to the smooth running of an organisation and it should be tailored to meet the needs of the learner. The service provides an induction for the learner to give them the opportunity to perform to the best of their ability and become part of a team.

Sometimes one staff member will guide you through all the information, and in some settings the manager/supervisor will allocate other members of staff to talk you through different sections. For example, a room leader in the toddler room might take you through all the activities that happen on a day-to-day basis because they will have more knowledge about what happens in that specific room.

An induction to a new service can be overwhelming. There is a lot of information to take in. You will need time to familiarise yourself with new surroundings, work practices of other staff and other learners. Be patient with yourself and take notes after each day, especially during the first week of professional practice placement. This is the beginning of you becoming a reflective practitioner on your ELC career path. (See Chapter 4, p. 38.)

As part of your planning skills you should have had an opportunity to research the ELC service online, identifying the following:

- Location
- Type of service, for example sessional service or full time
- Opening hours
- Facilities
- Number of children
- Number of staff
- Job description within the service.

If you have carried out this research, it will be to your advantage at your initial induction.

The following areas should be included in the induction checklist for learners:

- General operations
- Human resources
- Practice and room operations
- Work procedures
- Policies and procedures
- Health and safety.

(Adapted from the ECI 'Staff Induction Checklist')

GENERAL OPERATIONS

- A copy of the centre's code of ethics should be shared with the learner; if the service does not have a code of ethics, they may have a values statement or a mission statement
- The history of the service
- Introductions to all staff, supervisors and managers
- Tour of ELC service and all rooms including the kitchen/canteen/staff room
- Car park or bike/scooter lock area
- Smoking area (if any)
- Lockers or other storage area for personal belongings/coat hooks, etc.

HUMAN RESOURCES

Human resources refers to a set of strategies that ensure the effective management of an organisation, for example correct policies and procedures for recruitment, health and safety, child protection, etc. In addition, all ELC services registered with Tusla must have full compliance with the pre-school regulations. As part of this regulation, the following documents must be filed for every adult working in the setting, and it is your responsibility to ensure the placement has all of these documents in relation to you:

* Garda vetting
* Copy of your ID, e.g. driving licence, passport
* Two references.

PRACTICE AND ROOM OPERATION

* Introduction to the children in the service
* The curriculum approach that is used by the service
* The routines in the room
* How the service supports and manages emotional regulation with each child
* The role of the adult in the room
* The importance of interacting with the children
* Recording and documentation.

WORK PROCEDURES

* Signing in and out (if necessary)
* Punctuality and attendance
* Lunch and breaks
* Dress code
* Mobile phones policy
* Cleaning routines
* Communication: what is the best way to communicate if you are late, or cannot attend?
* Communication of service closures or CPD (which may be posted on the noticeboard or sent by email/text).

POLICIES AND PROCEDURES

All policies and procedures of the professional practice placement should be read by the learner who will then implement these with support from the ELC staff.

HEALTH AND SAFETY

The following should be made known to the learner:

* The health and safety statement
* Location of first aid boxes
* Information on risk assessment, lifting, etc.
* Location of fire extinguishers
* Location of fire exits and assembly points
* Accident and incident reporting procedures
* Identity of child protection designated liaison officer
* Identity of safety officer
* Identity of fire officer.

When induction is completed, the learner should be given an opportunity to ask questions and discuss their goals with the supervisor. (A short-term goal, for example, might be to get to know all the children's names by the end of the first week.)

For optimum learning and development throughout the professional practice placement, the learner should be partnered with an experienced member of staff who will become their mentor. The mentor should offer encouragement, support and guidance to the learner.

RECAP QUESTION

Is induction important? Make a short list of what should happen during the induction process.

Personal presentation in professional practice placement

15

This chapter will explore:
* conduct on professional practice placement
* code of ethics
* knowledge, skills and competence to work in professional practice placement
* reflection after the professional practice placement
* assessment of your learning.

Conduct on professional practice placement

First 5, Ireland's first ever whole-of-government strategy for babies, young children and their families (2019–2028) has set a target of achieving a graduate-led workforce by 2028. You are at the grassroots of this achievement. You are embarking on a career in ELC where you will embrace a new professional identity and become part of this graduate-led early years workforce. It is important that you behave in a professional manner at all times in the ELC setting. The most important thing is to arrive on placement early and to be prepared, both physically and emotionally. Thereafter, you should follow these guidelines:

1. Communicate effectively with the supervisor regarding all tasks to be completed on placement.
2. Read and review the centre's code of ethics, policies and procedures.

3. Be autonomous in your learning.

> **DEFINITION**
>
> To be **autonomous** means to be self-directing; in this case it means to be independent in your learning. Don't always wait to be asked; show initiative, show an eagerness to learn and try new things.

4. Demonstrate a positive attitude and willingness to participate in ELC setting.
5. Adhere to all policies and procedures of each ELC setting, for example:
   * Confidentiality
   * GDPR
   * Health and safety
   * Child protection
6. Be willing to take direction from the supervisor and other team members.
7. Discuss your progress to date and any issues arising with the professional practice supervisor.

> **DEFINITION**
>
> A **tripartite meeting** is a meeting involving three people. In this case, a meeting of the learner, the workplace monitor and the professional practice supervisor.

8. Take responsibility and ask to be assessed again if you are found incompetent in any given task.
9. Pay full attention to what other people are saying, take time to understand the points being made and ask questions if necessary.
10. Demonstrate the ability to take appropriate initiative in situations.
11. Show enthusiasm in finding opportunities to make decisions or influence events.
12. Be able to perform tasks effectively with minimum help.
13. Be reliable, responsible and dependable when carrying out tasks.

Code of ethics/values or mission statement

A code of ethics outlines the values and ethics underpinning the work of ELC educators. It offers a set of principles to provide a reference point in guiding day-to-day decision-making.

Professional responsibilities are an identifying feature of a profession. Consequently, the code of professional responsibilities recognises that ELC educators are in a unique position of trust and influence in their relationships with children, families, colleagues and the community. As such, the professional behaviour of ELC staff should be reflected in the commitment to respecting and maintaining the rights and dignity of children, parents and families, colleagues and communities. It is paramount that the ELC services provided to children, parents and families is of the highest possible standard. The conduct should be such that it places the profession in the highest possible esteem.

For the purpose of this chapter, we will focus on 'Professional Responsibilities Relating to the Early Childhood Education and Care Profession'. In relation to our profession, we will:

1. Present a positive demeanour including professional dress, good attendance and time keeping
2. Advocate for our profession and the provision of quality early childhood education and care
3. Engage in critical reflection and ongoing professional learning
4. Be proactive in remaining up to date with research, changes in legislation and policy, and take personal responsibility for our ongoing professional development and learning
5. Act with responsibility, accountability and integrity at all times
6. Value training and professional qualifications, and participate in continuous professional development, including the development of language and communication skills appropriate to the needs of children in our setting
7. Base our work on research, theory, content knowledge, practice evidence and understanding of the children and families with whom we work
8. Articulate our professional values, knowledge and practice, as well as the positive contribution our profession makes to society
9. In keeping with the requirements of the GDPR and this code of professional responsibilities, we will engage in respectful communication at all times, and resist any action that diminishes the good standing of our profession (which includes/extends to the use of social media, i.e. Facebook, Twitter etc.).

In relation to colleagues, we will:

1. Encourage colleagues to adopt and act in accordance with this code of professional responsibilities
2. Encourage colleagues to take action in the presence of inappropriate behaviour

3. Build a spirit of collegiality and professionalism through collaborative relationships, and teamwork based on trust, respect and honesty
4. Model quality practice
5. Respect colleagues' contributions
6. Acknowledge and support the diverse strengths and experiences of colleagues to build shared professional knowledge, understanding, skills and attitudes
7. Use constructive processes to address differences of opinion and to negotiate shared perspectives and actions
8. Collaborate with colleagues to generate a culture of continual reflection and renewal of best practices in early childhood education and care
9. Implement strategies that support and mentor colleagues (and students of early childhood education and care) to make positive contributions to the ECEC profession.

It is recommended the learner should read the full code, which includes the following:

* Professional responsibilities relating to children
* Professional responsibilities relating to parents and families
* Professional responsibilities relating to colleagues (see Chapter 4 Reflective Practice, page 38)
* Professional responsibilities relating to employers
* Professional responsibilities relating to communities.

Note: The full code is not yet available online from the DCEDIY website, but some CCC websites have adopted it, so a copy may be downloaded from, for example, limerickccc.ie or cavanccc.ie. Type 'Code of professional responsibilities and code of ethics for early years educators' into a search engine to find it.

Knowledge, skills and competence to work in professional practice placement

While on professional practice placement, you will be presented with lots of opportunities to learn and develop as an ELC professional. You will work alongside qualified, experienced practitioners and observe how they work with children and families on a daily basis. There will be opportunities to plan, implement and evaluate activities with babies, toddlers and young children. You can use your reflective journal to describe your experiences and to reflect on the daily routines in the ELC setting.

This can be a nervous but exciting time. The achievement of set objectives can be very rewarding.

Some objectives appropriate in ELC placement are as follows:

> By the end of placement I will:
> - know all the children's names and some of their favourite songs
> - be able to read a story, with confidence, using props and/or actions, to a small group of children
> - be competent in meeting the physical needs of babies under 12 months
> - be able to carry out observations of children to identify their holistic needs
> - be able to plan and implement inclusive activities for young children in the ELC setting
> - have an understanding of the role of the different people employed in the ELC setting
> - have knowledge of relevant legislation, policies and procedures.
>
> (Adapted from Mhic Mhathúna and Taylor, 2012)

Objectives may be revised while on placement and especially if the professional practice placement supervisor and the learner feel there is sufficient or insufficient knowledge and experience achieved. New learning objectives should be discussed, for example planning an outing for a group of children or talking to a parent about the child's day in the setting.

In order to achieve your objectives, it is important that you form a solid base for good practice.

TIME MANAGEMENT

In order to complete the full requirements of professional practice placement, attendance is compulsory. If, for whatever reason, you cannot make it to the ELC setting, you must contact the supervisor to explain your absence. Punctuality is also very important to demonstrate your reliability and respect for all other team members and service users. When managing your time, a good rule of thumb is to divide up your tasks into four categories:

> 1. Urgent and important, e.g. a baby crying
> 2. Urgent and not important, e.g. interruptions
> 3. Important and not urgent, e.g. planning a day trip with the children
> 4. Not urgent and not important, e.g. answering emails from marketing companies.
>
> (Covey, 2020)

PLANNING

The professional practice placement supervisor should be available to help you with planning. Communicating your intentions and organising a suitable date and time to carry out your plans is hugely important to the smooth running of the centre. This can be carrying out a child observation, a practical care skill or implementing an inclusive activity with a child/children.

> ### Think about
> Adults are often in a hurry when working or being with children. You may have seen an adult rushing the child/children to get to a certain point, for example walking to the park. The adult just cannot wait to get there so the child/children can play in the playground. But the child is having such an adventure on the way to the park. They are looking at the trees, pointing out nice flowers, stopping to pet a dog, etc. The adult, however, sometimes does not experience the same wonder and awe as the child.
>
> Think for a moment about looking at the world through the eyes of a child. Try to embrace every moment and slow down. As early years educators, we must be able to meet the child's needs in the present moment where all the value of learning is present rather than thinking about what will happen next.
>
> This important point was addressed by the French philosopher J. J. Rousseau in the eighteenth century when he wrote 'Nature wants children to be children before they are men. If we deliberately pervert this order, we shall get premature fruits which are neither ripe nor well flavoured and will soon decay.' (Hayes, 2005, p. 23)

IMPLEMENTATION OF ACTIVITIES

In order to carry out work-based assessments in professional practice placement, you must allow time for planning, implementing and tidying up. To work effectively with children, you must build respectful relationships. This is done over time and in many ways, the most important one of which is being present with the child in the form of actively listening, observing and taking turns. If this is achieved, the rewards will be fruitful.

> Good quality early years practice with children requires the attention of the adult in context to the whole child in context, highlighting the importance of being present in the now and not thinking of what you will be doing once the activity is over. (Hayes *et al.*, 2017, p. 118)

ROLE MODELLING

It is generally agreed that adults have a considerable influence in a child's life, whether they are a parent/guardian, grandparent, teacher, early years educator or student. It is crucial to ensure this influence is positive rather than negative. To be a positive role model in a child's life, it is important to think about the following:

* Take care of your health and wellbeing
* Show understanding

- Show compassion
- Show kindness
- Own your own emotions
- Take responsibility for your own actions
- Take deep breaths when you're stressed or worried
- Allow yourself space to be reflective
- Be patient
- Stop and think, and then rethink
- Reach out and ask for help when needed
- Offer help to others
- Make mistakes
- Try to look on the bright side of things.

MAKE POSITIVE USE OF SUPERVISION

Maintain a professional working relationship with the professional practice supervisor. The role of the supervisor is to coach, mentor, be an advocate for you as a learner and be an advocate for the ELC service. To be a coach the supervisor must provide you with opportunities to reach your goals. This will help you develop a sense of achievement and confidence in your role as a professional. The supervisor is also seen as your mentor. Because the supervisor has also been a learner at some point in their career, they can relate and empathise with the position you are in. This gives them an advantage as a supervisor to be a very supportive mentor to you. As an advocate for you, the learner, the supervisor should listen to any issues or concerns you may have. These concerns should be brought to the supervisor objectively, without bias and in a timely manner so that they do not escalate. In direct contrast to advocating on the learner's behalf, the supervisor must also be an advocate for the ELC service. This means that any messages or information coming from management must be delivered by the supervisor to the learner sensitively and without bias.

Making space and time for effective supervision in an ELC setting is sending a clear message that says 'quality is valued here'. It is important to engage in regular supervision sessions where the supervisor and the learner can develop honest and genuine relationships and where professional development can be identified through self and collective reflection. Over time, effective supervision will foster professional dialogue which will gradually lead to the formation of the professional identity of the learner.

Every part of the professional practice placement experience must be absorbed, and this is why keeping a reflective journal is very important. The learner should take full advantage of all opportunities for learning and personal development available on placement. 'Examining what went well, what did not go so well and what would be done if the situation arose in the future is the very essence of reflection' (Mhic Mhathúna and Taylor, 2012, p. 318).

Reflection after professional practice placement

When you have completed your professional practice your wealth of knowledge in ELC will be phenomenal and you should be very proud of yourself. Working professionally in ELC means being willing to recognise that there is always something more to learn about child development, learning experiences, inclusion, diversity, environments, working with team members, families and the community. You always need to ask yourself: Why am I doing this? What am I giving to my work? People are often resistant to this type of questioning and are hesitant to complete the thinking process. It is therefore very important to have support and guidance from your supervisor, mentor, teacher, peers, etc. when trying to develop the skill of reflective practice. Reflective models are a very helpful framework to help you get started. Once the skill is mastered you will adopt a style of your own.

Activity

Use either Gibbs' reflective cycle or Kolb's learning cycle to reflect on some or all of the following:

* Your learning goals and achievements
* Your experience of activities with the children, e.g. storytelling or caring for a baby
* Your emotional response to the children
* Observations of experienced practitioners
* Asking for help
* Challenges you faced
* Conflicts (if any)
* The supervision process, seeking and receiving feedback
* Professional development planning for further study and future career in ELC (CPD).

The following prompts might be helpful:

- **Description:** When and where did the experience take place, who was there and what happened?

- **Feelings:** Describe what you were feeling during this experience (both positive and negative feelings)

- **Evaluation:** What went well and why? What did not go well and why? What was your role in the experience? What was the role of others?

- **Action plan:** What will you do differently in the future? What skills do you need to develop to achieve this? Who and what will support your development in this area?

(See Chapter 4, p. 38 for more on reflective practice.)

DEFINITION

CPD stands for 'continuous professional development'. It refers to any work-related activity that prompts us to self-reflect and develop in our practice. It can be anything from a full-year course of study to a two-hour workshop on literacy and numeracy. (See page 69 for more detail on creating a CPD record.)

On completion of your placement, give a thank you card to the placement supervisor, the staff and the children. You could make a card and/or a picture of all the children's handprints as a memory for them to keep in the ELC service.

See Pinterest for lots of ideas!
www.pinterest.com

Professional practice placements are a fundamental part of your learning and you will always remember the time you spend in the placements. Be grateful for the wonderful opportunity that it is, because when you are qualified as an ELC practitioner, you will work with learners who are starting on their ELC journey. You will then realise the importance of offering unconditional support, guidance and encouragement.

> **"** The Child is curious. He wants to make sense out of things, find out how things work, gain competence and control over himself and his environment, and do what he can see other people doing. **"**
>
> (Holt, 1967)

What is worth noting about this quote is that even though it is dated 1967, the curious nature of children has been and will always be relevant to the work of early years practitioners. We must remember this when we are working with children, giving them freedom with guidance and helping them assess the risks of play. Hopefully you too will have been given the space and freedom to learn from mistakes.

Assessment of learning

The assessment of your learning takes place through a combination of college-based and work-based assessments during professional practice placement. Essential work-based professional competencies will be identified and they will be developed, practised and enhanced while you are on practice placement. The professional competencies to be demonstrated while on placement are:

Some of your assessments will rely on experiences and activities carried out while you are on professional practice placement and you are responsible for planning, implementing and requesting an appropriate time to carry out these activities.

Assessment activities may include:

* Child observations
* Practical holistic care activities
* Learning activities
* Promoting diversity and inclusion within the ELC service.

RECAP QUESTIONS

1. How can you prepare for professional practice placement?
2. What is a code of ethics/values or mission statement?
3. Why is it important to write a reflective journal?

16

Employment legislation

> **This chapter will explore:**
> * legislation relevant to professional practice and employment in ELC.

Introduction

This chapter will focus on relevant employment legislation which has been enacted to protect the rights of employers and employees within an organisation. As a future employee, it is important that you are familiar with the legislation and the protections it gives both employee and employer. It is also useful to know what to do if the employer is in breach of the employment legislation or what can happen if you are in breach of the law. Relevant legislation includes:

* Safety, Health and Welfare at Work Act 2005 (concerning responsibilities of employer and employee)
* Employment Equality Acts 1998–2015
* Equal Status Acts 2000–2018
* Terms of Employment (Information) Acts 1994–2014
* Minimum Notices and Terms of Employment Acts 1973–2005
* Organisation of Working Time Act 1997.

Safety, Health and Welfare at Work Act 2005

In all aspects of life, we are surrounded by things that can impinge on our health and our safety. These dangers can sometimes be very obvious, but at other times are not so easy to see. Preventing any health and safety issues is an essential part of planning in the workplace and it requires attention all year round. By implementing proper procedures, health and safety management can minimise and eliminate risks to employees and employers.

The main legislation providing for the health and safety of people in the workplace is the Safety, Health and Welfare at Work Act 2005. It applies to all employers, employees (including fixed-term and temporary employees) and self-employed people in their workplaces. It sets out the rights and obligations of both employers and employees. It also provides for substantial fines and penalties for breaches of the health and safety legislation. Almost all of the specific health and safety laws that apply generally to all employment are set out in the Safety, Health and Welfare at Work (General Application) Regulations 2007–2020.

For the purpose of this chapter, we will focus on sections 8 and 13 of the Safety, Health and Welfare at Work Act 2005.

Under Section 8, the employer has a duty to ensure the employees' safety, health and welfare at work as far as is reasonably practicable. In order to prevent workplace injuries, the employer is required to:

* provide and maintain a safe workplace which uses safe plant and equipment
* prevent risks from use of any article or substance and exposure to physical agents, noise and vibration
* prevent any improper conduct likely to put the safety, health and welfare of employees at risk
* provide training to employees on health and safety
* provide protective clothing and equipment to employees
* appoint a competent person as the organisation's safety officer.

Section 13 sets out the duties of employees while at work. These include the following:

* To take reasonable care to protect the health and safety of themselves and of other people in the workplace
* Not to engage in improper behaviour that will endanger themselves or others
* Not to be under the influence of drink or drugs in the workplace
* To undergo any reasonable medical or other assessment if requested to do so by the employer
* To report any defects in the place of work or equipment which might be a danger to health and safety.

The employer should tell employees about any risks that require the wearing of protective equipment. The employer should provide protective equipment (such as protective clothing, headgear, footwear, eyewear, gloves) together with training on how to use it, where necessary. An employee is under a duty to take reasonable care for his/her own safety and to use any protective equipment supplied. The protective equipment should be provided free of charge to employees if it is intended for use in the workplace only.

Think about

One of the reasons a service could be deemed non-compliant in a Tusla regulatory inspection report would be if the same gloves were used during nappy changing and redressing the child. This is an example of inadequate nappy-changing practices.

There is a risk of cross-contamination which is in breach of the infection control regulation. Therefore, it is imperative that an ample amount of protective clothing is made available to all staff members at all times.

This is a recurring theme in Tusla inspection reports. Why do you think this is so?

Health and safety procedures are very important for the workplace to ensure the safety of all employers and employees.

SAFETY STATEMENT

Under the Safety, Health and Welfare at Work Act 2005, every employer is required to carry out a risk assessment for the workplace which should identify any hazards present in the workplace, assess the risks arising from such hazards and identify the steps to be taken to deal with any risks.

ACCIDENTS IN THE WORKPLACE

All accidents in the workplace should be reported to the employer, who should record the details of the incident. Reporting the accident will help to safeguard social welfare and other rights which may arise as a result of an occupational accident. An employer is obliged to report any accident that results in an employee missing three consecutive days at work (not including the day of the accident) to the Health and Safety Authority.

VIOLENCE IN THE WORKPLACE

The possibility of violence towards employees should be addressed in the safety statement. Sometimes if there is cash on the premises, this may pose a risk to the staff. Proper safeguards should be put in place to eliminate the risk of violence as far as possible and the employee should be provided with appropriate means of minimising the remaining risk, for example, security glass.

BULLYING IN THE WORKPLACE

One of the employer's duties is to prevent improper conduct or behaviour, which includes bullying. An employer should have established procedures for dealing with complaints of bullying in the workplace and deal with such complaints immediately.

VICTIMISATION

Under the Safety, Health and Welfare at Work Act 2005, the employee may not be victimised for exercising his or her rights under safety and health legislation such as making a complaint. This means that the employer may not penalise an employee by dismissal or in any other way, for example by disciplinary action or by being treated less favourably than other employees.

> The Safety, Health and Welfare at Work Act 2005 is available from:
>
> https://www.hsa.ie/eng/Topics/Managing_Health_and_Safety/Safety,_Health_and_Welfare_at_Work_Act_2005/
>
> http://www.irishstatutebook.ie/eli/2005/act/10/enacted/en/print

Employment Equality Acts 1998–2015

The Employment Equality Acts 1998–2015 aim to outlaw discrimination in employment. They do this by:

* promoting equality
* banning discrimination across nine grounds
* banning sexual and other harassment
* banning victimisation
* making sure suitable facilities for people with disabilities are available in relation to access to employment, advancing in employment and taking part in training
* allowing positive action to ensure everyone gets full equality across the nine grounds.

THE NINE GROUNDS AND THEIR MEANING

1. **Civil status:** You are entitled to equal treatment whether you are single, married, separated, divorced or widowed, in a civil partnership or previously in a civil partnership.
2. **Family status:** You are entitled to equal treatment if you are the parent or the person responsible for a child under 18 years. This ground also protects those who are the main

carers or the parent of a person with a disability who is 18 years or over, where their disability requires care on an ongoing basis.

3. **Gender:** You are entitled to equal treatment whether you are a man, a woman or transgender.

4. **Sexual orientation:** You are entitled to equal treatment whether you are gay, lesbian, bisexual or heterosexual.

5. **Religion:** You are entitled to equal treatment no matter what your religious beliefs are or if you do not hold any religious beliefs.

6. **Age:** You are entitled to equal treatment if you are any age, so long as you are over 18. (The age ground only applies to young people under 18 if they hold a driver's licence and are buying car insurance.)

7. **Race:** You are entitled to equal treatment irrespective of your race, skin colour, nationality or ethnic origin.

8. **Traveller community:** You are entitled to equal treatment if you are a member of the Traveller community.

9. **Disability:** You are entitled to equal treatment if you have a disability.

The Acts apply to:

* full-time, part-time and temporary employees
* public and private sector employment
* vocational training bodies
* employment agencies
* trade unions, professional and trade bodies.

The Acts also extend in certain circumstances to self-employed people, partners in partnerships, and state and local authority officeholders.

OBLIGATIONS OF EMPLOYERS

The Equality Employment Acts 1998–2015 prohibit discrimination under the nine grounds in employment, including vocational training and work experience

LEGAL DEFINITION OF DISCRIMINATION IN THE WORKPLACE

Discrimination has a specific meaning in equality law. In the Employment Equality Acts the definition of discrimination focuses on whether a person has been treated less favourably in the workplace than another person in a similar situation on any of the nine grounds, including disability.

It is important to remember that discrimination can be direct or indirect. While direct discrimination is often more obvious, indirect discrimination has a similar impact on employees.

> **DEFINITIONS**
>
> **Direct discrimination** is when a worker is treated less well than another worker in the same situation or circumstances under any of the nine grounds covered in the Acts. Direct discrimination can also be, for example, always asking a young employee to open or close the workplace because it is known that they have no family responsibilities.
>
> **Indirect discrimination** happens where a worker or group of workers or job applicants are treated less favourably as a result of requirements that they might find hard to satisfy.

The Employment Equality Acts 1998–2015 are available from:

https://www.ihrec.ie/guides-and-tools/human-rights-and-equality-for-employers/what-does-the-law-say/eea-summary/

http://www.irishstatutebook.ie/eli/1998/act/21/enacted/en/html

Equal Status Acts 2000–2018

In 2016 the *Diversity, Equality and Inclusion Charter and Guidelines for Early Childhood Care and Education* was published by the DCEDIY (formerly DCYA). This was a welcome development because inclusion and equality go hand in hand in the early years sector. An inclusive environment, where equality is upheld and diversity respected, is fundamental in supporting children to build positive identities, develop a sense of belonging and realise their full potential. In order to comply with the law and meet the requirements of this charter, all ELC services should adhere to the Equal Status Acts so that all staff and service users can enjoy an inclusive environment.

Under the Equal Status Acts 2000–2018, discrimination in the supply of goods and provision of services is prohibited on nine grounds. In addition, the Acts prohibit discrimination in the provision of accommodation services against people who are in receipt of rent supplement, housing assistance or social welfare payments.

The Acts prohibit discrimination subject to some exemptions, in access to and use of goods and service, including indirect discrimination and discrimination by association, sexual harassment and harassment and victimisation. The Acts allow positive action to promote equality for disadvantaged persons or to cater for the special needs of persons.

> **Example of indirect discrimination:** An ELC service devising or having an enrolment policy that will only accept babies, toddlers and young children from a specific five-kilometre radius of the service or only from families who have a fixed address.

Activity

In groups, think of other examples of indirect discrimination.

Discriminatory advertising is also prohibited. It is prohibited to publish, display, or cause to be published or displayed, an advertisement that indicates an intention to discriminate, harass or sexually harass or might reasonably be understood as indicating such an intention.

The Equal Status Acts 2000–2018 are available from:

https://www.ihrec.ie/guides-and-tools/human-rights-and-equality-in-the-provision-of-good-and-services/what-does-the-law-say/equal-status-acts/#:~:text=The%20Equal%20Status%20Acts%202000,membership%20of%20the%20Traveller%20community

http://www.irishstatutebook.ie/eli/2000/act/8/enacted/en/html

Terms of Employment (Information) Acts 1994–2014

The purpose of the Terms of Employment (Information) Acts 1994–2014 is to ensure that all employers provide a written statement to employees setting out particulars of the employee's terms of employment.

The Acts apply to any person – working under a contract of employment or apprenticeship – employed through an employment agency or in the service of the state (including members of An Garda Síochána and the defence forces, civil servants and employees of any local authority, health board, harbour authority or vocational education committee). In the case of agency workers, the party who pays the wages (employment agency or client company) is the employer for the purposes of these Acts and is responsible for providing the written statement.

The Acts mandate that an employer must provide his/her employee with a written statement of the particulars of the employee's terms of employment. It also states that an employer must notify the employee of any changes in the particulars as given in the statement.

THE WRITTEN STATEMENT

The following particulars of the terms of employment should be included in the written statement:

1. The full names of the employer and the employee
2. The address of the employer in the state or, where appropriate, its principal place of business or the registered address of the employer as registered with the Companies Registration Office
3. The place of work or, where there is no main place of work, a statement indicating that the employee is required or permitted to work at various places
4. Job title or nature of the work
5. Date of commencement of employment
6. If the contract is temporary, the expected duration of employment
7. If the contract is for a fixed term, the date on which the contract expires
8. The rate of remuneration or method of calculating remuneration
9. The pay reference period for the purposes of the National Minimum Wage Act (2000)
10. Whether remuneration is paid weekly, monthly or otherwise
11. Terms or conditions relating to hours of work (including overtime)
12. Terms or conditions relating to paid leave (other than paid sick leave)
13. Terms or conditions relating to incapacity for work due to sickness or injury
14. Terms or conditions relating to pensions and pension schemes
15. Periods of notice which the employee is entitled to receive and required to give on termination of employment; where this cannot be indicated when the written statement is given, the written statement must state the method for determining the period of notice to be given
16. A reference to any collective agreements which affect the terms of employment. Where an employer is not a party to the agreement, the written statement must indicate the bodies or institution which made the agreement.

The Terms of Employment (Information) Acts 1994–2014 are available from:

https://www.workplacerelations.ie/en/publications_forms/terms_of_employment_information_act_-_explanatory_booklet.pdf

http://www.irishstatutebook.ie/eli/1994/act/5/enacted/en/html

Minimum Notice and Terms of Employment Acts 1973–2005

Under the terms of the Minimum Notice and Terms of Employment Acts 1973–2005, an employee or employer who intends to terminate a contract of employment must provide the other party with specified minimum notice.

Employees: Employees who have been in continuous employment for at least 13 weeks are obliged to provide their employer with one week's notice of termination of employment. If a greater amount of notice is specified in the employee's contract of employment, then this notice must be given.

Employers: Employers must give employees who have been in continuous service notice dependent on the length of the employee's service as follows:

Length of service	Notice period
13 weeks–2 years	One week
2–5 years	Two weeks
5–10 years	Four weeks
10–15 years	Six weeks
More than 15 years	Eight weeks

CONTINUOUS SERVICE

An employee's service is considered continuous unless he/she is either dismissed or voluntarily leaves his/her job. Continuity of service is not normally affected by strikes, lay-offs or lock-outs, nor by dismissal followed by immediate re-employment. The transfer of a trade or business from one person to another (a Transfer of Undertakings) does not break continuity of service, and in such cases an employee's service with the new owner includes service with the previous owner. However, for the purpose of these Acts, an employee who claims and receives redundancy payment in respect of lay-off or short-time is considered to have left his/her employment voluntarily.

CALCULATION OF SERVICE

Periods of absence from the employment due to service with the Reserve Defence Forces are deemed to be periods of service. Absences of up to 26 weeks between consecutive periods of employment count as periods of service if due to lay-offs, sickness or injury, or when taken by agreement with the employer. A week, or part of a week, when an employee was locked out by his/her employer, or when the employee was absent from work due to a trade dispute in another business, also counts when calculating periods of service. However, any period during which the employee has been absent from work because he/she was taking part in a strike relating to the business in which the employee is employed does not count.

> The Minimum Notices and Terms of Employment Acts 1973–2005 are available from:
>
> https://www.workplacerelations.ie/en/what_you_should_know/ending%20the%20employment%20relationship/minimum%20notice/
>
> http://www.irishstatutebook.ie/eli/1973/act/4/enacted/en/html

Organisation of Working Time Act 1997

The Organisation of Working Time Act 1997 sets out statutory rights for employees in respect of rest, working time and holidays and states that the maximum average working week for many employees cannot exceed 48 hours. This does not mean that a working week can never exceed 48 hours; it is the average that is important. The average may be calculated over one of the following periods:

* four months for most employees
* six months for employees in the security industry, hospitals, prisons, gas/electricity, airport/docks, agriculture or in businesses which have peak periods at certain times of the year (such as tourism)
* 12 months where this has been agreed between the employer and the employees (and this must be approved by the Labour Court).

The 48 hours of work do not include annual leave, sick leave or maternity or adoptive or parental leave.

The legislation lays down rules for night workers, minimum breaks and rest periods. There are also special provisions in relation to Sunday working.

EXCEPTIONS TO THE WORKING TIME LEGISLATION

The Organisation of Working Time Act 1997 in relation to working time and rest periods does not apply to all employees. It does not apply to the Gardaí, defence forces, employees who control their own working hours or family employees on farms or in private homes.

IMPORTANT POINTS TO NOTE

* Your employer must notify you of the starting and finishing times at least 24 hours before your first day of work.
* If you do not work every day, your employer must give you at least 24 hours' notice of your working hours for each day of the week that you have to work. They can do this by putting up a notice in a conspicuous place in your workplace on a day when you are working.
* If you have to work additional hours, your employer must give you 24 hours' notice in the same way. However, they can ask you to work at less than 24 hours' notice in unforeseen circumstances, such as when they need you to cover for another employee who is off sick.

OVERTIME

Overtime is work done outside normal working hours. Employers have no statutory obligation to pay employees for work completed in overtime. However, many employers pay employees higher rates of pay for overtime. Your contract of employment should state whether you are required to work overtime and should set out the rates of pay, if you are to be paid for it.

The Organisation of Working Time Act 1997 is available from:

https://www.workplacerelations.ie/en/publications_forms/owt-act-guide.pdf

http://www.irishstatutebook.ie/eli/1997/act/20/enacted/en/html

Think about

Q: I have an employee who has worked with me for a number of years and is on a term-time contract that's due to expire at the end of June. I haven't been happy with her work and so I don't think I will renew her contract in September. Can I do that?

A: A term-time contract is, in essence, a fixed-term contract and so you need to be very careful when making a decision not to renew. If the employee has had three or more fixed-term contracts in the past four years, then they must be employed under a contract of indefinite duration. So, it is important to look at how many years they have worked for you and how many term-time contracts they have had. If they fall within the above rules, then they are essentially permanent employees, so it is very risky not to 'rehire' them, as to do so would be considered a dismissal and would fall under the Unfair Dismissals Acts. Any issues with performance should therefore be managed by performance management, and if necessary, your disciplinary procedure.

See https://www.earlychildhoodireland.ie/wp-content/uploads/2019/06/EYES-Questions-of-the-Week.pdf for more questions and answers.

Activity

Map the relevant legislation to the context.

Context	Legislation
I would like gloves to wear while working in the ELC sector.	
I have worked every evening after closing time of the ELC service.	
I would like to know what the conditions of my employment are.	
I want to leave my job next month and return to college.	
I have been asked to open the ELC service every morning. Is this fair?	
I have been asked not to wear my nose stud to work.	

Communication

17

This chapter will explore:
* effective communication in ELC
* communication skills and barriers to communication
* confidentiality
* professional boundaries
* relationships and interaction in ELC.

Introduction

Communication and teamwork are essential elements of professionalism in ELC services. This chapter will focus on communication skills and the importance of working as part of a team, both of which contribute to providing high-quality ELC for children. Good communication facilitates working collaboratively to promote a democratic, inclusive and anti-bias approach in the ELC service.

Effective communication in ELC

Presenting yourself in a professional manner is a powerful form of non-verbal communication. As you prepare for professional practice placement there are many items to consider, many of which have been discussed in previous chapters. When you attend your placement, it is important to be aware that how you present yourself, including your dress and self-care, is a form of communication which is very powerful.

Activity

There is an old saying that 'first impressions are lasting impressions'. In small groups, discuss this statement. What does it mean? Do you agree or disagree with it? Feedback your views to the larger group.

> **Think about**
> Based on this discussion, think about how you would now prepare for professional practice placement and what you will be mindful of.

QUESTIONS TO ASK PRIOR TO PLACEMENT

Some question to ask prior to placement include:

* What is the dress code?
* What type of shoes should I wear?
* Is jewellery allowed?
* What is acceptable/unacceptable in relation to nails?
* What is the general hygiene policy?
* Is perfume allowed?

Answers to these questions can be resolved with a phone call or visit to the service prior to commencing placement. You can also do an online search of the service, which may provide images and photos that can also provide useful clues. Some course providers like their learners to wear appropriate dress which includes the college/centre logo. Similarly, some ELC services like their staff and students to wear a uniform with their logo, which may be provided by the service for a small fee. Working in ELC is very active and will require bending, lifting, squatting, sitting, standing and indoor and outdoor play with the children, therefore comfortable clothing is essential. Footwear should also be comfortable and flat to ensure safe play with children. Jewellery should be kept to a minimum, with no necklaces or earrings that could be pulled by the children. In general, you should appear well groomed, friendly and professional.

Communication skills

How you communicate is just as important as your personal presentation. Good communication skills can be acquired through practice and reflection and can promote better working and social relationships. When you consider the amount of time you will spend in study and placements, it is worth noting that forming good relationships with colleagues, children and families will make your work more enjoyable and rewarding. This does not mean that you must like all your work colleagues, but professionalism requires that you work in a collaborative way to provide the best possible ELC service for all concerned.

Communicating involves giving, receiving and making sense of information in the form of verbal, non-verbal and visual messages. Verbal person-to-person communication is perhaps the most efficient method of communication and includes speaking, tone and volume. Non-verbal communication is linked to visual clues including body language, gestures, facial expressions and touch. For example, a smile sends a friendly message to others. Therefore, verbal and non-verbal language are not exclusive but rather go together. It is this combination that makes person-to-person communication more effective.

Mehrabian (1966) proposes the following statistics for the effectiveness of spoken person-to-person communications:

* 7 per cent of meaning is in the words that are spoken.
* 38 per cent of meaning is paralinguistic (the way that the words are said).
* 55 per cent of meaning is in facial expression.

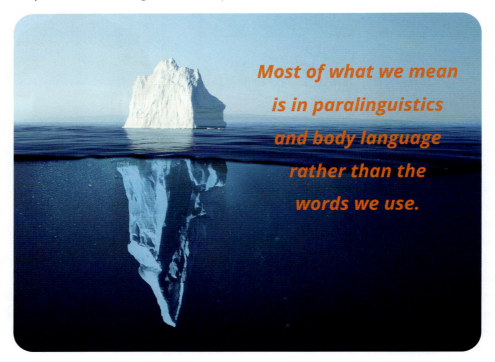

Most of what we mean is in paralinguistics and body language rather than the words we use.

As your work in pre-school services will involve direct communication with adults and children, it is useful to keep in mind Mehrabian's breakdown of meaning in communication. If you observe very young children, you will see how powerful their body language is and you will also observe that babies understand what is going on around them and can respond to tone of voice long before they understand the actual words, so it is essential to be aware of your body language and tone of voice around babies, toddlers and young children.

LISTENING AND SPEAKING SKILLS

For any conversation, knowing when to speak – and when to listen – is essential.

'The time to listen comes twice as often as the time to talk and there is a reason you have two ears and one mouth.' (Epictetus)

'Most people don't listen with the intent to understand; they listen with the intent to reply.' (Stephen Covey)

Skills required for active/mindful listening	
Do	**Don't**
1. Set an intention to listen mindfully.	1. Compare – it can make it hard to hear because the listener is too busy measuring themselves against the speaker.
2. Listen to understand rather than to answer.	2. Mind-read – it may turn the listener's focus on assumptions.
3. Notice the person's body language and tone of voice.	3. Rehearse how to reply – it can distract by shifting focus from what is being shared.
4. Allow the person to complete what they are saying.	5. Judge – it may lead to hastily writing someone off.
5. Practise not interrupting, finishing sentences, judging what is being said, or relating stories back to your experiences.	6. Daydream – it will suggest a lack of commitment to the conversation or relationship.
6. Recognise when your mind wanders and gently return your focus back to the speaker.	8. Spar – quick rebuttals and strong stands can foster hostility.
7. Pause and ask if the person has finished before asking questions or offering comments.	9. Advise – it prioritises problem solving over listening.
8. Ask for permission before giving advice.	10. Derail, which occurs through quick subject changes.
9 Give the gift of your presence and focused attention.	11. Placate, which is about people-pleasing rather than active or deep listening.
10. Just listen; often that is enough!	(Adapted from Shaffer, 2019)

Activity

Exercise 1: Listening exercise

Separating the group in two, half are instructed to leave the room, with the remaining half instructed to prepare a story to tell on a topic in which they are interested (e.g. family/TV series/film). When ready, the first half are instructed to return and class members pair up. The storyteller beings their story, with the listener actively listening for 30 seconds, after which they should feign a lack of interest (e.g. checking their phone, looking around them). The listener is then asked to repeat the story once the storyteller has finished.

* Were you able to relate the details?

The storyteller relays the experience of being half-listened to.

* When did you notice the other person had stopped listening?
* How did you feel about not being listened to?

Chinese whispers exercise

Sit in a circle and pass a (spoken) message to one person, who passes it on to the next, and so on until everyone has heard the message. The last person to receive the message says the message out loud. Has the message changed since it was first passed?

BARRIERS TO COMMUNICATION

As already noted, a prime barrier to effective communication is the inability to actively listen to others. You cannot engage with colleagues or children if you are not listening, because in the absence of listening you may make assumptions about their needs based on your perceptions rather than the reality of what is needed.

Confidentiality

ELC services routinely handle confidential information about the children enrolled, their families and the staff employed in the service. It is important to note that services maintain confidentiality on a 'need to know' basis. This is crucial, especially when there are specific health and safety concerns. When managing sensitive information, there is an ethical and legal responsibility to protect the privacy of individuals and families. This information is shared only when it is necessary. Relationships with staff, children and families are built on trust, and maintaining confidentiality builds that trust.

> **Síolta Standard 12:** 'Communicating effectively in the best interests of the child requires policies, procedures and actions that promote the proactive sharing of knowledge and information among appropriate stakeholders, with respect and confidentiality.' (*Síolta*, 2006, p. 85)

> **Sample confidentiality policy statement**
>
> 'ABC Childcare is committed to keeping confidential information in relation to families and children, staff and volunteers, unless there is an obligation for the common good to disclose such information or if the pre-school is legally obliged to do so.'

Confidentiality must remain central to information collection and storage and should be reflected in practices such as assurances to parents, compliance with relevant data protection legislation, consultation with parents regarding consent for the sharing of information about their child, and the use of secure storage facilities for records. (See p. 37 in relation to GDPR. See Síolta *Research Digest Standard 12: Communication*.)

Professional boundaries

Becoming an ELC professional will require you to use your judgement, skill and professional learning to develop boundaries in your work with babies, children, colleagues and families.

> " Boundaries are an integral part of the identity of every helping profession. Being aware of and honouring boundaries between practitioners and those they serve is an important professional responsibility."
>
> (Feeney, Freeman and Moravcik, 2020)

Professional boundaries are broader and less clear-cut than ethical principles. Ethical principles describe what professionals **must do** or **must not do** and are consistent across ELC services. For example, we must respect confidentiality and not endanger children. Professional boundaries are more situation-specific and may vary based on circumstances, community and the kind of service offered. ELC in Ireland is in the process of asserting its right to be called a profession and defining what this means. As a member of a profession, you need to be thoughtful about recognising and managing professional boundaries. It is essential to explore this area as currently there are no set rules for professional boundaries in ELC services. Guidelines set by other helping professions, for example social care professions, can help to identify boundaries for early years educators.

Activity

The following three scenarios highlight some possible boundary issues. In small groups, discuss what these issues might be.

Scenario 1: The parents of a child in your service live nearby and ask you to drop their child into the service on your way to work.

Scenario 2: You are involved in a charity fundraiser and you ask the parents in your service if they will buy tickets for this charity from you.

Scenario 3: The father of a child in your service asks if he can meet you after work for drinks to discuss his child's progress.

Perhaps you can think of other examples which you have come across. Share these with the class group, **being mindful not to disclose the names of individuals or services involved**.

Class Contract: It is a good idea to have a class contract in relation to group discussions and the information that emerges from these discussions.

WHY PROFESSIONAL BOUNDARIES ARE IMPORTANT

While relationships with families will vary, you must remember that the relationship between you and the family is not one of equals. Once you are qualified you will have specialised knowledge and access to sensitive and confidential information about the children attending the service. Families have less power in this relationship as most families may know less than you about young children's development and learning. They are required to share personal information with staff, who may come from a different ethnic, linguistic, cultural or socioeconomic background. Families entrust their children to teachers throughout their education, but in the early years, when children are most vulnerable, these relationships can have a particularly strong impact. Professional boundaries help to ensure that ELC educators use their power well and fairly. They understand that their purpose is to use their knowledge and skills to build relationships that support the development of children and that work in partnership with families in the task of child rearing. Families trust early childhood educators to act in the best interests of the child and family.

To maintain that trust, the *Code of Professional Responsibility and Code of Ethics for Early Years* (2020) provides guiding principles for your work and is designed to emphasise the professional nature of early childhood education. Value statements in this document include:

* Every child is unique and has inalienable rights as set out in the United Nations Convention on the Rights of the Child.

- Early childhood is a significant and distinct time in life that must be valued, respected, nurtured and supported in its own right.
- The young child is innately driven to learn and is an active agent in her/his own development through her/his interactions with the world. The young child is a competent and confident learner.
- Early childhood education and care takes place in the context of family, community and culture.
- Children thrive best in caring and democratic communities.
- Play is a key means of supporting young children's learning and development. Early years educators, in undertaking their roles and tasks, will seek to promote and maintain these values. (pp. 4–5)

It is proposed that early years educators will use this code as a foundation on which to develop policies, procedures and practice. It is designed to be applied in working with children, parents, services or within communities. Similarly, in emphasising the professional nature of ELC, it respects and encourages the educator's own judgements which are a fundamental part of early years pedagogy.

Building respectful partnerships

Children have a fundamental need to be with other people. They learn and develop through loving and nurturing relationships with adults and other children, and the quality of these interactions impacts on their learning and development (*Aistear*, NCCA, 2009, p. 9). Similarly, *Síolta*'s principle on relationships acknowledges that 'Responsive, sensitive and reciprocal relationships, which are consistent over time, are essential to the wellbeing, learning and development of the young child' (CECDE, 2006, p. 7).

Collaborative relationships between all those involved in ELC services, including children, staff, students and families, are key to the delivery of high-quality services. Of particular importance are:

- interactions between staff and children
- interactions within the adult team
- partnership with families.

INTERACTIONS BETWEEN STAFF AND CHILDREN

All areas of children's development are integrated and interdependent: physical, intellectual, language, emotional, social, moral and spiritual. It is therefore essential that all interactions with the adults in their lives should be positive and should support their development in all areas. Such adult–child interactions are evident when:

- adults interact frequently with children, speaking and listening to them at their eye level and showing positive body language while providing a warm secure environment

* adults respond to children's cues and maintain a focus on what children are doing
* adults try to ensure children do not have to wait for an adult response and will be aware of developmentally appropriate practice in their responses (for example, a baby's cry will be responded to immediately; a three-year-old will be verbally assured that the adult will respond to them even if it takes a few minutes to give the child their full attention)
* adults ensure a nurturing pedagogy which supports children's emotional wellbeing and ability to be comfortable, relaxed and involved in play
* adults help children deal with anger, sadness and frustration by comforting, identifying and helping children to name their feelings and use words rather than actions to solve their problems
* adults involve children in decision-making, encouraging and responding to their suggestions and comments.

(Adapted from Donohoe and Gaynor, 2011)

> *Síolta* **Standard 5 Interactions: Component 5.4**: 'The adult interactive style is focused on process as opposed to outcomes. It is balanced between talking and listening, offers the child a choice of responses and encourages expanded use of language. It follows the child's lead and interests, and challenges the child appropriately.' (CECDE, 2006, p. 42)

Studies have shown that when adults learn to effectively use a range of adult–child interaction strategies they can enhance the length and quality of children's interactions through 'sustained shared thinking'. This is where two or more individuals work together in an intellectual way to clarify an idea, solve a problem or evaluate an activity. It was found that this was most likely to occur when children were interacting individually with an adult or with a single peer partner, both contributing and participating equally as partners. Periods of 'sustained shared thinking' are essential for effective early years practice, extending child-initiated interactions and contributing to intellectual challenge. Furthermore, a balance between child-led and adult-led interactions is in evidence in the most effective ELC settings (Sylva, K., Melhuish, E., Sammons, P., Siraj-Blatchford, I. and Taggart, B., 2004).

> " Practitioners who are sensitive, attuned and responsive to children's cues, applying a nurturing pedagogy, are better able to engage in sustained shared thinking, assess what assistance children need, if any, and ensure their responses are respectful of the child. "
>
> (Hayes et al., 2017, p. 117)

ADULTS AS ROLE MODELS

In a high-quality ELC environment, the adults:

* model good communications, both verbal and non-verbal, and display appropriate ways of expressing feelings
* model fair and consistent behaviour with all children
* value all children equally and promote anti-discriminatory practice
* enjoy and value their work and that of their colleagues
* demonstrate professional practice in their work at all times.

(Donohoe and Gaynor, 2011, pp. 53-54)

INTERACTIONS WITHIN THE ADULT TEAM

> *Síolta* **Standard 5 Interactions: Component 5.5:** 'Interactions between the adults within, and associated with the setting, act as a model of respect, support and partnership for the child' (CECDE, 2006, p. 38).

The adult ELC team work together to meet the aims of the setting and take collective action for decisions made and implemented to ensure the effective running of the service. The adult team must be motivated towards common goals, be supported to achieve these goals and be able to communicate effectively within the team.

PARTNERSHIP WITH FAMILIES

Aistear's principle on parents states that parents are the most important people in children's lives:

> **The care and education that children receive from their parents and family, especially during their early months and years, greatly influence their overall development. Extended family and community also have important roles to play.** (NCCA, 2009, p. 9)

Similarly, *Síolta*'s principle on parents acknowledges:

> **Parents are the primary educators of the child and have a pre-eminent role in promoting her/his wellbeing, learning and development.** (CECDE, 2006, p. 6)

Síolta's Standard 3 Parents and Families highlights the importance of valuing and involving parents through a range of clearly stated, accessible and implemented processes, policies and procedures. The components focus on having informal and formal information sharing and communication with parents and on providing a variety of opportunities for parents to be involved in the setting.

Brostrom (2002) suggests establishing positive relations between the home and the setting, characterised by warm personal contact and followed by ongoing communication about the activities and the curriculum of the setting. Research demonstrates better outcomes for children in their cognitive and social development where child-related information between staff and parents is shared. In addition, parental collaboration in decision-making about their child's learning programme is reported as significant.

Parents/guardians and practitioners working together will ensure that the ELC setting is a microcosm of the wider society. Parents and practitioners working together can benefit the child, parents and the practitioners as follows.

Children will:

- feel more secure and benefit more from the educational opportunities provided for them
- transition from one setting to another with greater confidence
- view learning as more enjoyable when their home life is 'visible' in the setting
- enjoy hearing and seeing their home language in the setting when their home language is neither English or Irish
- experience more connections between the different services that support them.

Parents will:

- feel valued and respected
- be more involved in their children's learning and development
- share information about their children
- feel their family's values, practices, traditions and beliefs are understood and taken into account
- feel comfortable visiting the setting, talking to and planning with practitioners
- know more about their children's experiences outside the home and use this information to support their learning and development more effectively
- understand the importance of early learning and care
- gain increased confidence in their own parenting skills.

ELC practitioners will:

- understand the children and their families better and use this information to make learning more enjoyable and rewarding for all children
- help children develop a sense of identity and belonging in the setting by actively engaging with and finding out about family values, traditions and beliefs, and building on these where appropriate
- benefit from parents' skills and expertise
- provide a more emotionally secure environment for children.

(Adapted from *Aistear Guidelines for Good Practice*, 2009)

STRATEGIES FOR BUILDING PARTNERSHIPS WITH FAMILIES

* Share information about the curriculum with parents.
* Use a noticeboard to let parents know what activities children do on a particular day. Pictures might be useful in sharing this information with parents who have little English or Irish.
* Send home photographs of the children with captions that describe what they have been doing and learning.
* Let parents know about topics that interest their children. Find out what their interests are at home and build on these.
* Invite parents to share information about their culture and traditions that might be useful in supporting their children's learning and development.
* Organise information sessions for parents especially before and/or after children join the setting. A session might focus on Aistear's four themes and what you do to support children's learning and development in these areas. Another session might highlight the importance of play and how children learn through it.
* Invite parents to spend time in the setting so that they can join in with activities and learn about what their children do.
* Develop a regular newsletter that provides useful information such as the words of songs and rhymes that the children are learning, important dates, updates on policies and snippets of theory followed by ideas for activities to do at home that are fun and inexpensive.
* Engage members of the extended family and the wider community.

(Adapted from *Aistear Síolta: Building Partnerships*, pillar-overview-building-partnerships-with-parents1.pdf)

Activity

In groups, considering *Síolta* Standard 3 Parents and Families, discuss how the ELC setting could best meet the needs of the following parents, both in terms of the service the ELC setting offers and in its capacity as advisor about other services available in the community.

1. Hannah and Mark: 'Our nanny is excellent. She drops Chloë (3 years) into the pre-school every morning and collects her at 12.30 p.m. We both have to be at work by 8.30 a.m. and Mark often works late into the evening. We rarely get to talk to the ELC staff. We'd both like to be more involved in the pre-school but it's very difficult with our work commitments.'

2. Kirsty: 'It's very difficult for me to leave my baby (10 months) in the mornings. I phone the staff often during the day to find out how he's getting on; I think I am sometimes annoying them. I would love to call in sometimes to see him. Although I know he is being well looked after, I sometimes find myself in tears after these phone calls.'

3. Michael: 'Since I split up with Rishi's mother and he doesn't live with me anymore, I'm very conscious that he needs to have more male influences in his life. I'd like to get a bit more involved with the service too, but I can't face all those women!'

4. Mr and Mrs Nasim: 'We came here to live six months ago, and Fatima (2.5 years) has settled in very well to the crèche. She is now starting to speak English, and we are both concerned that she is not getting enough support in this from us, as we don't speak English at home.'

RECAP QUESTIONS

1. In what way has your knowledge of communication changed having read this chapter?
2. Why is personal presentation part of communication?
3. Identify why boundaries are important when working in ELC.

18

Teamwork

> **This chapter will explore:**
> * the purpose and functions of teams, and teamwork skills
> * stages of group formation using Tuckman's group formation model
> * team roles and responsibilities, identifying roles in the professional practice placement
> * communicating a democratic, inclusive and anti-bias approach.

Purpose and function of teams

Most teams are not teams at all but merely collections of individual relationships with the boss. Each individual vying with the others for power, prestige and position. (Douglas McGregor)

Activity

In groups, think of a time when you were part of a team (e.g. in a club, playing sport, organising an event). What is your memory of working as part of this team? What did you learn? Did some members participate more than others? Consider the positive (what made it a good team) and negative (why it was not good) aspects. Share your own personal experiences and learning as a result of your involvement.

Working with young children in ELC settings requires a high level of teamwork which in turn provides better services for children and families and provides opportunities for personal and professional growth.

SKILLS NECESSARY FOR WORKING IN AN ELC TEAM

* Excellent communications, with staff being open with and trustful of each other and communication 'moving up and down'
* Willingness to cooperate
* Clear roles and expectations

- Goal setting with staff working together to set and achieve goals
- Decision-making; with many alternatives discussed and time to reflect
- Clear communication of decisions to all affected
- Recognition of conflict, with problems dealt with openly and creatively
- Cooperation in relations and sharing of ideas
- Use of resources, with people knowing each other's strengths and those particularly skilful in certain areas using those skills
- Regular evaluation and reflection of teamwork, with time regularly scheduled to collectively reflect on and evaluate personal and group efforts and make new team goals.

GROUP/TEAM DEVELOPMENT

Effective teamwork contributes to the quality of pre-school services by improving the self-esteem, job satisfaction and morale of educators, which in turn reduces stress and burnout. It is also crucial in achieving goals and accomplishing tasks. Tuckman (1965) discovered that teams normally go through five stages of growth: forming, storming, norming, performing and adjourning.

Forming — Specification of common goals
Storming — Conflicts and negotiation
Norming — Consensus and team spirit
Performing — Finding balance of conformity and deviance
Adjourning — Feedback and dispersion

FORMING

In this stage, team members are introduced. They state why they were chosen for the team and what they hope to accomplish within the team. Members cautiously explore the boundaries of acceptable group behaviour. This is a stage of transition from individual to member status, and of testing the leader's guidance both formally and informally. Forming includes these feelings and behaviours:

- Excitement, anticipation and optimism
- Pride in being chosen for the project
- A tentative attachment to the team
- Suspicion and anxiety about the job
- Defining the tasks and how they will be accomplished
- Determining acceptable group behaviour
- Deciding what information needs to be gathered.

Activities include discussions of the concepts and issues, and for some members, impatience with these discussions. There is often difficulty in identifying some of the relevant problems as there is so much going on that members get distracted. The team often achieves very little concerning its goals. This is perfectly normal.

STORMING

Storming includes these feelings and behaviours:

- Resisting the tasks
- Resisting quality improvement approaches suggested by other members
- Sharp fluctuations in attitude about the team's chance of success
- Arguing among members, even when they agree on the real issues
- Defensiveness, competition and choosing sides
- Questioning the wisdom of those who selected the project and appointed the members of the team
- Establishing unrealistic goals
- Disunity, increased tension and jealousy.

These pressures mean that team members have little energy to spend on progressing towards the intended goal, but they are beginning to understand each other. It can often take three or four meetings before the next phase is arrived at.

NORMING

Norming includes these feelings and behaviours:

- An ability to express criticism constructively
- Acceptance of membership in the team
- An attempt to achieve harmony by avoiding conflict
- Friendliness, confiding in each other and sharing personal problems
- A sense of team cohesion, spirit and goals
- Establishing and maintaining team ground rules and boundaries.

As team members work out their differences, they have more time and energy to spend on the project.

PERFORMING

By now the team has settled its relationships and expectations. They can begin performing by diagnosing, problem solving and implementing changes. At last, team members have discovered and accepted each other's strengths and weaknesses. In addition, they have learned what their roles are. Performing includes these feelings and behaviours:

- Members have insights into personal and group processes
- An understanding of each other's strengths and weakness
- Constructive self-change
- Ability to prevent or work through group problems
- Close attachment to the team.

The team is now an effective, cohesive unit. You can tell when your team has reached this stage because you start getting a lot of work done.

ADJOURNING

The team shares the success of the project having worked together. Once the team breaks up (e.g. a member moving on), there is always a bittersweet sense of accomplishment coupled with a reluctance to say goodbye. Many relationships formed within these teams continue long after the team disbands (Tuckman and Jenson, 1977).

When team members leave the ELC setting and new members join, the team leader needs to be mindful that these changes require attention to the overall team development process to ensure it reaches the performing stage once more.

BENEFITS OF TEAMWORK IN ELC

Essentially, good teamwork allows all members of the group to feel ownership of what happens within the group and feel empowered to speak up and act when problems arise.

- Roles are clearly identified and staff know what is expected of them.
- Staff recognise their own and each other's strengths.
- Common goals for the children and the service are identified.
- Staff members feel they are a part of a group and have a sense of loyalty to the service and feel valued.
- Staff members cooperate and share resources, ideas and experiences.
- Communication flows freely and accurately in all directions — plans, problems, decisions and developments are shared freely by the leader/manager and problems, suggestions and criticisms are routinely brought to their attention by team members.

Activity

In relation to *Síolta* Standard 3 Parents and Families and Standard 4 Consultation, role play the following scenario.

> You are working as part of a team in an ELC service that is planning an open day for parents and members of the local community.

- Assign roles to different members of the team.
- Draw up an agenda.
- Through discussion, reach decisions on:
  - when and how the open day will be organised
  - how it will be advertised/promoted
  - duties of different team members on the day
  - how the children will be involved.

Record the meeting for your Professional Practice Placement module.

Communicating a democratic, inclusive and anti-bias approach

In promoting a democratic, inclusive and anti-bias approach in ELC, it is useful to examine what these words mean.

> **DEFINITION**
>
> **Democracy** for adults means having your say, for example, voting in elections. Being democratic is generally linked to fairness.

To be democratic in your work in ELC means actively listening to all stakeholders and being willing to work with others in the best interests of children. It also means being fair to all the children and not favouring individuals or groups of children. Children are good at recognising if something is unfair even though they may not yet be able to verbalise it. For children, democracy is about helping them to understand that their opinions are important, and that each child's thoughts and feelings should be listened to and valued. It is also about children having a say in matters that affect them, which is in line with Article 12 of the United Nations Convention on the Rights of the Child (1989), ratified by Ireland in 1992, which states that the child's view must be taken into account in matters affecting him/her.

DEFINITION

Bias is a tendency to lean in a certain direction, either in favour of or against a particular thing, view or person.

To have personal biases is a natural tendency based on life experience, beliefs, values, education, family, friends, peers and others.

DEFINITION

Inclusion refers to a process involving a programme, curriculum or educational environment where each child is welcomed and included on equal terms, can feel they belong and can progress to their full potential in all areas of development. (National Childcare Strategy, 2006–2010)

Activity

In groups, read this case study and discus how the pre-school leader handled Farid's arrival in the pre-school. How might this influence your work in the future?

> **Farid, aged 3.5 years, recently migrated to Ireland with his family from Syria. Farid started in a local ELC service in late October while many of the children had commenced in September. On his first day the other children were curious about Farid and commented on his skin colour and the way he spoke with a different accent. In anticipation of Farid coming to the service the pre-school leader had completed some research on Syria and the situation there and why there was mass emigration from Syria as a result of the war. She had collated a book of pictures for all the children, including Farid, to view, with appropriate images from Syria including images of people with the same skin colour as Farid. She also explained that English was not Farid's first language and that is why he spoke with an accent.**

Being aware of your bias is vital to both your personal and professional development. As you will make several decisions every day in your placements, some of which are more important than others, make sure that the ones that do matter are not made based on bias but rather on reflective judgement and critical thinking.

Anti-bias education provides opportunities for students, educators and families to learn from and about one another and explore ways to address bias and prejudice through awareness, intervention and personal action. 'The heart of anti-bias work is a vision of a world in which all children are able to blossom, and each child's particular abilities and gifts are able to flourish' (Derman-Sparks and Olsen Edwards, 2010).

The anti-bias education approach establishes four goals in relation to adults and four goals in relation to children. Each goal addresses a particular area of growth and builds on and interacts with the others. From these specific goals, an anti-bias and inclusive approach to race, ethnicity, disability, gender, family structure and class can be built.

Goals for adults	Goals for children
1. To be conscious of one's own culture, attitudes and values, and how they influence practice.	1. To support each child's identity (individual and group) and their sense of belonging.
2. To be comfortable with difference, have empathy and engage effectively with families.	2. To foster children's empathy and support them to be comfortable with difference.
3. To critically think about diversity, bias and discrimination.	3. To encourage each child to critically think about diversity and bias.
4. To confidently engage in dialogue about issues of diversity, bias and discrimination and work to challenge individual and institutional forms of prejudice and discrimination.	4. To empower children to stand up for themselves and others in difficult situations.

(Diversity, Equality and Inclusion Charter, 2016)

PHYSICAL ENVIRONMENT

The physical environment plays a crucial role within the ELC setting. It provides a first impression to families and children, and it plays an important role in building each child's individual and group identity. The creation of a physical environment that represents all the children attending the service at any given time makes it clear that it is an inclusive environment.

Pointers for considering the physical environment

1. The physical environment sets the scene for all children to be recognised, respected and valued, and for discussing diversity, equality and inclusion topics with children.
2. The materials should initially depict the children who are attending the service and materials that represent the broader community should also be used.
3. Children from other countries should be represented accurately. For instance, many Black children are born Irish with, for example, Nigerian, Kenyan or other heritage. Therefore, materials need to support their identity appropriately.
4. A child with a disability should be able to see themselves represented in the materials in the environment.
5. It is important to provide a rich, accurate, non-stereotypical environment with regard to gender, race, culture, ethnicity, including Travellers and those with a disability.

6. Responding to children's play comments while they are interacting with the materials can form the basis of the curriculum content regarding diversity, equality and inclusive practice.

7. A child whose background, language, ability or culture is not represented in the environment may feel less confident, less comfortable and less able to participate. Children will not tell you 'I'm not here' when they are presented with materials that accurately represent their identity and background; instead, they will respond openly and positively.

8. A physical environment that depicts all children can offer reassurance to families that their child will be given due recognition and have equal status.

9. Draw on children's 'funds of knowledge' to acknowledge children's home and community experiences which can inform the curriculum, enhance the material environment and support the children to have pride in their lifestyle and their individual and group identity.

10. Bear in mind that even in a service where there appears to be a homogenous group, e.g. all two-year-old girls of a similar ethnicity, there will be diversity. One may wear glasses, another may be the child of a same-sex couple, another may speak two languages, and this should be reflected in the physical environment. Children will come across differences in the wider world and need to be positively supported and aware of diversity in our society.

11. Children have multiple identities, thus enriching the environment with images that make up the diversity in the early childhood service. Broader society creates a space for open discussion and learning.

12. Children rely on adults to provide the necessary physical environment for development and learning. Early childhood practitioners are central to shaping these environments and the powerful messages and opportunities that they engender.

(Diversity, Equality and Inclusion Charter, 2016)

INCLUSION OF CHILDREN WITH ADDITIONAL NEEDS

While inclusion terminology refers to all children, there is a different focus on including children with additional needs, for example where English is not their first language or where there are special needs as a result of a physical or intellectual impairment. The Education for Persons with Special Educational Needs Act 2004 (EPSEN) enshrined a commitment to inclusive education.

> A child with a special education need shall be educated in an inclusive environment with children who do not have such needs, unless the nature or degree of those needs of the child is such that to do so would be inconsistent with (a) the best interests of the child and (b) the effective provision of education for children with whom the child is to be educated. (EPSEN Act, 2004, Section 2)

Promoting an anti-bias approach to children with disabilities should include:

* providing an inclusive education environment in which all children can succeed
* enabling children with disabilities to develop autonomy, independence, confidence and pride
* providing all children with accurate, appropriate information about their own and others' disabilities, and fostering an understanding that a person with a disability is different in one respect, but similar in many other respects
* enabling all children to develop the ability to interact knowledgeably, comfortably and fairly with people who have various disabilities
* showing children with disabilities how to handle and challenge name-calling, stereotypical attitudes and physical barriers
* showing children how to resist and challenge stereotyping, name-calling and physical barriers directed against children or adults with disabilities.

(Derman-Sparks and ABC Task Force, 1989, p. 40)

The non-representation of diversity is as powerful in influencing children's attitudes and understanding as what is represented. It is vital that negative stereotypes are not reflected in the material and images portrayed in the environment. A rich, diverse physical environment will not, on its own, change attitudes or support children to be comfortable with difference, it is the interaction and discussion associated with the materials that drives development and change. Every aspect of the programme should actively address diversity and inclusion issues, using the environment as a learning tool.

ROLE OF THE ADULT IN PROMOTING CHILDREN'S INDIVIDUAL AND GROUP IDENTITY

Identity and belonging is one of the four Aistear themes. It concerns children developing a positive sense of who they are and feeling they are valued and respected as part of their family and the community. Giving children messages of respect, love, approval and encouragement enables them to develop a positive sense of who they are and a feeling that they have a valuable contribution to make wherever they are. Positive messages about their families, backgrounds, cultures, beliefs and languages help children to develop pride in who they are. These messages also give them confidence to voice their views and opinions, to make choices and to help shape their own learning and development.

Babies, toddlers and young children need a secure attachment to at least one of the adults in their setting. This relationship, which is known as the **key worker** system, provides comfort, reassurance and security for the child. In addition, interactions that are nurturing, respectful and consistent increase the child's confidence and competence to explore, develop and learn.

Promoting positive peer interactions supports children's learning and development and encourages the formation of a group identity. You can support this by ensuring all children and their families feel welcome in the centre. Providing children with their own named space for storing their coats, bags, lunch, etc. provides them with a sense of identity and belonging as soon as they arrive, while a warm welcome showing you are happy to see them encourages children to have a sense of security.

This chapter focused on the role of communication, partnerships and teamwork in building an inclusive, democratic and anti-bias setting which is required to support families and to enable all children to develop their full potential.

RECAP QUESTIONS

1. Discuss how Tuckman's teams can be utilised in ELC.
2. What particular areas does the Diversity, Equality and Inclusion Charter 2016 cover?

Current developments in early learning and care

19

> **This chapter will explore:**
> * the TOY project
> * Aistear: planned update
> * the *Better Start* strategy
> * the *First 5* strategy.

Together Old and Young – the TOY Project

Dr Anne Fitzpatrick

An interesting and innovative approach to introducing inclusive and anti-bias practice in ELC services is through intergenerational learning (IGL). Simply stated, IGL can be understood as the way people of all generations can learn with, from and about each other (ENIL, 2012). Intergenerational learning between young children and older adults can take place in services for young children, services for older adults and in a wide range of community settings such as libraries and community centres (Kernan and Cortellesi, 2020).

IGL involves bringing children and older adults together to share experiences, have fun, learn from each other and develop meaningful relationships. Successful IGL experiences reported in the research include children and older adults singing together, storytelling, participating in creative activities including painting, playdough and crafts, games, gardening, sharing snack time and celebrating special occasions (The TOY Project Consortium, 2013). Importantly, IGL creates opportunities for children to experience diversity in real-life, community contexts.

Social changes including increasing separation of generations as young and old spend more time in age-segregated settings such as ELC services and care centres for older adults, increasing cultural diversity, migration, smaller families and older people living longer have highlighted the importance of social engagement between generations as a key factor for the wellbeing of all. COVID 19 has further highlighted the interdependence of all age groups and drawn attention to the many benefits of intergenerational solidarity.

The research shows that IGL has wide-ranging benefits including the development of positive self and group identities (Cartmel *et al.*, 2018). Intergenerational learning promotes understandings and knowledge of the 'other' which benefits young and old and contributes to social inclusion in communities. The values underpinning IGL include positive perspectives on diversity, equity and inclusion and bringing children and older adults together promotes respect, embraces differences and supports an anti-bias approach in ELC services. Positive changes in perceptions and attitudes about older people and realistic understandings of the strengths and challenges of the ageing process (Cohen-Mansfield and Jensen, 2017), as well as an appreciation of the diversity of persons in all stages of life are significant benefits of IGL for children. Interacting with people of mixed ages, abilities, cultures and experiences creates rich opportunities for children's cognitive and socio-emotional learning and supports children as critical thinkers and problem solvers. Importantly, IGL creates in children a sense of belonging and helps them to build positive identities as they contribute to their own lives and learning as well as to the lives and learning of older adults (The TOY Project Consortium, 2013). Offering children IGL opportunities at a critical stage in their developing sense of identity and belonging enriches the contexts in which children build a range of images of themselves and the worlds to which they belong (Nimmo, 2008). Children learning about difference in environments that promote respectful views of themselves and others has been found to be particularly empowering (Derman-Sparks and Edwards, 2010). Most important, positive experiences of identity and belonging in one context, such as through IGL experiences, have been associated with promoting inclusive attitudes and behaviours in other contexts (Tillett and Wong, 2018). Intergenerational learning aligns closely with theories and principles underpinning Aistear, Síolta and the Regulations and offers an innovative strategy in implementing democratic, inclusive and anti-bias values and practice in ELC services. Now read about the TOY project and how to introduce successful intergenerational learning in ELC services.

The TOY project researches and develops good practice in IGL involving young children and older adults (**www.toyproject.net**). The original TOY project took place in seven European countries including Ireland. TOY has two overarching goals: improved health and wellbeing for all generations and the development of all-age-friendly communities. The TOY project identifies five goals of intergenerational learning:

1. Building and sustaining relationships
2. Enhancing social cohesion in the community
3. Facilitating older people as guardians of knowledge
4. Recognising the roles of grandparents in young children's lives
5. Enriching the learning processes of both children and older adults.

TOY created a compendium of 21 case studies of intergenerational initiatives involving young children and older people in seven European countries and published a guide to community-based intergenerational initiatives in Europe. The importance of training for practitioners who wish to introduce IGL was acknowledged, and TOY offers a short introductory online training course and an accredited course introducing innovative and digital approaches to IGL. TOY also offers a toolkit for anyone who wants to organise a training workshop about intergenerational learning involving young children and older people.

TOY FOR INCLUSION

The TOY for Inclusion project, a sister project of TOY, addresses issues of discrimination and segregation that oppress minority, migrant and vulnerable young children (**www.toyproject.net/project/toy-inclusion-2/**). TOY for Inclusion combines two approaches – it promotes IGL opportunities between older adults and young children as well as community-based early childhood education and care. It does so by creating community-based early childhood education and care Play Hubs, where relationships between young children and families from different backgrounds are built. They are located in areas that are reachable for all families and are designed and run by multi-sectoral teams composed of representatives of communities, school and pre-school teachers, health services, parents and local authorities. The 'TOY for Inclusion Toolkit – A step-by-step guide to creating inclusive Early Childhood Education and Care (ECEC) Play Hubs for all generations' provides information to enable trainers and practitioners of different sectors to set up and run play spaces for children, families and communities (**https://www.reyn.eu/toy4inclusion/**).

REFERENCES

Cartmel, J., Radford, K., Dawson, C., Fitzgerald, A., and Vecchio, N. (2018). Developing an evidenced based intergenerational pedagogy in Australia. *Journal of Intergenerational Relationships*, 16(1–2), 64–85.

Cohen-Mansfield, J. and Jensen, B. (2017). Intergenerational programs in schools: Prevalence and perceptions of impact. *Journal of Applied Gerontology*, 36(3), 254–276.

Derman-Sparks, L., and Edwards, J. O. (2010). *Anti-bias Education for Young Children and Ourselves*. National Association for the Education of Young Children.

[ENIL] European Network for Intergenerational Learning (2012). *Report on intergenerational learning and volunteering*. http://envejecimiento.csic.es/documentos/documentos/enil-ilv-01.pdf

Fitzpatrick, A. (2019). Towards a Pedagogy of Intergenerational Learning. In M. Kernan and G. Cortellesi (eds), *Intergenerational Learning in Practice: Together Old and Young,* pp. 40–54. Routledge.

Kernan, M., and Cortellesi, G. (eds). (2020). *Intergenerational Learning in Practice: Together Old and Young.* (pp. 40–54). Routledge.

Nimmo, J. (2008). Young Children's Access to Real Life: An Examination of the Growing Boundaries between Children in Childcare and Adults in the Community. *Contemporary Issues in Early Childhood, 9*(1), 3–13.

The TOY Project Consortium (2013). *Intergenerational Learning Involving Young Children and Older People.* The TOY Project http://www.toyproject.net/wp-content/uploads/2016/01/TOY-literature_review_FINAL.pdf

Tillett, V., and Wong, S. (2018). An Investigative Case Study into Early Childhood Educators' Understanding about 'Belonging'. *European Early Childhood Education Research Journal, 26*(1), 37–49.

Activity

Discuss the TOY project in terms of benefits for children, families and the wider community.

Aistear: Planned update

Aistear: The Early Childhood Curriculum Framework (NCCA, 2009) is now 12 years old and the NCCA is preparing to update this framework.

> The central tenet of the updating process is that Aistear is fundamental to children's lived experiences of early childhood education in Ireland and has become the bedrock of good practice in many settings. It is crucial that we nurture and develop the early childhood curriculum framework into the future to ensure its continued relevance and impact in enhancing quality provision for our youngest children. (NCCA, 2021, p. 3)

The framework will be updated

a. in light of all the changes that have taken place since it was first introduced and

b. taking account of feedback from all stakeholders, including children.

A. POLICY INITIATIVES

* Literacy and Numeracy for Learning and Life: The National Strategy to Improve Literacy and Numeracy among Children and Young People 2011–2020 (DES, 2011)

* The National Strategy on Education for Sustainable Development (ESD) 2014–2020 (DES, 2014)
* The Education for Sustainable Development Action Plan Q4 2018–Q4 2020
* *First 5: A Government Strategy for Babies, Young Children and their Families 2019–2028* (Government of Ireland, 2018)
* The Policy on Gaeltacht Education/Polasaí don Oideachas Gaeltachta 2017–2022 (DES, 2016)
* The STEM Education Policy Statement (DES, 2017).

DEVELOPMENTS IN CURRICULUM AND ASSESSMENTS

Aistear was the first early childhood curriculum framework developed in Ireland. It was followed by a curriculum framework developed for the Junior Cycle of post-primary education (2015). Currently, a similar framework for primary education is under way. The Primary Language Curriculum/Curaclam Teanga Bunscoile (PLC/CTB) (DES, 2019a) is also built on the principles of Aistear.

> **Aistear is a critical part of the curriculum and assessment infrastructure in the education system, and in the updating process it will be vital to consider how curriculum and assessment continuity is conceptualised, articulated and achieved. (NCCA, 2021, p. 7)**

B. STAKEHOLDERS

The stakeholder base has increased greatly since 2009, including:

* mentors working on the *Better Start* strategy whose work is underpinned by the principles of Aistear and Síolta
* those carrying out pre-school inspections under the Tusla inspectorate
* numerous educators in colleges and institutes who have introduced new ELC programmes from Level 4 through to Level 8.

Additionally, practitioners have now had the opportunity to use the frameworks and resources as listed in the *Aistear Síolta Practice Guide*, introduced by the NCCA in 2015, and develop their practice with the support of expert mentors under the *Better Start* initiative. Therefore, there will be an opportunity to undertake the review with feedback from these practitioners.

Feedback will also be forthcoming from the ELC workforce development, where the percentage of staff with a Level 5 or above qualification has increased from 71 per cent in 2010 to 94 per cent in 2019. As noted in Chapter 6, there is considerable ongoing work to professionalise this sector. It is a requirement of the Pre-school Regulations 2016 that all staff must have a minimum QQI Level 5 childcare qualification.

The changes that have occurred in Ireland since 2009 mean that children's lived experience is also changing. Changes include increased diversity (socially, culturally, ethnically and linguistically), while supports provided through the AIM model mean that more children with additional needs are now able to access ELC services.

Finally, the experience of living through a pandemic will also inform updates to the framework.

Given the breadth of change, it is now timely to pause and reflect on these, and other developments, with a view to ensuring that Aistear continues to be effective in providing enjoyable and meaningful learning experiences for every child throughout the early childhood period. (NCCA, 2021, p. 9)

PLANS FOR THE UPDATE

The update will be carried out over two phases, both of which will involve consultation and research.

- Phase, 1 May–December 2021: all stakeholders will be consulted and feedback will be sought on what is working well and what can be improved. Of course, this will include gathering the views of children.
- Phase 2 will begin towards the end of 2022. Proposals developed after Phase 1 will be shared and feedback gathered.

It is projected that the update to *Aistear* will be published towards the end of 2023.

Better Start

Better Start is a National Early Years Quality Development initiative of the Department of Children, Equality, Disability, Integration and Youth (DCEDIY) in collaboration with the Early Years Education Policy Unit of the Department of Education and Skills (DES). *Better Start* is hosted by Pobal and aims to bring an integrated national approach to developing quality in early childhood education and care (ECEC). This work will be underpinned by the national quality frameworks from both Aistear and Síolta. (See relevant sections of this book for details.)

There are three strands to the *Better Start* strategy:

1. The Quality Development (mentoring) Service to enhance quality of practice in ELC settings
   - Professional mentoring and coaching delivered by a highly skilled and experienced Early Years Specialist team.
   - Expert early learning and care advice.

2. Supporting Access and Inclusion of Children with Disabilities in ECCE (AIM)
   - To empower service providers to deliver an inclusive early years experience
   - To ensure provision of timely advice and supports to parents and guardians.

3. As part of Level 3 of AIM (which is to develop a qualified and confident workforce)
   - *Better Start* will coordinate the provision of specialised training programmes in relation to disability and inclusion.

The *Better Start* Quality Development Service is an additional resource to support and drive quality improvement. It provides a highly skilled and experienced Early Years Specialist team to work directly in a mentoring capacity with ELC services, complementing and adding to other quality resources such as training, continuing professional development programmes, networking, cluster-type support groups and individual or team-based development work provided by the City and County Childcare Committees (CCCs) and the voluntary childcare organisations.

The Quality Development Service operates on a national rather than regional or county basis. Requests for the service are made directly to *Better Start* from the CCCs. The steps involved when your request has been granted are listed as follows.

FIRST STEPS
- Introductory phone call from your Early Years Specialist
- Letter of Engagement is sent out, along with information leaflets for Providers and Parents
- First Visit Appointment Made

FIRST VISIT
- Discuss Quality priorities with manager
- Talk through the Quality Development Agreement
- Consent Forms provided
- Exchange Child Safeguarding policies
- Quality Liaison Person discussed and identified
- Timing and frequency of visits discussed (at least every 2 weeks for 6 months)

NEXT STEPS?
- Observe practice using self-evaluation tools of *Aistear and Síolta Practice Guide* and video observation
- Provide Feedback on observations
- Discuss, identify and agree quality development goals
- Document goals and actions
- Share goals and actions with Quality Liaison person, management and staff
- Revisit, review and develop goals and actions with relevant staff and management on regular visits and at team meetings
- Share a Final Report detailing the quality development goals with the service
- Make recommendations for sustaining and continuing the quality development work

Steps to Quality Development; what to expect if your service is allocated the support of a Better Start Early Years Specialist (Source: www.betterstart.ie)

The broader aim of *Better Start* is to bring coordination, cohesion and consistency to the provision of state-funded ECCE quality supports and to work in alignment with statutory ECCE systems.

Alongside other bodies, *Better Start* is also involved in developing and delivering online courses and training as part of an initiative to promote continuous professional development for those working in the ELC sector. Online resources include:

- Supporting Transitions Back Into Pre-school – Social Story
- *Aistear Síolta Practice Guide*
- AIM Inclusive Play Resources
- Lámh
- The Hanen Organisation

* Barnardos e-learning course: Learning Environments in Early Years
* Tusla Early Years Inspectorate e-learning training – Managing Unsolicited Information
* Inside Education
* Early Childhood Ireland – Practice Blog
* Early Arts UK.

For further information on *Better Start* National Early Years Quality Development, refer to the dedicated website: betterstart.ie. (Note that *Better Start* uses ECCE as an acronym for ELC services.)

First 5 Strategy 2019–2028

In November 2018 the Government introduced the first ever cross-departmental strategy to support babies, young children and their families. This is a welcome support in Ireland as up to now society has had a diminished capacity to support parents in doing what society expects them and needs them to do. *First 5* is a 10-year strategy based on the appreciation that the early years of a child's life are a critical and distinct period when well-structured inputs and supports can have long-term and lasting effects on the outcomes of children's' lives.

The development of *First 5* has been informed by *Right From the Start*, the report of the expert advisory group on the Early Years strategy.

Right from the Start: Report of the Expert Advisory Group on the Early Years Strategy
https://www.gov.ie/en/publication/ba2572-right-from-the-start-report-of-the-expert-advisory-group-on-the-earl/

The principles underpinning the *First 5* strategy taken from the *Right From the Start* report are that:

* early childhood is a significant and distinct time in life that must be nurtured, respected, valued and supported in its own right
* relationships and interactions with significant others, and the environments in which they take place, play a central role in the quality of children's experiences in early childhood
* services and supports to children and their families should be of a high quality, affordable and accessible to all, while recognising that some children and families will need additional support
* the provision of quality services requires everyone working with children and families to communicate and cooperate with one another and with children and families in an atmosphere of mutual respect and common purpose/partnership
* society must value and support parents, guardians, families and everyone who promotes the wellbeing, learning and development of young children

* government policies pertaining to children should be informed by evidence, by international standards of best practice and by children's rights.

The *First 5* strategy envisages an overarching effective early childhood system and sets out the 'First 5 Big Steps' (see below) involved in creating an integrated, high-quality and supported early years system.

First 5 adopts the term early learning and care (ELC) and defines it as:

> **any regulated arrangement that provides education and care from birth to compulsory primary school age – regardless of the setting, funding, opening hours or programme content – and includes centre and family day care; privately and publicly funded provision; pre-school and pre-primary provision. (EU Quality Framework)**

It excludes care by family members such as grandparents and also the early primary school classes.

FIRST 5 BIG STEPS

1. Access to a broader range of options for parents to balance working and caring. This will include extending parental leave and developing more flexible working arrangements
2. A new model of parenting support – streamlining and improving existing supports; provision of guidance and information on health and early learning; a new Parenting Unit to be established
3. New developments in child health; the development of a dedicated child health workforce focusing initially on the greatest areas of need and disadvantage; to integrate and extend existing programmes
4. Reform of the ELC system; introduction of the Affordable Childcare Scheme, progression towards a graduate-led professional ELC workforce; extending regulations and supports to all paid childminders and school-age childcare services; and the introduction of a new funding model for ELC
5. A package of measures to tackle early childhood poverty, to include free and subsidised ELC, introducing a meals programme to ELC services and other measures to narrow the gap created by poverty.

There are four goals set out in the strategy:

A. Strong and supportive families and communities
B. Optimum physical and mental health
C. Positive play-based early learning
D. An effective early childhood system.

Each of the goals A, B and C has set objectives:

A.
1. Balance working and caring during the first year
2. Information, services and supports for parents
3. Practical and material resources

B.
1. Positive health behaviours
2. High-quality health services
3. Positive mental health

C.
1. Positive home learning
2. Affordable, high-quality early learning
3. Supported transitions

Goal D has five building blocks:

* Building Block 1: Leadership, governance, collaboration
* Building Block 2: Regulation, inspection, quality assurance
* Building Block 3: Skilled and sustainable workforce
* Building Block 4: Research, data, monitoring and evaluation
* Building Block 5: Strategic investment

Thirty-two strategic actions have been set in order to achieve these goals and objectives.

Implementation will first include a *First 5* trial programme, which will be reviewed, and thereafter the whole initiative will be reviewed after three years.

This is a very ambitious programme as it puts babies, toddlers and young children at the centre of the whole plan. As an integrated strategy, it will constitute a significant development in policy services for families with children in Ireland.

References

AIM (2016) *Access and Inclusion Model (AIM): Better Pre-school Access for Children with Disabilities Access and Inclusion Model*. Available from https://aim.gov.ie/ [accessed 6 June 2021].

Aubrey, C. and Dahl, S. (2008) *A Review of the Evidence on the Use of ICT in the Early Years Foundation Stage*. Coventry: University of Warwick. Available from https://dera.ioe.ac.uk/1631/2/becta_2008_eyfsreview_report.pdf [accessed 10 June 2021].

Barnardos (2018) *Protecting Children: A Child Protection Guide for Early Years and School Age Childcare Services*. Dublin: Barnardos.

Better Start (n.d) *National Early Years Quality Development*. Available from https://www.betterstart.ie/

Bolstad, R. (2004) *The Role and Potential of ICT in Early Childhood Education*. Wellington: Ministry of Education. Available from https://www.nzcer.org.nz/system/files/ictinecefinal.pdf [accessed 2 June 2021].

Boud, D., Keogh, R. and Walker D. (1985) *Reflection: Turning Experience into Learning*. UK: Routledge.

Brostrom, S. (2002) Transitions from Kindergarten to School. In: Fabian, H. and Dunlop, A. (eds) *Transitions in the Early Years: Debating Continuity and Progression for Children in Early Education*. London: RoutledgeFalmer, pp. 146–154.

Canavan Corr, A. (2006) *Children and Technology: A Tool for Child Development*. Dublin: National Children's Resource Centre. Available from https://www.barnardos.ie/media/1496/chidlren-and-technology.pdf [accessed 15 June 2021].

Centre for Early Childhood Development and Education (2006) *Síolta: The National Quality Framework for Early Childhood Education*. Dublin: CECDE. Available from https://www.siolta.ie/about.php [accessed 2 June 2021].

___ (2006) *Síolta Handbook*. Dublin: CECDE. Available from https://siolta.ie/media/pdfs/final_handbook.pdf [accessed 2 June 2021].

___ (2006) *Síolta Research Digest Standard 11 Professional Practice*. Available from https://siolta.ie/media/pdfs/Research%20Digest%20-%20Professional%20Practice.pdf [accessed 2 June 2021].

___ (2006) *Síolta Research Digest Standard 12 Communication*. Available from https://siolta.ie/media/pdfs/Research%20Djgest%20-%20Communication.pdf [accessed 2 June 2021].

Covey, S. (2020) *The 7 Habits of Highly Effective People*, revised and updated. London: Simon and Schuster.

___ 'Most people don't listen' [quote]. Available from http://www.richardbandrews.com/most-people-dont-listen-with-the-intent-to-understand-they-listen-with-the-intent-to-reply-stephen-r-covey/ [accessed 21 June 2021].

Crann Support Group and National Childhood Network (2016) *Skills and Competencies Framework for Early Years Professionals*. Available from https://www.ncn.ie/images/PDFs/Proposed-Core-Skills-and-Competencies-Framework-071116.pdf [accessed 7 June 2021].

Department of Children, Equality, Disability, Integration and Youth (2016) *Child Care Act 1991 (Early Years Services) Regulations 2016*. Dublin: Stationery Office.

___ (2016) *Diversity, Equality and Inclusion Charter and Guidelines for Early Childhood Care and Education*. Available from https://www.gov.ie/en/publication/b1a475-diversity-equality-and-inclusion-charter-and-guidelines-for-early-ch/ [accessed 11 June 2021]

___ (2020) *Early Childhood Care and Education Programme* (ECCE). Available from https://www.gov.ie/en/publication/2459ee-early-childhood-care-and-education-programme-ecce/ [accessed 4 June 2021].

___ (2021) *First 5 – A Government Strategy for Babies, Children and Their Families 2019–2028*. Available from https://first5.gov.ie/ [accessed 8 June 2021].

Department of Children and Youth Affairs (2016) *Diversity, Equality and Inclusion Charter and Guidelines for Early Childhood Care and Education*. Available from https://assets.gov.ie/38186/c9e90d89d94b41d3bf00201c98b2ef6a.pdf [accessed 11 June 2021].

___ (2017) *Children First: National Guidance for the Protection and Welfare of Children*. Dublin: Stationery Office. Available from https://www.tusla.ie/services/child-protection-welfare/children-first/ [accessed 15 June 2021].

___ (2017) *Addendum to Children First: National Guidance for the Protection and Welfare of Children*. Dublin: Stationery Office.

___ (n.d.) *Workforce Development Plan for the ELC/SAC Sector: Background Note and Draft Terms of Reference for the Steering Group*. Available from https://assets.gov.ie/26650/a384c2888749488d8e93badc501507b3.pdf [accessed 10 June 2021].

Department of Education and Skills (2010) *A Workforce Development Plan for the Early Childhood Care and Education Sector in Ireland*. Available from https://www.education.ie/en/schools-colleges/information/early-years/eye_workforce_dev_plan.pdf [accessed 5 June 2021].

___ (2017) *Síolta User Manual*. Dublin: Early Years Education Policy Unit. Available from https://www.siolta.ie/media/pdfs/siolta-manual-2017.pdf [accessed 2 June 2021].

___ (2019) *Professional Award Criteria and Guidelines for Initial Professional Education (Level 7 and Level 8) Degree Programmes for the Early Learning and Care (ELC) Sector in Ireland*. Dublin: DES. Available from https://www.gov.ie/pdf/?file=https://assets.gov.ie/30316/784a2158d8094bb7bab40f2064358221.pdf#page=1 [accessed 23 June 2021].

Department of Justice, Equality and Law Reform (2002) *Quality Childcare and Lifelong Learning: Model Framework for Education, Training and Professional Development in the Early Childhood Care and Education Sector*. Available from https://www.education.ie/en/Schools-Colleges/Information/Early-Years/Model-Framework-for-Education-Training-and-Professional-Development-in-the-Early-Childhood-Care-and-Education-Sector.pdf [accessed 5 June 2021].

Department of Social Protection (2020) *After School Childcare Scheme*. Available from https://www.gov.ie/en/service/2e0c5d-after-school-childcare-scheme/ [accessed 4 June 2021].

Department of Education and Science (2004) *The Education for Persons with Special Educational Needs Act 2004* (EPSEN). Available from https://www.oireachtas.ie/en/bills/bill/2003/34/ [accessed 16 June 2021].

Derman-Sparks, L. and ABC Task Force (1989) *Anti-bias Curriculum: Tools for Empowering Young Children*. Washington DC: National Association for the Education of Young Children.

Derman-Sparks, L. and Olsen Edwards, J. (2010) *Anti-bias Education for Young Children and Ourselves*. Washington DC: National Association for the Education of Young Children.

Dewey, J. (1910) *How We Think*. Boston: D.C. Heath and Company.

Donohoe, J. and Gaynor, F. (2011) *Education and Care in the Early Years*, 4th edition. Dublin: Gill and Macmillan.

Doyle, A. (2021) *How to Use the STAR Interview Response Method*. Available from https://www.thebalancecareers.com/what-is-the-star-interview-response-technique-2061629 [accessed 2 June 2021].

Durrow Communications (2020) *Reach+: Career and College Preparation Programme*. Dublin: Durrow Communications Ltd.

Dweck, C.S. (2017) *Mindset: Changing the Way You Think to Fulfil Your Potential*, revised edition. London: Robinson.

Early Childhood Ireland (2019) *Finance and Funding*. Available from https://www.earlychildhoodireland.ie/eyes/operating-a-childcare-setting/finance-and-funding/ [accessed 17 June 2021].

____ (2019) Staff Induction Checklist. Available from https://www.earlychildhoodireland.ie/product/staff-induction-checklist/ [accessed 28 June 2021].

____ (2019) *Types of Childcare Settings*. Available from https://www.earlychildhoodireland.ie/eyes/operating-a-childcare-setting/types-of-childcare-settings/ [accessed 4 June 2021].

____ (n.d.) *Current Learning Story Winners*. Available from https://www.earlychildhoodireland.ie/work/quality-practice/awards/learning-stories/current-learning-story-winners/ [accessed 23 June 2021].

Feeney, S., Freeman, N.K. and Moravcik, E. (2020) Focus on ethics: professional boundaries in early childhood education. *Young Children*, 75(5). Available from https://www.naeyc.org/resources/pubs/yc/dec2020/professional-boundaries [accessed 16 June 2021].

Fogg, S. (2019) *GDPR for Dummies: Simple GDPR Guide for Beginners* [graphic]. Available from https://termly.io/resources/articles/gdpr-for-dummies/ [accessed 2 June 2021].

Gibbs, G. (1988) Reflective Cycle [graphic]. Available from https://www.toolshero.com/management/gibbs-reflective-cycle-graham-gibbs/ [accessed 14 June 2021].

Graham, I. and McDermott, M. (2010) *Your Learning and Development: Continuing Professional Development in Early Childhood Care and Education*. Dublin: Barnardos.

Hayes, N. (2005) *Early Childhood: An Introductory Text*. Dublin. Gill and Macmillan.

Hayes, N., O'Toole, L. and Halpenny, A. (2017) *Introducing Bronfenbrenner: A Guide for Practitioners and Students in Early Years Education*. UK: Routledge.

Hays (n.d.) *Interview tips*. Available from https://www.hays.ie/resources/career-advice/handling-an-interview [accessed 2 June 2021].

Health Service Executive (2018) *Mindfulness* [online]. Available from https://www2.hse.ie/wellbeing/mental-health/mindfulness.html [accessed 2 June 2021].

Hill, S. and Broadhurst, D. (2001) Technoliteracy and the Early Years. In: L. Makin and C. Jones Diaz (eds) *Literacies in Early Childhood: Changing Views, Challenging Practice*. Eastgardens, NSW: MacLennan and Petty, pp. 269–287.

Holt, J. (1967) *How Children Learn*. New York: Pitman Publishing Company.

Iberdrola (n.d.) *Do You Know How Educational Robots Can Help Your Children to Develop?* Available from https://www.iberdrola.com/innovation/educational-robots [accessed 2 June 2021].

Kolb, D. (1984) Experiential Learning Cycle [graphic]. Available from https://www.simplypsychology.org/learning-kolb.html [accessed 22 June 2021].

Landon, K. (2014) *Impact of Parent Involvement on Child Development*. Available from https://hubbli.com/impact-of-parent-involvement/ [accessed 20 June 2021].

Lear, E. (1917) 'The Jumblies'. Available from https://www.poetryfoundation.org/poems/54364 [accessed 13 June 2021].

Lindon, J. (2012) *Reflective Practice and Early Years Professionalism*, 2nd edition. London: Hodder Education.

Marsh J., Brooks G., Hughes J., Ritchie L., and Roberts S. (2005) *Digital Beginnings: Young Children's Use of Popular Culture, Media and New Technologies*. Available from www.digitalbeginnings.shef.ac.uk/DigitalBeginningsReport.pdf. Sheffield: University of Sheffield.

McHugh, J. and Zappone, K. (2019) *Guidelines for professional education degree programme for the early learning and care sector*. Press release. Available from https://www.education.ie/en/Press-Events/Press-Releases/2019-press-releases/PR19-04-12.html#:~:text=A%20working%20group%20was%20established,the%20ELC%20sector%20in%20Ireland [accessed 8 June 2021].

Mehrabian, A. (1966) *Mehrabian's Communication Theory: Verbal, Non-Verbal, Body Language* [online article]. Available from https://www.businessballs.com/communication-skills/mehrabians-communication-theory-verbal-non-verbal-body-language/ [accessed 21 June 2021].

Mhic Mhathúna, M. and Taylor, M. (2012) *Early Childhood Education and Care: An Introduction for Students in Ireland*. Dublin: Gill and Macmillan.

Ministry of Social and Family Development, Singapore (2012) *Achieving Excellence through Continuing Professional Development: A CPD Framework for Early Childhood Educators*. Singapore: MSF. Available from http://impressie.xs4all.nl/ecwi/node/86 [accessed 30 June 2021].

National Council for Curriculum and Assessment (2009) *Aistear: The Early Childhood Curriculum Framework: Guidelines for Good Practice*. Dublin: NCCA. Available from https://ncca.ie/media/4151/aistear_theearlychildhoodcurriculumframework.pdf [accessed 2 June 2021].

____ (2009) *Aistear: The Early Childhood Curriculum Framework: Principles and Themes*. Dublin: NCCA. Available from http://www.ncca.biz/Aistear/pdfs/PrinciplesThemes_ENG/PrinciplesThemes_ENG.pdf [accessed 2 June 2021].

____ (n.d.) *Aistear and Siolta in action Research Digest – Communication*. Available from https://siolta.ie/media/pdfs/Research%20Djgest%20-%20Communication.pdf [accessed 10 June 2021]

____ (2015) *Aistear Síolta Practice Guide*. Available from https://www.aistearsiolta.ie/en/ [accessed 11 June 2021].

____ (2015) *Aistear Síolta Practice Guide: Building Partnerships with Parents Pillar: Overview*. Available from https://www.aistearsiolta.ie/en/building-partnerships-with-parents/overview/pillar-overview-building-partnerships-with-parents1.pdf [accessed 15 June 2021].

____ (2015) *Aistear Síolta Practice Guide: Element 4: Professional Practice*. Available at https://www.aistearsiolta.ie/en/curriculum-foundations/element-4-professional-practice/activity-a-professional-role.pdf [accessed 11 June 2021].

____ (n.d.) *Curriculum Online*. Available from https://www.curriculumonline.ie/Early-Childhood/ [accessed 2 June 2021].

____ (2021) *Updating Aistear: Rationale and Process*. Available from https://ncca.ie/media/5053/updating-aistear_rationale-and-process_background-paper_2021.pdf [accessed 4 June 2021].

Pastor, E. and Kerns, E. (1997) A digital snapshot of an early childhood classroom. *Educational Leadership*, 55(3), pp. 42–46.

Pobal (2021) *Voluntary Childcare Organisations*. Available from https://www.pobal.ie/programmes/voluntary-childcare-organisations-vcos/ [accessed 3 June 2021].

Positive Psychology [n.d.] 'Help other people with this science-based positive psychology toolkit to create a more meaningful and fulfilling life and career' [online article]. Available from https://positivepsychology.com/toolkit-exclusive/?gclid=Cj0KCQjwlMaGBhD3ARIsAPvWd6j1m73w4qbjmBJ5ZXJcmjQzBjkwN7OPvvr7bw51ewlbQQPre0dlSR0aAnqOEALw_wcB [accessed 22 June 2021].

Professionalisation Sub-Group of the Early Years Forum (2020) *Code of Professional Responsibility and Code of Ethics for Early Years Educators*. Available from http://www.limerickchildcare.ie/wp-content/uploads/2015/06/Code-of-Professional-Responsibilities-and-Code-of-Ethics-for-Early-Years-Educators.pdf [accessed 19 June 2021].

RCSI Centre for Positive Psychology and Health (2021) *The Science of Health and Happiness* (online public course). Available from https://www.rcsi.com/dublin/about/faculty-of-medicine-and-health-sciences/centre-for-positive-psychology-and-health/science-of-health-and-happiness [accessed 7 June 2021].

Schön, D. (1983) Reflective Model [graphic]. Available from https://nursinganswers.net/reflective-guides/schon-reflective-model.php [accessed 22 June 2021].

Shaffer, D.K. (2019) *Feeling lonely? Listen carefully* [online article]. Available from https://www.alive.com/lifestyle/feeling-lonely/ [accessed 11 June 2021].

Siraj-Blatchford, I. and Siraj-Blatchford, J. (2000) *More than Computers: Information and Communications Technology in the Early Years*. London: Early Education (British Association for Early Childhood Education). Available from http://www.327matters.org/Docs/DATEC7.pdf [accessed 3 June 2021].

Siraj-Blatchford, J. and Siraj-Blatchford, I. (2002) Developmentally appropriate technology in early childhood: 'Video conferencing'. *Contemporary Issues in Early Childhood*, 3(2), pp. 216–225. Available from https://journals.sagepub.com/doi/pdf/10.2304/ciec.2002.3.2.5 [accessed 22 June 2021].

Skills You Need (n.d.) *Reflective Practice* [online article]. Available from https://www.skillsyouneed.com/ps/reflective-practice.html) [accessed 19 June 2021].

Sullivan, A. and Bers, M.U. (2015) Robotics in the early childhood classroom: Learning outcomes from an 8-week robotics curriculum in pre-kindergarten through second grade. *International Journal of Technology and Design Education*, 26, pp. 3–20. Available from https://ase.tufts.edu/DevTech/publications/robotics%20paper.pdf [accessed 22 June 2021].

Sylva, K., Melhuish, E., Sammons, P., Siraj-Blatchford, I. and Taggart, B. (2004) *The Effective Provision of Pre-School Education (EPPE) Project Technical Paper 12: The Final Report – Effective Pre-School Education*. Available from https://www.researchgate.net/publication/320194757_The_Effective_Provision_of_Pre-School_Education_EPPE_Project_Technical_Paper_12_The_Final_Report_-_Effective_Pre-School_Education/citation/download [accessed 13 June 2021].

Tuckman, B.W. (1965) Development sequence in small groups. *Psychological Bulletin*, 63(6), pp. 384–399. Available from http://www.communicationcache.com/uploads/1/0/8/8/10887248/developmental_sequence_in_small_groups_-_reprint.pdf [accessed 22 June 2021].

Tuckman, B.W. and Jensen, M.A.C. (1977) Stages of small-group development revisited. *Group & Organization Studies*, 2(4), pp. 419–427. Available from http://faculty.wiu.edu/P-Schlag/articles/Stages_of_Small_Group_Development.pdf [accessed 14 June 2021].

Tusla (2015) *Questions and Answers on Management and Staffing in Early Years/Pre-School Services Giving Particular Attention to: Employee References, Qualifications and Garda Vetting*. Available from https://www.tusla.ie/uploads/content/Q_and_A_Vetting_December_2015.pdf [accessed 8 June 2021].

___ (2017) *Child Care Regulations*. Dublin: Stationery Office. Available from https://www.tusla.ie/services/preschool-services/early-years-pre-school-inspection-services/child-care-regulations/ [accessed 4 June 2021].

___ (2017) *A Guide for the Reporting of Child Protection and Welfare Concerns*. Dublin: Stationery Office. Available at https://www.tusla.ie/uploads/content/4214-TUSLA_Guide_to_Reporters_Guide_A4_v3.pdf [accessed 5 June 2021].

___ (2018). *Quality and Regulatory Framework: Full Day Care Service and Part-Time Day Care Service*. Dublin: Early Years Inspectorate. Available at: https://www.tusla.ie/services/pre-school-services/early-years-quality-and-regulatory-framework/ [accessed 6 June 2021].

___ (2019) *Child Safeguarding: A Guide for Policy, Procedure and Practice*, 2nd edition. Dublin: Stationery Office. Available at https://www.tusla.ie/services/child-protection-welfare/ [accessed 5 June 2021].

___ (2021) *Early Years (Pre School) Inspectorate: Types of Pre-school Services.* Available from https://www.tusla.ie/services/family-community-support/pre-school-services/ (accessed 4 June 2021].

University of Portsmouth (n.d.) *Reflective Writing* [online article]. Available from https://www.port.ac.uk/student-life/help-and-advice/study-skills/written-assignments/reflective-writing-introduction [accessed 12 June 2021].

Urban, M., Vandenbroeck, M., Lazzari, A., Van Laera, K. and Peeters, J. (2012) *CORE: Competence Requirements in Early Childhood Education and Care – A Study for the European Commission Directorate-General for Education and Culture*. Available from https://files.eric.ed.gov/fulltext/ED534599.pdf [accessed 30 June 2021].

Waddell, M. (1996) *Farmer Duck*. UK: Walker Books Ltd.

Wheatley, M.J. (2005) *Finding Our Way: Leadership for an Uncertain Time*. San Francisco: Berrett-Koehler.

Appendices

Appendix 1 Tusla Early Years Inspection Process

A GUIDE TO REGULATORY ENFORCEMENT IN EARLY YEARS SETTINGS

WHAT HAPPENS ONCE AN INSPECTION OF A SERVICE HAS TAKEN PLACE?

Following any inspection of an Early Years' Service, the Early Years Inspectorate develop a draft inspection report which lists compliant and non-compliant findings. This is sent to the service and the provider is invited to submit a Corrective and Preventive Action (CAPA) response. The CAPA provides the service with an opportunity to detail and provide evidence in relation to what corrective and preventive actions they have taken to ensure that the non-compliant issue is resolved and how they will prevent the non–compliance from occurring again. If the Early Years Inspectorate is satisfied that the submitted information and evidence effectively addresses the issue this will be recorded on the inspection report. If satisfactory evidence is not provided, then the Early Years Inspectorate may propose to attach a condition to the registration of the service. The service then has a further opportunity to submit information and evidence in relation to the issue. If satisfactory evidence is not provided, then the condition will be attached to registration. If there is no response made to a proposal to add a condition by a provider, then the condition will be automatically applied after the statutory allowed period of 21 days without further notice to the provider.

WHAT IS A CONDITION OF REGISTRATION AND HOW DO I KNOW IF A SERVICE HAS A CONDITION APPLIED TO ITS REGISTRATION?

A condition is applied to a service registration in order to assist it to address the noncompliance identified. They are usually very specific and time limited and will be followed up by the Early Years Inspectorate either through another inspection or direct request for information and evidence regarding compliance with the condition.

Details concerning attached conditions are made publically available via two sources via the Early Years Section on the Tusla website. The information is made available in the inspection report section and is available on the national register of early years providers, which is also available on the website.

HOW CAN A CONDITION BE REMOVED OR ALTERED?

A provider can submit Information and evidence in relation to the condition to the Inspectorate at any time and it will be considered for removal or alteration. However, requests to alter the terms of an attached condition will only be considered where the provider has provided the required and verified evidence that they are now compliant with the relevant regulations.

WHAT IF A CONDITION OF REGISTRATION HAS NOT BEEN ADHERED TOO OR IS FOUND NOT TO HAVE BEEN MET ON A FOLLOW UP OR SUBSEQUENT INSPECTION?

If the condition remains attached the provider is legally required to adhere to it until advised to the contrary. If it is found on subsequent inspection (which may be triggered through the submission of Unsolicited Information) that the provider has breached or has not adhered to one or more condition, enforcement actions will be taken by the inspectorate. Enforcement actions will include consideration of removing the service from the Register of Early Years Services. It is an offence under legislation not to comply with a condition of registration.

(Source: https://www.tusla.ie/services/preschool-services/a-guide-to-regulatory-enforcement-in-early-years-settings/)

Blank Tusla inspection and blank Tusla Capa reports are available at https://www.tusla.ie/services/preschool-services/focused-inspection-tool-and-outcome-reports/#Inspection%20Tool

All Tusla registered providers inspection reports are available to view at https://www.tusla.ie/services/preschool-services/creche-inspection-reports/

Appendix 2 Tusla Child Safeguarding Statement Sample Template

Note: This is a sample template provided as a guide only. It is not a standardised format for a Child Safeguarding Statement. Please see the following documents for more information about developing a Child Safeguarding Statement:

* Children First: National Guidance for the Protection and Welfare of Children
* Guidance on Developing a Child Safeguarding Statement (www.tusla.ie)
* Child Safeguarding: A Guide for Policy, Procedure and Practice (www.tusla.ie)

1. **Name of service being provided:** _____

2. **Nature of service and principles to safeguard children from harm** *(brief outline of what our service is, what we do and our commitment to safeguard children):* _____

   _____

   _____

3. **Risk Assessment**

   We have carried out an assessment of any potential for harm to a child while availing of our services including the area of online safety when accessing the internet. Below is a list of the areas of risk identified and the list of procedures for managing these risks.

	Risk identified	**Procedure in place to manage identified risk**
1		
2		
3		
4		
5		

4. **Procedures**

   Our Child Safeguarding Statement has been developed in line with requirements under the Children First Act 2015, *Children First: National Guidance for the Protection and Welfare of Children* (2017), and Tusla's *Child Safeguarding: A Guide for Policy, Procedure and Practice*. In addition to the procedures listed in our risk assessment, the following procedures support our intention to safeguard children while they are availing of our service:

   * Procedure for the management of allegations of abuse or misconduct against workers/volunteers of a child availing of our service;

* Procedure for the safe recruitment and selection of workers and volunteers to work with children;
* Procedure for provision of and access to child safeguarding training and information, including the identification of the occurrence of harm;
* Procedure for the reporting of child protection or welfare concerns to Tusla;
* Procedure for maintaining a list of the persons (if any) in the relevant service who are mandated persons;
* Procedure for appointing a relevant person.

All procedures listed are available upon request.

5. Implementation

    We recognise that implementation is an on-going process. Our service is committed to the implementation of this Child Safeguarding Statement and the procedures that support our intention to keep children safe from harm while availing of our service.

This Child Safeguarding Statement will be reviewed on _____, or as soon as practicable after there has been a material change in any matter to which the statement refers.

Signed: _____ (Provider)

[Provider's name and contact details]

For queries, please contact _____ Relevant Person under the Children First Act 2015.

Guidance Notes

Section 2: Nature of service and principles to safeguard children from harm: Describe the nature of your services and specify the principles that you will observe to keep children safe from harm while they are availing of your service.

Section 3: Risk assessment: *Children First: National Guidance for the Protection and Welfare of Children* (2017) provides additional guidance on carrying out the risk assessment component of your Child Safeguarding Statement.

Section 4: Procedures: As this is only a sample list, you will need to add to this list as appropriate, based on the outcome of your risk assessment. Please see also Tusla's *Child Safeguarding: A Guide for Policy, Procedure and Practice.*

Section 5: Implementation: At a minimum, reviews must be carried out every 24 months. The provider is the individual with overall responsibility for the organisation. This may be the chief executive officer, chairperson of a board of management, owner/operator, etc.

Relevant Person: You should include the name and contact details of the Relevant Persons, who are the first point of contact regarding your Child Safeguarding Statement.

(Source: https://www.tusla.ie/uploads/content/4214-TUSLA_Guidance_on_Developing_a_CSS_LR.PDF)

Appendix 3 Sample forms

Childcare Accident Report

Name of Child: _____

Date of Accident: _____ Time of Accident: _____

Nature of Injury: _____

Describe the Accident: _____

_____

_____

_____

Caregiver Name: _____

First Aid Given: _____

_____

Was the parent contacted?   Y   N   How? _____

Which parent was contacted? _____

Who contacted the parent? _____

What time were they contacted? _____

Additional Contacts or Actions: _____

_____

_____

Additional Notes: _____

_____

_____

Provider signature: _____ Date: _____

Baby Daily Log

Name: _____   Date: _____

Time	Food eaten	Fluids ml/oz	Nappies Wet/Dry?	Sleep	Extra notes

My Day at Daycare

Name: _____   Date: _____

Arrival: _ _:_ _ am/pm

Today I am feeling: _____

During the day: I last ate at _ _:_ _ am/pm

I slept:	I need: _____
from _ _:_ _ am/pm to _ _:_ _ am/pm	Notes: _____
from _ _:_ _ am/pm to _ _:_ _ am/pm	_____
from _ _:_ _ am/pm to _ _:_ _ am/pm	_____
	_____

I was changed:				I ate:	
at: _ _:_ _ am/pm	dry	wet	dirty	_____ at	_ _:_ _ am/pm
at: _ _:_ _ am/pm	dry	wet	dirty	_____ at	_ _:_ _ am/pm
at: _ _:_ _ am/pm	dry	wet	dirty	_____ at	_ _:_ _ am/pm
at: _ _:_ _ am/pm	dry	wet	dirty	_____ at	_ _:_ _ am/pm

Index

accidents (workplace), see Safety, Health and Welfare at Work Act 2005, 178
AIM Access and Inclusion Programme, see *Better Start*, 141, 217–8
Aistear, 23, 25, 121–32
   3 groups, 122
   4 themes, 122–3
   12 principles, 122
   guidelines for good practice, 123–4
   guidelines on assessment, 124–8
   planned update, 215–8
   reflective practice, 41
Aistear Siolta Practice Guide, 132–4
   4 curriculum foundations, 132–3
   6 curriculum pillars, 133
Algorithms, 29
allegations of abuse (against staff), 111
appendix, 13
application letter, 152–4
assessment, see Aistear, 26–7, 124–31
   assessment for learning 125
   assessment of learning 125, 175
   documenting, 128–31
   formative assessment, 26
   guidelines on, 124–6
   methods of, 126–8
   summative assessment, 26
assessment methods, 126–8
   conversation, 126
   observation, 126
   self-assessment, 126
   setting tasks, 127
   testing, 127
autonomous learning, 163

basic care needs, 83,
Better Start National Early Years Quality Development, 217–9
Bias, anti-bias, 206–8

bibliography, 9
Bronfenbrenner, 48–9

calculation of service, see Minimum Notices and Terms of Employment Acts 1973–2005, 184–5
child abuse, 94–101
   child factors, 99–101
   parental factors, 97–9
   physical abuse, 94–5
   emotional abuse, 94, 96,
   neglect, 95, 96
   sexual abuse, 95, 96–7
Child Care Act 1991, 110
   Child Care Act 1991 (Early Years Services) Regulations 2016, 72, 76
   Pre-school regulations (2016), 76–109
child observations, 17–22
   aim and rationale, 20
   evaluation, 20–1
   recommendations, 22
   reflection on personal learning, 21–2
child protection, 92, 101–4
   designated child protection officer, 103
   child safeguarding, 92, 101, 103
   mandated persons, 104
   record-keeping, 30
   role of practitioner, 101
   role of manager of ELC service, 102
   Tusla Children First e-Learning Programme, 93
   Tusla Report Form, 105–109,
child safeguarding statement, 93, 102, 103
Child Safeguarding: A Guide for Policy, Procedure and Practice 232
Childminding Ireland, 68, 138, 143
Children First e-Learning Programme, 93
Children First: National Guidance for the Protection and welfare of children 92–112, 137

Children's Ombudsman, 136
code of ethics, 164
communication, see written communication, 188–201, 115, 116, 122
   barriers to 193
   confidentiality 193
   effective 188
   listening and speaking skills 191
   professional boundaries 194–6
   respectful partnerships 196
   skills 189
   verbal/non-verbal, 63
conclusion, 16, 17
confidentiality, see communication, 193
Continuous Professional Development (CPD), 68–70
   CPD record, 68–70
continuous service, see Minimum Notices and Terms of Employment Acts 1973–2005, 184
core beliefs, 58–9
Criminal Justice Act 2006, 110
Criminal Justice (withholding of Information on Offences against Children and Vulnerable Persons) Act 2012, 110
Criminal Law (Sexual Offences) Act 2017, 110
curriculum vitae (C.V.), 146–152

daily record, 30, 32
data protection, see GDPR, 37, 194,
Developmentally Appropriate Technology in Early Childhood Project (DATEC), 34
   8 principles, 34
democracy, 206
designated child protection officer, see child protection, 101, 103
digital footprint, 158
direct discrimination, see discrimination, 181
discrimination 180
   direct discrimination, 181
   indirect discrimination, 181
   Equality Employment Acts 1998–2001, 180–6
Diversity, Equality and Inclusion Charter, 181, 208–9
documentation, 7 types of, 128–131
   checklists, 130
   children's work, 129
   daily diaries, 130
   ICT, 129
   notes, 129
   reports, 130
   stories, 130
Domestic Violence Act 2018, 110

Early Childhood Ireland (ECI), 27, 138, 219
ECCE scheme, 139
education and qualifications, 146, 147–8
ELC Sector, professionalising, 70–3
ELC services, 137–140
   private, 139
   statutory, 139
   voluntary, 139
emotional abuse, 94
   signs and symptoms, 96
employment legislation, 176–186
   Safety, Health and Welfare at Work Act 2005, 77, 176–9
   Equal Status Acts 2000–2018, 176, 181–2
   Terms of Employment (Information) Acts 1994–2014, 176, 182–5
   Minimum Notices and Terms of Employment Acts 1973–2005, 184–185
   Organisation of Working Time Act 1997, 185
employment written statement, 183
Equal Status Acts 2000–2018, 176, 181–2
Equality Employment Equality Acts 1998–2015
   employers obligations, 180
   discrimination 180
   nine grounds, 179–180

fire safety measures, 89
First 5: A Government Strategy for Babies and Young Children, 71, 137, 166, 219–21
first aid, 69, 88–9,165
five stages of growth, see group/team development, 203–5
formal professional development, see personal & professional development, 68–9
formative assessment, 26

Gaelscoileanna, 138, 140
General Data Protection Regulation (GDPR), 37, 81, 167
   information usage, 37
   privacy and security breaches, 37
   rights, 37
   storage of information and data, 37
Gibbs' Reflective Cycle, 42–5
   action plan, 44
   conclusion, 44
   description, 43

evaluation, 43–4
feelings, 43
glossary, 12–3
goal setting career goals, 67, 203
SMART, 67
governance, 78–82
assessment, 81
management, 78
notification of incidents, 82
parent information, 81
procedures & statements, 78
records, 81
staffing, 79
group/team development, 203–5
five stages of growth, 203–5
Tuckman, 203
Guidance on Developing a Child Safeguarding Statement, 93

health, welfare and development of the child, 82–5
basic care needs, 83
relationship with children, 83
inclusion & diversity, 84
behaviour policy, 84
learning, development & well-being, 84
support programme & care practices, 85
technology use, 85,
rest & play facilities, 85
high five principles, see stress, 56–57

Ikigai, 57–8
inclusion of children with additional needs, 209–10
role of adult in promoting, 210–1
index, 12–3
indirect discrimination, see discrimination, 180–2
induction, 162–5
general operations, 163
human resources, 164
work procedures, 164
policies and procedures, 164
practice and room operation, 164
health and safety, 165
information communication technology (ICT), 28–37
effects of ICT in ELC, 36
IoToys, 33
robotics, 35–6

uses of, in ELC, 31–5
inspection process, 78
attendance records (checking in/out), 88
governance, 78–82
health, welfare and development of child, 82–7
safeguarding safety, health and welfare of child, 88
insurance, 89, 162
internet search, 28, 29, 30

IoToys, see ICT, 33
benefits of, 33
Irish Steiner Waldorf Early Childhood Assoc, 68, 138

job interview, 155–8
preparing for interview questions, 156–8
STAR interview method, 156
knowledge, skills and competencies, 169–172
implementation of activities, 171
planning, 170–1
relationship with supervisor, 172
role modelling, 171–2
time management, 170
Kolb's Experiential Learning Cycle, 45–6
stage 1: concrete experience, 45
stage 2: reflective observation, 45
stage 3: abstract conceptualisation, 45
stage 4: active experimentation, 46

learning, 54–5, 124–8
centre-based learning, 54
directed learning, 54
experiential learning, 54
self-directed learning, 54,
work-based learning, 54
learning story, 26–7
assessment for learning, 26, 124–5,
impact of, 27
storytelling format, 27
letter of application
listening and speaking skills, see communication, 191

mandated persons, see child protection, 101, 104
Tusla Child Protection and Welfare Report Form, 105–9
Maslow's Hierarchy of Needs, 60–1

medicine administration, 30
methodology, 15
mindsets, 62–3
   fixed mindset, 62
   growth mindset, 62
Minimum Notice and Terms of Employment Acts 1973–2005, 184–5
   calculation of service, 184–5
   continuous service, 184

National Childhood Network, 68, 72–3, 138
National Early Years Inspectorate, 137
National Parents Council, 68, 138
National Tusla Early Years Inspectorate, see Tusla, 70
National Vetting Bureau (children and Vulnerable Persons) Act 2012–16: Children First Act, 110
neglect, 95
   signs and symptoms, 96
non-formal professional development, see personal & professional development, 68–9

Organisation of Working Time Act 1997, 185–7
   exceptions, 185
   overtime, 186
overtime, see Organisation of Working Time Act 1997, 186

partnerships 196
   with adult team 197
   with children 196
   with families 197
peer mentoring, 50
people skills, 63–5
   intrapersonal skills, 63
   interpersonal skills, 63
personal and professional development, 54–65
   Siolta Standard 11, 40, 55, 116–8
   showcasing, 68–9
   formal professional development, 69
   non-formal professional development, 68–9
personal development, 55–6
personal presentation, 158–9, 166–175, 189
personal profile, 147
physical abuse, 94
   signs and symptoms, 95
physical environment, 208–9
placement, 160–5
   first visit, 162

   induction, 162–5
   personal conduct 162
preparation for placement, 136–145
plagiarism, 9
planning, 66–7
   importance of, 66
   short term, 67
   medium term, 67
   long term, 67
play activity, 22–6
   writing a plan for 23
policy, definition, 31
Pre-school Regulations 2016, 76–91
   Child Care Act 1991, 110
presentation of findings, 16
primary research, see research methods, 6–7
   case study, 7
   checklist, 7
   interview, 7
   questionnaire, 6
   questionnaire design, 6
   survey, 6
procedure, definition, 31
process, definition, 25
product, definition, 25
professional boundaries, see communication, 194–6
professional development, 54–65
professional practice placement, 160–5
   first visit, 162
   induction, 162–5
   personal conduct, 162
   preparation for placement, 136–145
professional responsibilities, 168–9
   relating to our colleagues 168–9
Protections of Persons Reporting Child Abuse Act 1998, 110

qualitative research, 8–9
Quality & Regulatory Framework, see Tusla, 70, 72, 76–91
quantitative research, 8–9

record-keeping, 30–1
referees, 148–9
reference list, 9–12
references, 9
referencing, 10–12
   book, 11
   chapter in edited book, 11

citations, 10
edited book, 11
electronic sources, 11
journal article, 11
quotations, 10
reflection, 39,
  after professional practice placement,
  on learning & development for children 25
  on personal learning, 21–2, 26
  reflective learning journal, 51–3
reflective practice
  Aistear and reflective practice, 41–2
  models of, 42–7
  Siolta and reflective practice, 40
Reflective practice models, 42–7
  Gibbs' Reflective Cycle, 42, 44
  Kolb Experiential Learning Cycle, 45–6
  Schön Reflective Model, 46–7
research methods, 6–9
  primary research, 6–8
  secondary research, 8
robotics, 35–6
  development of cognitive skills, 35
role modelling, see knowledge, skills and competences, 171–2

safeguarding children, 93–4
  principles of best practice 93
safety statement, see Safety, Health and Welfare at Work Act 2005, 165, 178
Safety, Health and Welfare at Work Act 2005, 176–9
  accidents in the workplace 178
  bullying in workplace, 179
  safety statement, 178
  victimisation, 179
  violence in the workplace, 178
scaffolding, 23
  Zone of Proximal Development, 23
  Vygotsky, 23
Schön's Reflective model, 46–7
  reflection in action, 46
  reflection on action, 46
search engine optimisation (SEO), 29,
secondary research, 8
sessional services, 140–4
  after-school services, 144
  city & county childcare committees, 143
  drop-in centre, 143
  early start pre-school programme, 141
  ELC services for children with additional needs, 141
  family day care, 142–3
  full-time services, 142
  Montessori pre-schools, 140
  naíonraí, 140,
  overnight services, 143
  parent & toddler groups, 140
  playgroups, 140
sexual abuse, 95
  signs and symptoms, 96–7
Siolta, 113–120
  12 principles, 114–5
  16 standards, 115–7
  75 components, 117
  practical application of, 118–9
  quality indicators, 119–20
skills and personal qualities, 148–9
skills audit, 64
space requirements, 90–1
St. Nicholas Montessori Teachers' Association, 68, 138
stress, dealing with, 56–7
  parents with, 98
summative assessment, 26
supervision, learning from, 49–50
  positive use of, 172–4

teams, 202–6
  skills necessary to work in, 202–3
teamwork, 202–11
  benefits of 205
technology-enhanced learning (TEL), 31, 33
  Internet of Toys (IoToys), 33–4
  benefits of, 33–4
Terms of Employment (Information) Acts 1994–2014, 182–4
The Jumblies, 4
  Edward Lear, 4
time-keeping/ management 159 166
Together Old and Young TOY Project, 212–4
  TOY for Inclusion, 214
transversal skills, 64
tripartite meeting 163
Tuckman, see five stages of growth, 203
Tusla, 30, 69, 70, 76–91, 93, 103–4
  Child Protection and Welfare Report Form, 105–9
  Tusla Children First e-Learning Programme, 93

Tusla Report Form, 105–9
Tusla National Tusla Early Years Inspectorate Quality & Regulatory Framework, 70

UN Convention on the Rights of the Child, 136
unique selling point (USP), 147

voluntary childcare organisations, 68, 138

work experience, 148
written communication, forms, of, 4–6
   creative writing, 4
   academic writing, 4–13
   reflective writing, 4–5
   report compilation, 4
   form completion, 4
   letter writing, 4
   research undertaking, 4
writing for assessment, 14–27